American Broadcasting
and the First Amendment

American Broadcasting and the First Amendment

LUCAS A. POWE, JR.

UNIVERSITY OF CALIFORNIA PRESS
Berkeley   Los Angeles   London

University of California Press
Berkeley and Los Angeles, California

University of California Press, Ltd.
London, England

© 1987 by
The Regents of the University of California
First Paperback Printing 1988
Printed in the United States of America
1 2 3 4 5 6 7 8 9

Library of Congress Cataloging-in-Publication Data

Powe, L. A. Scot.
American broadcasting and the First Amendment.

Includes index.
1. Freedom of the press—United States. 2. Broadcasting—Law and legislation—United States. I. Title.
KF4774.P68   1987   343.73′0998   86–19254
347.303998
ISBN 0-520-06467-4 (alk. paper)

For my parents who provided the love and perspective

Contents

Acknowledgments

This book was started in the fall of 1980 when I had a semester research grant from the University Research Institute at The University of Texas. That grant provided me with the opportunity, for the first time in my career, to reflect at length on where my scholarship had been leading me. I decided that it pointed to this book, for two reasons. First, I wanted to intertwine different disciplines as well as different areas within law to explain how broadcasting had been separated from the print tradition of almost complete freedom. Second, and more fundamentally, I wanted to explore the consequences of that separation and bring this academic debate to a wider audience. In so doing I have tried to explain legal decisions with perfect accuracy but at the same time avoid the anesthetizing language of law: I wanted to write a book that is easy—and fun—to read. I hope I have succeeded. To the extent I have, a great debt is owed to Mary Barrow, now of the Austin office of Vinson & Elkins. During her final year at The University of Texas Law School she was my editor. She took my style as she found it and provided the best editing I have ever seen, maintaining my style but adding to its clarity.

Once I began, Roy Mersky's staff at the Tarlton Law Library at The University of Texas became my ablest associates. They know my strong dependence on their seemingly unlimited talent to find what I think I need. Barbara Bridges, the indispensable documents librarian at Tarlton, is a constant joy in her ability to find immediately whatever I ask for. Three other librarians, all of whom have moved on to higher positions (unfortunately elsewhere), were especially helpful: Mickie Voges, the law librarian at the University of Oklahoma; Eleanor DeLashmitt, associate librarian for research at the George Washington National Law Center; and Georgia Chadwick, manager of library services for Jenkens & Gilchrist in Dallas.

Four friends made major contributions. Thomas Krattenmaker of Georgetown University Law Center, my frequent collaborator and occasional coauthor, with whom I had originally hoped to write this book, was always available with helpful suggestions, and he materially improved chapter 12 by telling me succinctly what was wrong with an earlier draft. Sanford Levinson has throughout been the perfect colleague in every sense of the word. And David Anderson, who shares with me the teaching of mass communications at the law school, likewise offered helpful comments and support throughout my writing. Finally, Robert Post of the University of California Law School gave me encouragement and a needed organizational suggestion at a time when I was at a particularly low point. Without his intervention this book might not have been written.

Serious scholarship is made so much easier by a supportive environment. Together, deans and colleagues combine to create just such an environment. My deans, John Sutton and Mark Yudof, saw that summer research grants from our Law School Foundation were always forthcoming. My colleagues offered comments and assistance. Finally, my secretaries, Karen Sacratini Buslett and Betty Tanenbaum, consistently kept the preparation of my manuscript up-to-date.

I thank them all.

Introduction

The ancestors of the modern press are men whose names are inseparable from the freedom and fierce independence of the press: John Peter Zenger, Thomas Paine, Elijah Lovejoy. We automatically associate them with the tradition, enshrined in the First Amendment, that the press may not be licensed. In the ringing words of Justice Black's last opinion,

> the press [is] to serve the governed, not the governors. The Government's power to censor the press was abolished so that the press would remain forever free to censure the Government. The press was protected so that it could bare the secrets of government and inform the people. Only a free and unrestrained press can effectively expose deception in government. And paramount among the responsibilities of a free press is the duty to prevent any part of the government from deceiving the people and sending them off to distant lands to die of foreign fevers and foreign shot and shell.[1]

Thus rather than condemning (as did Chief Justice Burger and Justice Blackmun) the *New York Times,* the *Washington Post,* and other papers that published the Pentagon Papers, Justice Black praised them as "nobly" doing "precisely that which the Founders hoped and trusted they would do."[2]

It was no accident that Justice Black was praising newspapers and not broadcasters. Every network was offered the Pentagon Papers, and each turned down the opportunity to air them.[3] That was no accident either. Just a few years earlier Harry Kalven had suggested that what broadcasting needed was its own Zenger case.[4] But the corporate con-

1

glomerates had no desire to enshrine their names and logos in the Zenger pantheon.

Nor has broadcasting produced any John Miltons. The intellectual underpinnings for a free press begin with Milton's plea in *Areopagitica:*

> Give me the liberty to know, to utter, and to argue freely according to conscience, above all liberties. . . .
>
> And though all the winds of doctrine were let loose to play upon the earth, so Truth be in the field, we do injuriously, by licensing and prohibiting to misdoubt her strength. Let her and Falsehood grapple; whoever knew Truth put to the worse in a free and open encounter?[5]

Milton was demanding an end to licensing of the press. He wanted all authors to have the right to put forward their ideas without first having to clear them with a government licensor. Milton's notion of a free press became English law a half century later, and by the time of the framing of the First Amendment it was so widely accepted that all agreed that, at a minimum, the First Amendment prohibited licensing of the press.[6]

Seven years after the publication of *Areopagitica,* Milton was one of Cromwell's licensors of newsbooks. It is thus tempting to conclude that his protestations concerning freedom of the press were directed more toward his desire to print a pamphlet about his divorce than toward any generalized view of the merits of freedom. But the temptation should be resisted, however neatly it fits with our post-Freudian views of individual behavior. More likely, Milton did not find the licensing of newsbooks inconsistent with freedom of the press. Newsbooks were, at the time, a relatively young phenomenon, initially introduced only thirty years before to provide information about the Thirty Years War and to encourage English support for the Protestant side. As the country prepared for civil war in the early 1640s, the need for information on the activities of Parliament increased the importance of the newsbooks. But Milton could easily distinguish newsbook authors from thoughtful, serious people who gave, as he himself did, time and care to their work. In making such a distinction, Milton accorded freedom of the press to serious authors, even though they might hold differing opinions, but not to lesser persons writing hastily about current events. He would not be the last to uphold freedom of the press while excluding, perhaps thoughtlessly, a large group of claimants to that freedom.[7]

Three hundred years later, another new member of the press was excluded from the tradition of free expression because it looked different and frivolous. The new medium was radio broadcasting, and its exclusion from the tradition has given the United States well over a half century of a regulated First Amendment. This book is about the American experiment with a licensed press.

The English experiment with licensing ended in the late seventeenth century with the conclusion that it had not worked.[8] Decisions had been inconsistent and overly political. Such has not been the generally accepted view of American licensing, with the exception of the aberrant Nixon administration. The Communications Act created safeguards that were designed to prevent abuses. First, the licensors were members of the Federal Communications Commission, who would, as an overall group, be nonpartisan; with the exception of the chairman, the remaining commissioners were to be balanced so that neither political party had a majority. Second, the Commission would be forbidden to censor. Section 29 (now §326) of the Act reads: "Nothing in this Act shall be understood or construed to give the Commission the power of censorship over the radio communications or signals transmitted by any radio station, and no regulation or condition shall be promulgated or fixed by the Commission which shall interfere with the right of free

speech by means of radio communication." Although broadcasting was not considered part of the press, Congress saw
the potential for censorship on the part of the Commission
and wanted none of that on American soil. Finally, to ensure that the safeguards would in fact work, all important
decisions of the Commission were appealable to the ultimate guardians of American liberty: the federal courts, including, with the assent of the Supreme Court, final review
at the highest court in our land.

This is a book about the First Amendment and broadcasting. It evaluates the safeguards imposed by the Communications Act over almost sixty years of regulation. It is not a
complete history of broadcasting, and many important aspects of broadcasting will be neglected. For example, I will
not discuss the effects of commercialism on programming
quality, the issues of network dominance of our broadcasting landscape, or whether and how the Commission has
been captured by the industry it was designed to regulate.
Nor is this a book extolling the successes of American broadcasting, although to be sure there have been many. All of the
above topics have been treated, and treated well, in available
literature.

This book is written against the background of two seminal law review articles that have dominated the debate on
regulation of the mass media for the past two decades. The
first, Jerome Barron's "Access to the Media—A New First
Amendment Right,"[9] published in 1967, argued that newspapers and broadcasting had become indistinguishable and
that we should apply the broadcast model of regulation to
newspapers. The broadcast model would provide a means
of countering the growing concentration of ownership of
the press and enable underrepresented or ignored voices to
be heard. Barron's thesis was highly controversial because it
required taking away a right—editorial control over what
goes into a newspaper—that had long been associated with

freedom of the press. Thus, although Barron was able to set the agenda for debate, many scholars avoided his embrace. Then in 1974 the Supreme Court mooted the debate by concluding, in *Miami Herald v. Tornillo*,[10] that newspapers were constitutionally free to print whatever they desired.

Two years later, in 1976, Lee Bollinger's "Freedom of the Press and Public Access" appeared.[11] Like Barron, Bollinger rejected the prevailing wisdom that there was a relevant constitutional distinction between print and broadcasting. But Bollinger went one step further, to the provocative thesis that "the very similarity of the two major branches of the mass media provides a rationale for treating them differently."[12] The separation of broadcasting from print provides the nation with "the best of two worlds": "access in a highly concentrated press and minimal government intervention."[13] Access and balance are important goals, but governmental regulation always brings with it the risks of censorship, either private or public. The fact that print is unrestrained, however, provides a check on those risks: information not disseminated by broadcasters will be available in newspapers, and the very existence of an unregulated press will provide a competitive spur to offset any tendency of broadcasters to be excessively timid.[14]

Bollinger's article explained that there was no reason to be uneasy about the print-broadcast duality created by *Tornillo*—indeed, the duality was a good thing. This ingenious solution allowed Bollinger to avoid the issue on which Barron had floundered both in the legal academy and ultimately at the Supreme Court: Bollinger's thesis required no changes in the legal status quo. It was the right idea at the right time, and it swept the legal academy, being immediately and impressively embraced in Laurence Tribe's treatise *American Constitutional Law* and becoming the standard citation in any discussion of the topic.[15]

Bollinger's subtitle, "Toward a Theory of Partial Regulation of the Mass Media," recognized that his thesis was, after all, a theory. The theory asserted that we have the best of two worlds, that an unregulated print medium serves to minimize any adverse consequences of the regulation of broadcasting. Part of the theory's power was that it fit so well within the prevailing view that American broadcasting had escaped the traditional evils associated with licensing. This fit within the prevailing view illustrates an often overlooked facet of the theory: it is contingently based on facts.[16] Neither at the time Bollinger wrote nor subsequently has anyone explored the question of abuses in broadcasting regulation. This book is designed to fill that void.

The existing literature about broadcasting contains no serious analysis of our deviation from the First Amendment tradition—just what happens when a society licenses its press? This book suggests that licensing has had precisely the effects that might have been postulated by a student of the English experience: the privilege to broadcast has been granted to friends of the government and withheld from its foes; efforts at censorship have been employed to back the political agenda of the party in power; and abuses have occurred with unfortunate frequency. It is thus my conclusion that the prevailing academic view, which holds to the Bollinger thesis, is wrong. Although print remains unregulated, the regulation of broadcasting has not brought us the best of two worlds.

This is not to say that on all issues through all presidencies the power of licensing and supervision has been abused, because it has not. I argue, rather, that abuses in the licensing scheme have existed almost since the beginning and are not aberrational. Consistent with the English experience, abuses of licensing are an inevitable by-product of the decision to license and to supervise the licensees. It is naive to assume that the safeguards presumed to be built into the system or some uniqueness in the American character could spare us from the political abuses of licensing a part of the press.

The book is divided into four parts. Part I, The Setting, demonstrates that broadcasting has been treated differently from the print media since the beginning and explores the various reasons that have been offered for that distinction. Part II, Licensing, discusses why licensing was placed under the Communications Act and how the decisions to award licenses to various applicants have been made; it concludes with a discussion of whether there has ever existed a credible threat that, once licensed, broadcasters could lose their privileges. Part III, Supervision, looks at politics and morality in FCC decisions concerning what the American people may and may not hear and see. Finally, Part IV, The Present and the Future, explores current theories on the differential treatment of broadcasting and other media and then turns to the significant problem of the future: the licensing and potential censorship of cable television and the other new technologies.

I
THE SETTING

OVERVIEW

To understand the legal status of broadcasting it is necessary to understand the assumption made at the very beginning of discussion about this issue: that broadcasting is not entitled to the full range of First Amendment privileges enjoyed by the print media. This point was made early on and with crystal clarity. In 1932, just as the Supreme Court was launching its era of protecting the First Amendment claims of both individuals and the press, the U.S. Court of Appeals for the District of Columbia Circuit upheld the removal of the Reverend Robert Shuler's broadcast privilege because of his attacks on Los Angeles public officials, in which he alleged corruption and dereliction of duty. This ruling came but a year after the Supreme Court's decision, in *Near v. Minnesota,* that the government could not legally threaten to close down a newspaper simply because of the newspaper's persistent allegations of official corruption. The striking contrast between these virtually identical cases is detailed in chapter 1.

Once the fact of the difference between broadcasting and the print media is established, it becomes necessary to explore the source and rationale of the distinctive treatment accorded broadcasting. Chapter 2 opens with a story epitomizing the differences, that of the famous Dr. Brinkley, the "goat gland doctor" from Milford, Kansas, and his KFKB, in the late 1920s the most popular radio station in the United

States. It is hard to think of Brinkley's popular radio quackery as a respectable relative of the print medium: whereas newspapers and magazines were attempting serious discussion of the news, the medicine men and entertainers of radio, by contrast, were aiming to alleviate the boredom of the public and exploit its naïveté. Congress and the Federal Radio Commission mirrored the views of thoughtful Americans in recognizing the profound difference between the two media, a perception buttressed by a 1915 Supreme Court decision stating out-of-hand that motion pictures, including newsreels, were not part of the press. At the beginning of the broadcast era, just making the distinction was sufficient analysis.

With time, however, simply "knowing" there was a difference proved inadequate. More than simple assertion was necessary to sustain the point. Two major Supreme Court cases, *NBC v. United States* in 1943 and then *Red Lion Broadcasting v. FCC* in 1969, set forth the modern theory of differences between the two media. Furthermore, *Red Lion,* as the Supreme Court's leading decision detailing the constitutional status of broadcasting, went on to articulate a "new" First Amendment, one befitting this "new" method of communication. The rationale and explanation of the "new" First Amendment take us through chapter 3 and establish unequivocally that the protections extended to the print medium would not be fully available for broadcasters. The remainder of the book will look at the consequences of that decision.

1

A DIFFERENT MEDIUM

"Back in the Tennessee Mountains, where I come from, they would not allow city doctors to strip young girls seeking restaurant employment."[1] The Reverend Bob Shuler made that observation blasting the Los Angeles Board of Public Health. It was but one example of the style that earned him his nickname "Fighting Bob"—a "scrapper for God," as he summed up his career in a farewell sermon to his Trinity Methodist Congregation in 1953.[2]

Shuler was a rigid moralist with an intense dislike for vice, especially prostitution and alcohol, the twin evils of the era of Prohibition. During an early ministry in Austin, Texas, he energetically worked to dry up Texas counties but also concluded that political and civic corruption were important targets for his wrath. And he had plenty of that; he was one of those men who cannot sit quietly by when something around him meets with his disapproval. A transfer to a debt-ridden church in Los Angeles in 1920 gave him a virtually unlimited array of targets, for, like many other American cities during Prohibition, Los Angeles was mired in corruption.

In 1926 a wealthy widow from Berkeley, impressed after hearing some of Shuler's indignant sermons, gave him $25,000 to purchase a better forum. KGEF, a one-kilowatt station broadcasting twenty-three and one-quarter hours a week on a shared frequency, was born. The license was granted in the name of Shuler's Trinity Methodist Church, and Shuler's sermons were broadcast each Sunday. Shuler took two additional hours of airtime for himself, one on Tuesday and one on Thursday evening, for the "Bob Shuler Question Hour" and "Bob Shuler's Civic Talk." It was during these two hours that Shuler waged war on local corruption. In so doing, he built a vast audience for his small station, which within a few years was rated the fourth most popular in the market. Commercial stations were unable to sell time opposite Shuler's two evening programs. A recent study states that he had an audience of six hundred thousand listening to him lash out at an imperfect world.[3]

Shuler's application for renewal of KGEF's license in September 1930 stated that KGEF had "thrown the pitiless spotlight of publicity on corrupt public officials, and on agencies of immorality, thereby gladly gaining their enmity and open threats to bring pressure to bear to 'get' this station's license." He was right. The Federal Radio Commission decided to hold a hearing on the renewal. The chief hearing examiner was sent to Los Angeles and presided over a sixteen-day hearing where for the first time in the Commission's short three-year history an outside party was allowed to handle the opposition to a licensee. Indeed, the opposition's counsel was a former city prosecutor whom Shuler had driven from office.[4]

The hearing procedure placed Shuler on the defensive. He was confronted with a thousand typewritten pages of his on-the-air statements taken down in shorthand or by mechanical devices over a three-year period. The hearing thus provided a replay of Shuler's charges: the mayor let a gangster run the city and once had the course of a boulevard changed so that it would run past the gangster's property; the chief of police protected the underworld by allowing commercialized vice to flourish even when informed of where the illegal activities were occurring; the police framed the head of the Morals Efficiency Association and killed a woman to cover the frame-up; the district attorney and his chief deputy took bribes; the bar association wanted to elect judges who would go easy on vice. Also included were attacks on the Catholic religion, some disparaging remarks about Jews, and finally, an incident in which Shuler allegedly stated that if a prominent (unnamed) figure did not give him one hundred dollars, "I will go on the air next Tuesday night and tell what I know about him." Interestingly, in many cases Shuler's side of the story was compelling. The chief of police had resigned, and the mayor had chosen not to run for reelection. Shuler's story of the murder cover-up was corroborated and uncontradicted. The hundred-dollar story (which allegedly brought forth several contributions), according to Shuler, was a humorous reference to a member of the Trinity congregation whose name he had mentioned minutes earlier in the context of a fund drive at the church. The member in question corroborated Shuler.[5]

Two convictions for contempt of court—for critically commenting during his radio programs on pending court cases—could not be explained away as easily, although today the convictions would be instantly overturned as based on perfectly legitimate exercises of the right to criticize governing agencies, even courts.

The chief hearing examiner ruled in favor of renewing KGEF's license, but the opponents appealed to the full Commission, where their challenge was sustained. KGEF was ordered off the air, effective immediately. The principal thrust of the FRC decision against Shuler was that he used his station as a forum for outrageous and unfounded attacks on public officials. This view comes out clearly in the

Commission statement prepared for the judicial appeal to the D.C. Circuit:

> [Shuler] has repeatedly made attacks upon public officials and courts which have not only been bitter and personal in their nature, but often times based upon ignorance of fact for which little effort has been made to ascertain the truth thereof. . . .
>
> [Shuler] has vigorously attacked by name all organizations, political parties, public officials, and individuals whom he has conceived to be moral enemies of society or foes of the proper enforcement of the law. He has believed it his duty to denounce by name any enterprise, organization, or individual he personally thinks is dishonest or untrustworthy. Shuler testified that it was his purpose "to try and make it hard for the bad man to do wrong in the community."[6]

The Commission's overall conclusion was that Shuler's broadcasts "were sensational rather than instructive."[7]

The Commission attempted to capitalize on the *Shuler* case by convincing the courts to sustain its power to regulate broadcasting on the widest possible grounds. It had refused to renew Shuler's license because it disapproved strongly of his attacks on public officials. There could be no way around the issue, and the Commission intended a frontal victory.

It put forward a two-pronged argument. First, broadcast speech was not "speech" within the meaning of the First Amendment—that is, nothing said over the air was entitled to any First Amendment protection. Second, Commission scrutiny of programming to determine if it was in the public interest did not constitute censorship within the meaning of the no-censorship provision of the Radio Act, section 29; accordingly, a Commission determination that a licensee's programming did not serve the public interest would justify termination of the right to broadcast. The Commission won the second argument, but no decision was made on the first, as the D.C. Circuit never reached the issue.

The beginning of the court's opinion is somewhat ambiguous, possibly because of indecision about how to deal with the Commission's argument that the First Amendment has no place in broadcasting. The opinion stated that it would not "stop to review the cases construing the depth and breadth" of freedom of speech. This was partly because it was clear that the "constitutional guarantee should be given liberal and comprehensive construction," but it is no doubt also relevant that the court concluded that Shuler's case had nothing to do with freedom of speech.

Here the court turned to the Commission's arguments. Knocking a station off the air was "merely the application of the regulatory power of Congress in a field within the scope of its legislative authority." The First Amendment does not bar the government from refusing to renew a "license to one who has abused it" by broadcasting "defamatory and untrue matter." From the court's perspective, it was clear that the Commission had the duty to scrutinize a licensee's past programming in order to ascertain whether future programming was likely to be in the public interest. Yet that scrutiny could be focused exclusively on offending programming, with no attention given to overall programming. There was no indication that either the Commission or the court cared what went out over KGEF during the 86 percent of airtime that Shuler did not have the mike. If there was offending programming, good programming simply could not balance the injury.[8]

Once the court concluded that the Commission had the duty to refuse to renew a license to a station that so exceeded the bounds of propriety, treatment of Shuler's argument that taking away the license violated the no-censorship provision of the Radio Act was perfunctory. The court felt this argument bordered on the frivolous and concluded that the facts "abundantly" sustained the Commission's conclusion that Shuler's programming was not in the public interest. It would be horrible if this "great [new] science" of broadcasting were used in the way Shuler used his station. Fortunately, no censorship had been involved:

> [Shuler] may continue to indulge his strictures upon the characters of men in public office. He may just as freely as ever criticize religious practices of which he does not approve . . . but he may not, we think, demand, of right, the continued use of an instrumentality of commerce for such purposes, or any other, except in subordination to all reasonable rules and regulations Congress, acting through the Commission, may prescribe.[9]

Both the court and the Commission had concluded that Shuler's broadcasts exceeded all bounds of propriety. He concentrated on the wrong material and expressed his views in a defamatory way; public officials ought not to have their reputations sullied so easily. It evidently did not occur to the court or the Commission that "Fighting Bob" was basically correct. Although intemperate and all too willing to provide a wide audience with unfounded rumors of wrongdoing, Shuler was hardly off target. There was ample corruption in Los Angeles, and Shuler was highlighting it; not surprisingly, those earning their livings off the corruption were hardly pleased by his broadcasts. By their success within the legal system, those very people were able to silence an important voice demanding reform.

Shuler requested that the Supreme Court review his case and return his license. The Court refused, as always without opinion.[10] This was not because the Supreme Court had concluded that critics of local corruption using defamatory and heightened rhetoric could be silenced. Far from it. Just before Shuler lost in the D.C. Circuit Jay Near was winning a major victory in the Supreme Court.[11]

Near was the publisher of the *Saturday Press,* a Minneapolis weekly. Because of his scurrilous articles attacking local corruption, he had been the first test of Minnesota's

Gag Law of 1924.[12] In 1927 the *Saturday Press* had printed a series of articles charging "in substance that a Jewish gangster was in control of gambling, bootlegging and racketeering in Minneapolis, and that law enforcing officers and agencies were not energetically performing their duties."[13] The paper was charged and convicted under the Gag Law as a "malicious, scandalous, and defamatory" publication.[14] Under the statute, such publications were public nuisances, and their abatement by means of local suits was the hoped-for outcome of the law. On conviction, the paper was perpetually enjoined from issuing any publication whatsoever that was a malicious, scandalous, or defamatory newspaper, as defined by law. In *Near v. Minnesota,* however, the Supreme Court reversed that conviction, in the first major Supreme Court case wherein a First Amendment claim prevailed.

The Court's essential point in *Near* seems obvious today: Minnesota was engaging in censorship. But this fact was not as obvious in 1931—and therein lies the significance of *Near*. The Court's analysis begins by separating the statute in *Near* from more usual statutes. It was not a defamation law, because remedies for libel were available and unaffected by the Gag Law's passage. Nor was it a law to protect private citizens from the press, as the facts involved charging public officials with neglect of their duties. Nor was the statute concerned with false charges, because truth was not a defense unless the publisher could also show that the material was published with good motives and for justifiable ends.

Once it was clear what the statute wasn't, it was also pretty clear what it was. The Minnesota Supreme Court had pointed out that it was not a criminal libel statute, because such statutes do not result in "efficient repression or suppression of the evils of scandal"[15]—something the Gag Law did. The law was in fact an efficient suppression scheme in which, after the initial court order, subsequent enforcement was by contempt—that is, tried only to a judge without a jury, and in all probability to the judge who issued the permanent injunction in the first place. It is the subsequent enforcement that constitutes the "effective censorship."[16] Should the publishers resume publication they would run the risk that any article published might run afoul of the terms of the injunction, which was written in the terms of the statutory language. And those terms were nowhere defined: not in the statute, not in the injunction.

The Supreme Court, through Chief Justice Hughes, determined that the Minnesota statute was analogous to the infamous prior licensing, that is, requiring a publisher to seek permission of a censor prior to publication. From the Court's perspective, if Near had the right to publish the first attacks on the officials without censorship, it followed that, because he had exercised the right to publish in the first place, he did not lose the right to publish subsequently. Furthermore, if a prior restraint were proper, it could have been exercised before Near published any of his attacks. However, the Constitution forbids prior restraints except in the most limited circumstances (such as publishing the sailing dates of troop ships, the court suggested).[17] Finally, although attacks on public officials who are attempting to faithfully discharge their duties are unfortunate and deserve the severest condemnation by public opinion, the Court found that

> the administration of government has become more complex, the opportunities for malfeasance and corruption have multiplied, crime has grown to most serious proportions, and the danger of its protection by unfaithful officials and of the impairment of the fundamental security of life and property by criminal alliances and official neglect, emphasize the primary need of a vigilant and courageous press, especially in great cities.[18]

That liberty of the press might be abused could not make less necessary the press's immunity from censorship when it was dealing with allegations of official misconduct. As Vincent Blasi would note fifty years later, the emphasis is on the fact that the Gag Law, as applied, suppressed criticism of public officials, and Chief Justice Hughes rightly sounded the theme that the government must not attempt to censor charges of misconduct and malfeasances of those charged with governing.[19]

It is difficult to ignore the similarities between what happened to Near and what happened to Shuler. Near was enjoined, Shuler stripped of his station—and thereby forbidden to continue. Each attacked public officials for dereliction of duty and so was perceived locally as a scandal-monger. Neither was sued for libel by the affected officials. Near was enjoined because his articles were supposedly "malicious, scandalous, and defamatory"; Shuler's license was not renewed because his broadcasts were "sensational rather than instructive." Near could not publish without fear of a judge's constant oversight; Shuler could not broadcast—period. And, although no court knew it then—or likely would have believed it—both Near and Shuler made charges that carried more than a little truth to them. They were shrill, undisciplined, alone, but they both screamed corruption and demanded that responsible officials act.

In the case of Jay Near, the Supreme Court knew that censorship of criticism of government officials was at stake. Not so for Bob Shuler. *Near*, decided a year earlier, was seen as having no relevance to Shuler when the D.C. Circuit decided the case, and when Shuler requested that the Supreme Court review his case, the Court declined. Although there may be many reasons for the Supreme Court to decide not to review a case, the principal one is that the case was rightly decided by the lower court. It is impossible to say for sure, but the overwhelming likelihood is that the Supreme Court left Shuler alone for precisely that reason: the court of appeals had gotten it right. How that could be so is the subject of the next chapter.

2

DR. BRINKLEY AND
THE PEEP SHOW IMAGE

The short answer to why Near and Shuler received differ-ent treatment is found in the Federal Radio Commission's major argument to the D.C. Circuit: broadcasting was not included under the First Amendment. Americans simply perceived broadcasting to be different from publishing a newspaper.

Unlike the positions argued on many agency trips to a re-viewing court, the Commission's legal argument had not been created on the spot to fit the facts of a questionable case. Almost from the inception of the FRC, once it began the tough task of deciding who should broadcast and who should not, the Commission determined that it must look at the programming on the air. And "look at" meant evaluate critically. If Fighting Bob Shuler had praised the mayor of Los Angeles and the chief of police and had urged his lis-teners to back these officials fully, he would have continued as the licensee of KGEF. The Commission had already pointed this way when it stripped two Chicago stations of their licenses to share a frequency, giving the frequency in-stead to a Gary, Indiana, station (as part of an effort to move stations to states with fewer radio operations) and in the process noting the Gary station's service to the immigrant community, with programs that were "musical, educational and instructive in their nature and [that stressed] loyalty to the community and the Nation." Its facilities were offered free to the "local police department and to all fraternal, charitable and religious organizations" in the area.[1]

Of course, Shuler's criticisms and the Main Street boosterism that characterized the Chicago-Gary move were not at all alike. The Commission members had no trouble reaching a decision in either case, however: since the First Amendment had nothing to do with their actions, they could not violate it. As the Commission expressed it in its Second Annual Report in 1928, "The Commission is unable to see that the guarantee of freedom of speech has anything to do with entertainment programs as such."[2] That conclusion was not startling in the slightest. Few, if any, Americans would have disagreed. Just as adults today would hotly and easily deny that a child is having a First Amendment experience playing Pac-Man, so the adults of 1928 knew that radio was not included under the First Amendment. The perception of radio as a thing apart could be justified and illustrated in a number of ways, but the famous "goat gland doctor" of Milford, Kansas, John R. Brinkley, probably illustrates the point better than anyone.

Although Milford was but a tiny hamlet west of the present-day Fort Riley, connected by a dirt road to Junction City, its radio station KFKB was one of the most powerful in the United States, blanketing the area between the Rockies and the Mississippi, but extending far beyond. It was also one of the most popular stations in the nation, as illustrated by its having won *Radio Digest's* nationwide listeners' poll in 1929 by a four-to-one margin over the runner-up.[3] This overwhelming popularity was due to the fine combination of fundamentalist theology and medical information provided by Brinkley, a small, dapper, bespectacled doctor who sported a Vandyke and diamonds. When Dr. Brinkley, the licensee, would intone into the microphone, "Greetings to

my friends in Kansas and everywhere," radio's most successful medicine man was about to increase his revenues.[4]

Brinkley, the doctor, and KFKB, the station, were inseparable, from their successes to their defeats. Brinkley had
settled in Milford before the end of World War I to practice
medicine in one of the eight states that would recognize his
degree from Eclectic Medical University of Kansas City.[5]
Within a year after his arrival he had performed the first of
the hundreds of operations that soon earned him his nickname, the "goat doctor." To pep up the declining male sex
life, Brinkley would implant the gonads of a young Ozark
goat in the patient's scrotum. In the early days the patient
would supply his own goat, but as time passed and "successes" accumulated, the Milford operations took on a
higher price—$750—and a more professional air.[6] Thus,
just as a good seafood restaurant will have a lobster tank
from which customers can choose their dinners, so in Milford the patient could pick, from among many, his donor
goat.

By 1928 Brinkley's hospital was grossing $150,000, and
Milford had electricity and a promise of pavement to Junction City.[7] KFKB's popularity ensured its prosperity as well.
This prosperity had been assisted in part by a change in emphasis. Whereas the number of likely recipients of goat
glands is limited, enlargement of the prostate could potentially affect any man over forty. That was an audience more
of Brinkley's dimension, and his medical business focused
increasingly on the prostate. Not content to rely on a single
medium for communication, Brinkley flooded the mails
with circulars addressed to "the prostate man."[8] Like his
smooth radio presentations, these pamphlets were designed
to convince the recipient that he had a problem and that,
fortunately, Brinkley was in a position to solve it. "It certainly behooves a man who has an enlarged prostate to con-

sider it, and we are indeed glad to hear from such men for we are convinced we can render him a real, genuine and lasting service."[9] A superb detail man, Brinkley also provided easy directions on how to get to Milford.

KFKB was a happy adjunct to Brinkley's promotion. A typical day would find Brinkley on the air twice (after lunch and after dinner) to speak on medical problems. The evening discussion was a gland lecture, explaining the male change of life. "Our bodies are not holding up as well as those of our forefathers did. . . . Enlargement of the prostate is on the increase"[10]—a situation that he could correct.

Brinkley's other program was his "Medical Question Box," a program that grew out of the ever-increasing daily mail. Usually he would pick up some letters on his way to the mike, leaf through them, and make an instant diagnosis.[11] On the air he would read the listener's symptoms, quickly give the diagnosis, and then prescribe the medicine required.

> Here's one from Tillie. She says she had an operation, had some trouble ten years ago. I think the operation was unnecessary, and it isn't very good sense to have an ovary removed with the expectation of motherhood resulting therefrom. My advice to you is to use Women's Tonic numbers 50, 67, and 61. This combination will do for you what you desire if any combination will, after three months' persistent use.

Or

> Now here is a letter from a dear mother—a dear little mother who holds to her breast a babe of nine months. She should take number 2 and number 16 and—yes—number 17 and she will be helped. Brinkley's 2, 16, and 17. If her druggist hasn't got them, she should write and order them from the Milford Drug Company, Milford, Kansas, and they will be sent to you, Mother, collect. May the Lord guard and protect you, Mother. The postage will be prepaid.[12]

As the use of numbers rather than names on the "Medical Question Box" illustrates, Brinkley had expanded into the pharmacy business. Indeed, he had even organized a National Dr. Brinkley Pharmaceutical Association, which would fill listeners' "prescriptions." The numbers also usefully concealed the common agents, such as aspirin and castor oil, that he would prescribe. At a dollar a sale kickback to Brinkley, this adjunct brought in hundreds of thousands of dollars. No small thinking here.[13]

But no small enemies, either. Between his constant attacks on doctors, his unorthodox practice, and his financial successes, he had managed to curry the wrath of organized medicine. In 1930 he faced a two-pronged attack on his operations: in Topeka, the Kansas Board of Medical Examiners put at issue his right to practice; and in Washington, D.C., the Federal Radio Commission challenged his right to broadcast. On Friday, June 13, 1930, he effectively lost both battles.[14] The Kansas Supreme Court turned away his efforts to enjoin the medical board proceeding, and the FRC, finding the operation of KFKB a "mere" adjunct to his medical practice and hospital and insufficiently attuned to the needs of Kansas—making wheat grow, not prostates shrink—refused to renew his license.[15] His enemies had found allies. Goat gland recipients may have been too embarrassed to talk, but not so disgruntled prostate patients and pharmaceutical customers.

Still, Brinkley was not without supporters and resources. In a stunning effort begun in late September after the ballot was printed, Brinkley ran as a write-in candidate for governor of Kansas—and may even have "won." Unfortunately, he lacked poll watchers, and somewhere between ten thousand and fifty thousand of his votes were thrown out. In the middle of those figures was the margin of defeat. (He also polled twenty thousand write-ins in the Oklahoma election.)[16]

Brinkley was down but not out. He acquired a Mexican border station with even more power than KFKB and began phoning his broadcasts across the Rio Grande. With so many loyal followers, it was just like the old days. Eventually he moved his operations to Del Rio, Texas, just across the border from his powerful station XER.[17] But Texas provided only a temporary respite from his adversaries. In 1938 he lost a libel suit against a prominent AMA doctor on his new home ground, which disillusioned him about Del Rio, leading him to make an ill-conceived move to Little Rock, where huge claims by Uncle Sam for back taxes awaited him.[18] An unhappy bankruptcy would have been the end result but for a timely move back to Del Rio, where the liberal exemptions under Texas law could be put to good use as he saved his diamonds from creditors.

Events were taking their toll, however. In 1941, after years of effort, the U.S. government finally succeeded in silencing the flamboyant pioneer when Mexico agreed to knock him off the air. A few days later he suffered a heart attack, and within a year, at the age of fifty-six, he was dead.[19]

The demise of KFKB, however popular the station was with the American listening public, was entirely predictable once the Commission turned its attention to the perceived value of the programming offered. Furthermore, Dr. Brinkley could not be taken as a part of the press tradition no matter how hard one argued. And it was not just Brinkley: no one using radio was a part of that tradition—a fact Shuler would soon learn.

Yet the Commission was not on a frolic. The idea being expressed—that radio was an entertainment medium and that since entertainment was not entitled to First Amendment protection neither was radio—could be traced directly to a U.S. Supreme Court decision of a little more than a decade earlier. The Supreme Court's syllogism, although referring to a different medium, was effectively indistinguishable: entertainment is not part of the First Amendment; motion pictures are entertainment; therefore, motion pictures are not entitled to First Amendment protection.

In 1915, Mutual Film Corporation came to the Court in a trio of cases involving two state censorship commissions for motion pictures.[20] Mutual was a major film distributor, its output including a weekly news film, "Mutual Weekly," and the censorship commissions would at a minimum impose uncertainty, delays, and costs on Mutual's business. The cases, which were diversity-of-citizenship actions in federal court,[21] raised a number of challenges to the censorship commissions. The most significant of these challenges was that the statutes involved infringed the liberty of speech, opinion, and the press guaranteed by both the applicable state constitutions and the federal Constitution. The Supreme Court did not choke on the word "censorship"; it used it unhesitatingly. And it found nothing wrong with censorship of motion pictures.

In the lead case, from Ohio, the Court ignored Mutual's reliance on the federal Constitution (probably from legitimate doubt whether it was applicable to a state statute restricting freedom of speech)[22] and concentrated instead on the applicable provision of the Ohio constitution guaranteeing freedom of speech and press. The Court began with what for the era was an unusual acknowledgment that freedom of speech was an important value:

> We need not pause to dilate upon the freedom of opinion and its expression, and whether by speech, writing or printing. They are too certain to need discussion—of such conceded value as to need no supporting praise. Nor can there be any doubt of their breadth nor that their underlying safeguard is, to use the words of another, "that opinion is free and that conduct alone is amendable to the law."[23]

But however great freedom of speech was, moving pictures were not included within the principle. They might be

mediums of thought, but so too were a lot of other things—
such as "shows and spectacles." And the Court was convinced the latter could claim no protection. "The first impulse of the mind is to reject the contention. We immediately feel that the argument is wrong or strained." The
initial impulse was also the final conclusion. "Judicial sense"
supports "common sense" in rejecting the conclusion that
motion pictures were part of freedom of expression. "It
cannot be put out of view that the exhibition of moving pictures is a business pure and simple, originated and conducted for profit, like other spectacles, not to be regarded,
nor intended to be regarded by the Ohio constitution, we
think, as part of the press of the country or as organs of
public opinion."[24] In the Kansas case, the result was identical. To the argument that the statute "violates the bill of
rights of the United States and of the State of Kansas," the
Court tersely responded that censorship of motion pictures
did not "abridge the liberty of opinion."[25]

Thus in the first cases involving a new technology that
claimed the protections of freedom of speech, the Court
almost summarily rejected the argument. These were not
newspapers: they were much closer to circus acts. And no
one thought making a tiger jump through a flaming hoop
had anything to do with the traditions of John Milton and
John Peter Zenger. When the problems of radio arose a
little more than a decade later, an identical conclusion was
carried over. Radio programming was entertainment and
thus no part of the exposition of ideas entitled to the protection of the First Amendment.

The point was so obvious that it really needed no discussion. When it was discussed, as Alexander Meiklejohn did
near the end of his seminal work on freedom of expression,
it was to the same effect. Meiklejohn felt it necessary to devote a concluding section of his "Reflections" chapter specifically to stating that radio had no claim to the principles of
freedom of speech to which he attached his "passionate de-

votion." Radio had "failed" in its promise to assist in our national education; it was engaged in making money, not in "enlarging and enriching human communication." Because in Meiklejohn's view the First Amendment was intended "only to make men free to say what, as citizens, they think, what they believe, about the general welfare," radio flunked the test and forfeited its claim to protection.[26]

Most often, of course, no discussion was needed to reach the same conclusions. Common sense dictated the difference between a newspaper and a radio station. Perhaps the political scientist V. O. Key, Jr., put it best: the owners of broadcast stations were the "lineal descendants of operators of music halls and peep shows."[27] Thus a First Amendment protecting John R. Brinkley would be as seriously out of whack as a First Amendment protecting the Ringling Brothers Circus or any like "spectacle." Broadcasting passed into our legal and then judicial systems without so much as a pause—from a circus, to the goat gland doctor, to Fighting Bob Shuler. Differences in speech content there may have been, but these were irrelevant. The media themselves simply were not within the system of freedom of expression. And that is why the Supreme Court saw no point in reviewing Shuler's case. That he should lose was obvious. Common sense.

3

THE SUPREME COURT SPEAKS:
NBC AND *RED LION*

The governing principle, whether overt or *sub silentio,* that radio, as an entertainment medium, was excluded from First Amendment protections could dominate only so long as both broadcasting and First Amendment doctrine remained embryonic. When broadcasting began to engage in serious debate (as distinguished from Shuler's inveighing), or when First Amendment theory was pushed to deal with issues involving serious literary works, such as *Ulysses,* an analysis more sophisticated than the "broadcasting is entertainment and not protected speech" litany became necessary to justify the separation of broadcasting from the print traditions. The new justification was introduced by the Supreme Court in 1943 in *NBC v. United States*[1] and elaborated extensively a quarter of a century later in *Red Lion Broadcasting v. FCC.*[2]

Gone was the FRC (now the Federal Communications Commission) claim that broadcasting was unworthy of First Amendment protections. In its place had sprung up a newer and more elaborate version of the same claim: broadcasting was entitled to some First Amendment protections, but its special characteristics demanded a different First Amendment, one regulated by the federal government. The difference in the form of the argument, however, could not disguise the substantive constancy. Neither the FRC nor the FCC had the slightest doubt that the traditions of the print media did not apply to broadcasters. The argument was simply recast to suit a new era.

The two Supreme Court cases advancing the new constitutional theory were tailor-made for big wins by the Commission, which was graced with perfect timing for both cases. The 1943 Court decision in *NBC* was handed down just six years after the New Deal judicial revolution, whereby all constitutional protection for big business had vanished at the hands of justices who were erstwhile architects of the New Deal. Twenty-five years later, the right-wing radio station involved in *Red Lion* got to the Supreme Court just before the Court began its period of questioning administrative agencies. Furthermore, the facts and setting of each of the cases were like manna from heaven. The Commission could not have written a better script to test and strengthen its authority—it had every litigator's dream: great facts and a disreputable opponent. Thus, although the style of argument changed from *Shuler* to the subsequent cases, the Commission's real goal did not: take the facts and construct a legal argument to give a total victory. This is exactly what the Commission did, and a pair of accommodating, enthusiastic Supreme Courts complied fully. The FCC was not merely two for two; it hit grand-slam homers each time at bat.

NBC was an outgrowth of the first FCC attempt to come to grips with the development and apparent dominance of commercial broadcasting networks. In pursuit of the goals of increased competition and fostering of localism in broadcasting, the Commission passed a number of rules (the Chain Broadcasting Rules) designed to decrease network power over local affiliates.[3] Essentially, the rules were an effort to allow the affiliates to select programming free of network constraints. The Commission believed that if left to their own choices, affiliates would produce more "good" local programming and use less of what the networks offered.

The entire broadcast establishment, with the exception of the dwarf Mutual Network (the seeming nonpublic beneficiary of the rules), prepared to battle the Commission to prevent what they feared would be the end of the American system of broadcasting.[4] CBS President and owner William Paley, who had the most at stake financially, was especially apoplectic. He predicted that the "networks will become mere catch-as-catch-can, fly-by-night sellers of programs. Performance and stability will have departed from the industry and incentive to public service will have been removed. . . . Worst of all, the first paralyzing blow will have been struck at freedom on the air."[5] The rules would make broadcasters "impotent vassals" of the government.[6]

Their power apparently at stake, the networks mounted a full attack on the rules. Their best argument, that the Communications Act of 1934 did not give the Commission power to regulate the networks, was, strange as it may seem, technically accurate. The Communications Act carried over the Radio Act's provisions, including its most glaring regulatory deficiencies: failure to anticipate both how vital a role the networks would play and just how commercial radio was to become. Any excuse available to the Congress that adopted the Radio Act cannot be extended to the Congress that adopted the Communications Act. By 1934, the importance of both commercials and networks was clear. However, the Communications Act's sole acknowledgment of networks was section 303(i), which tersely stated that the Commission had "authority to make special regulations applicable to radio stations engaged in chain [network] broadcasting."[7] The Commission tried to build on this slight foundation by drafting each of the rules to forbid licensing any station affiliated with a network that did any of eight specified activities the Commission found contrary to the public interest. In other words, the Commission intended to regulate the networks by threatening their affiliates. The Chain Broadcasting Rules were thus a wonderful example of form controlling substance.

Because the Commission was stretching to reach what Congress had not placed within its grasp, the networks were able to mount a strong attack. A second, and decidedly weaker, attack on the rules was that they were simply antitrust holdings without any adjudication of antitrust violations. Weakest of all was the networks' argument that the rules violated First Amendment guarantees of freedom of speech and the press; this argument was factually untenable, because the rules did not prohibit a station from airing any materials any time it wished.

The Supreme Court was unimpressed with any of the three arguments, and it wholly endorsed the Chain Broadcasting Rules in a five-to-two opinion written by Justice Frankfurter[8] and based on the lessons of history. The years prior to the Radio Act had been chaotic, and "Congress acted upon the knowledge that if the potentialities of radio were not to be wasted, regulation was essential." Although Justice Frankfurter noted that, "true enough, the Act does not explicitly say that the Commission shall have power to deal with network practices found inimical to the public interest," Congress nevertheless granted the Commission "expansive powers." These "expansive powers," many of which the Court named separately, seemingly placed a gloss on the public-interest standard of the Act and provided a "comprehensive mandate" to, in the language of section 303(g), "encourage the larger and more effective use of radio." The Chain Broadcasting Rules, having the potential to accomplish this, were therefore not beyond the scope of the Commission's powers.[9]

The networks' principal argument was thus dispersed in the space of six pages in the *U. S. Reports*. In the end, it appears that the Commission's victory was based simply on the absence of specific statutory prohibitions on its actions. Indeed, the Court referred to the generalities of the Communications Act with some of the reverence it usually reserved for the Constitution's vague provisions. Congress, it was said, did not wish to "frustrate the purposes" for which regulation was created; it did not "stereotype the powers of the Commission to specific details in regulating a field of enterprise the dominant characteristic of which was the rapid pace of its unfolding."[10] A more complete victory on the point is hard to imagine.

With the strongest argument out of the way, the rest was easy. The networks' antitrust argument was a combination of two strands: first, the Commission was permitted to deny licenses only to those who had previously been found in violation of the antitrust laws; and second, the Commission was arrogating to itself the powers of the Justice Department to enforce the antitrust laws. Both lines of reasoning were disposed of by the simple—and correct—conclusion that "nothing in the provisions or history of the Act lends support to the inference that the Commission was denied the power to refuse a license to a station not operating in the 'public interest,' merely because its misconduct happened to be an unconvicted violation of the antitrust laws."[11]

In the next-to-last paragraph, the Court's opinion came "finally, to [the networks'] appeal to the First Amendment."[12] As noted, this was hardly a persuasive argument, since the Chain Broadcasting Rules allowed a station to air any programming it wished at any time it wished. In fact, the rules made it easier for a station to choose programming by making it easier for an affiliate to reject network programming when the affiliate wished to air alternatives. The networks argued nonetheless that the First Amendment forbade any governmental interference whatsoever in the choice of programming, even for the asserted purpose of fostering freedom of expression. They argued further that if network contracts with affiliates were intolerably anticompetitive, as the FCC claimed, the sole remedy was in enforcing the antitrust laws, "not in expanding the power of the licensor of instruments of free speech. Only by circumscribing the power of the licensor with the strictness required by the guarantees of the First Amendment can freedom of the press be preserved."[13]

While the networks' argument was not without strength, it simply did not fit the facts. The terse rejection of the argument follows in full.

> The regulations, even if valid in all other respects, must fall because they abridge, say the appellants, their right of free speech. If that be so, it would follow that every person whose application for a license to operate a station is denied by the Commission is thereby denied his constitutional right of free speech. Freedom of utterance is abridged to many who wish to use the limited facilities of radio. Unlike other modes of expression, radio inherently is not available to all. That is its unique characteristic, and that is why, unlike other modes of expression, it is subject to governmental regulation. Because it cannot be used by all, some who wish to use it must be denied. But Congress did not authorize the Commission to choose among applicants upon the basis of their political, economic or social views, or upon any other capricious basis. If it did, or if the Commission by these Regulations proposed a choice among applicants upon some such basis, the issue before us would be wholly different. The question here is simply whether the Commission, by announcing that it will refuse licenses to persons who engage in specified network practices (a basis for choice which we hold is comprehended within the statutory criterion of "public interest"), is thereby denying such persons the constitutional right of free speech. The right of free speech does not include, however, the right to use the facilities of radio without a license. The licensing system established by Congress in the Communications Act of 1934 was a proper exercise of its

power over commerce. The standard it provided for the licensing of stations was the "public interest, convenience, or necessity." Denial of a station license on that ground, if valid under the Act, is not a denial of free speech.[14]

The dissent in the case was written by Justice Murphy, the most liberal justice, who was joined by Justice Roberts, the most conservative. It avoided the constitutional issue and relied instead on the simple, and probably accurate, point that if the Commission should have these powers, they ought to be granted by Congress, not the courts.

The dissent underscored the stunning victory: the majority had found all necessary powers in the Communications Act. Statutorily, then, the Commission had a free hand. More significant was the removal of the constitutional impediment. Because the scarcity of frequencies requires the government to allocate rights to broadcast, some mechanism of allocation was necessary. In selecting the public interest, convenience, or necessity as the mechanism, Congress did not violate the First Amendment. Thus all First Amendment rights are intact—but significantly, these rights do not include use of radio without a government license.

As long as the Commission avoided choosing applicants on the basis of their political views, it was safe. But in order to know whether the public interest is being served, the Commission must scrutinize programming, and, under the terms of *NBC*, such scrutiny is not subject to First Amendment strictures. The result was just the same as in the *Shuler* case, but this time the Supreme Court spoke frankly and wrapped up licensing and the First Amendment with a ribbon of necessity flowing directly from spectrum scarcity.

No further constitutional developments with regard to broadcasting had intervened by the time the Supreme Court returned to the constitutional issue in *Red Lion*. This case involved a blatant personal attack on liberal writer Fred

Cook by the Reverend Billy James Hargis during his "Christian Crusade," a fifteen-minute program for which Hargis purchased airtime on a small AM station, WGCB, in Red Lion, Pennsylvania. The owner of the station stubbornly refused to provide Cook with free time to rebut the attack even though Commission doctrine, subsequently codified, clearly required the station to do so.

The Supreme Court spoke unanimously, through Justice White.[15] As the Court saw it, the issue was whether Congress had the power to impose on broadcasters certain affirmative duties (such as the duties under the fairness doctrine, of which the personal-attack rules were a modest offshoot) that would require them to air programming they did not wish to air. *Red Lion* thus presented an opportunity to decide an issue that had been festering for most of the decade in circumstances unencumbered with factual nuances.

The opinion found that fairness-type obligations had been imposed on licensees since *Great Lakes Broadcasting* in 1929.[16] Broadcasters had the duty to give adequate coverage to controversial issues; moreover, such coverage must be "fair in that it accurately reflects the opposing views."[17] The duties imposed by the personal-attack rules were quite similar, differing from fairness obligations only on the inconsequential point that the licensee did not have the option of choosing the spokesman to present the other side of the issue. Although the opinion is not explicit on why it discusses the fairness doctrine rather than the newly codified personal-attack rules, the only logical purposes for this discussion were, first, to show that the FCC was not concocting a new rationale out of thin air, and second, and more interesting, to imply that a practice so historically rooted and so long unchallenged could hardly be unconstitutional.

Red Lion found the fairness doctrine to be doubly authorized. First, the Federal Radio Commission had from its inception been sufficiently authorized to act by the broad powers conferred on it to regulate in the public interest. The Court made its mandatory bow to *NBC* to demonstrate that these powers are "not niggardly but expansive."[18] In addition, when Congress in 1959 modified section 315, the equal-opportunities provision, it adopted language stating that this section provided no exception "from the obligation imposed upon them [broadcasters] under this Act to operate in the public interest and to afford reasonable opportunity for the discussion of conflicting views on issues of public importance." Administrative construction going back thirty years was thus expressly adopted by Congress. An agency can't do much better than that, and, although Justice White took several pages to say it, the conclusion that the Commission had acted within the sphere of congressionally delegated authority was obvious. This conclusion then set the stage for the real issue in *Red Lion:* broadcasting and the First Amendment.

The constitutional question was simply put and agreed on by all: does the rule that "no man may be prevented from saying or publishing what he thinks, or from refusing in his speech or other utterances to give equal weight to the views of his opponents" apply "equally to broadcasters"? This, it turned out, comprised two further questions. First, was there a relevant constitutional distinction between broadcasting and the print medium? If so, was there an applicable theory of freedom of speech that could separate broadcasting from print? The answer to both questions had remained constant over time: it was an unambiguous yes.[19]

The certainty of this answer was based on the following (and by now familiar) line of reasoning. On the one hand, broadcasting was different. Even in 1969, the Court still seemed somewhat perplexed by this newer and better means of communication. Print media, on the other hand, were well understood. Every person in the United States could, for example, simultaneously publish a book or magazine without any necessary conflict. Likewise, every single person could sit down and read something at the same moment without mutual interference. But only a tiny fraction of those having the resources can broadcast at the same time if intelligible communication is to be had.

The Court referred the reader to the pages of Justice Frankfurter's *NBC* opinion discussing the chaos prior to the Radio Act of 1927. And, playing up the notion of scarcity, it noted: "Where there are substantially more individuals who want to broadcast than there are frequencies to allocate, it is idle to posit an unabridgeable First Amendment right to broadcast comparable to the right of every individual to speak, write, or publish." The Court would return to this theme at the end of the opinion to refute the broadcasters' last point, that whatever scarcity existed in 1927 had vanished. To this claim Justice White responded, "Scarcity is not entirely a thing of the past." There was, he noted, competition between types of spectrum uses: hearings for competing applications for the same channel were still held, and even though there were gaps in spectrum utilization, existing broadcasters had acquired a dominant position "over new entrants even where new entry is technologically possible."[20]

Although the conclusion is somewhat ambiguous, the major point is clear enough: scarcity justifies content regulation. But Justice White also hints that, even if that were not the case, the broadcasters' position of entrenched power exists by virtue of government regulation; therefore, further government regulation to restrict that power is justifiable. Discovering this last point requires an exegetic reading of a very cryptic sentence, but the oblique approach is consistent with Justice White's opinion-writing habit of defeating a party's best argument frontally and then adding a throwaway point to show that they would have lost even if their major point had prevailed.

The conclusion that scarcity distinguishes broadcasting

from print answered only the first question of whether there could be different First Amendment standards. The second question—whether any available theory granted radio some First Amendment protections (say, against blatant government censorship) while denying them others—was more difficult. *NBC* had been decided during the relatively early stages of First Amendment development. *Red Lion,* decided during the last term of Earl Warren's tenure, was set against a fairly aggressive buildup of First Amendment doctrine that held that the government could prevail in only the rarest and most extraordinary circumstances.

Furthermore, looming towerlike on this horizon was *New York Times v. Sullivan,* the centerpiece of First Amendment theory that had constitutionalized the law of libel.[21] It was not difficult to picture *New York Times* as the logical culmination of refined First Amendment thought; indeed, Harry Kalven, the leading First Amendment scholar of the period, stated just that. Kalven emphasized that *New York Times* had brought the ideas of the very persuasive philosopher Alexander Meiklejohn to the forefront of First Amendment jurisprudence.[22]

Although the Court did not adopt either Meiklejohn's public speech/private speech distinction (as regards public affairs) or his absolute protection of public speech, it did implement Meiklejohn's principal notion that the state may not penalize controversial speech about public issues. Justice Brennan imaginatively combined this thesis with his own conclusions in *Speiser v. Randall*[23] about the potential "chilling effect" of mistaken factfinding on speakers' choices. (The "chilling effect," coined by Justice Goldberg but traditionally associated with Justice Brennan, stands for the proposition that the very existence of the legal rule in question will cause would-be speakers to shy away from the legitimate exercise of their First Amendment rights because they will fear the possibility of either criminal or civil liability.) This integration resulted in the conclusion that even civil jury scrutiny of news decisions regarding what to publish presents too fearsome a governmental intrusion into public debate because, unless strictly limited, such scrutiny is too likely to promote self-censorship rather than vigorous debate.

Not surprisingly, the broadcasters in *Red Lion* offered a similar theory to argue that the fairness doctrine and the personal-attack rules cast a pall over broadcast decisions. Yet although *New York Times* was but five years old and had been forcefully proclaimed by Kalven as *the* First Amendment decision, it was to have no influence on the outcome in *Red Lion*. Indeed, it was cited but a single time, in conjunction with a reference to an early dissent by Justice Holmes and in the context of an assertion that the purpose of the First Amendment is "to preserve an uninhibited marketplace of ideas in which truth will ultimately prevail."[24]

It did not follow that because *New York Times* was to be insignificant to *Red Lion*, Meiklejohn, too, must be. Meiklejohn's First Amendment demanded that rational citizen-governors consider the options fully and then "vote wise decisions."[25] With his town-meeting analogy, Meiklejohn focused not on "the words of the speakers, but the minds of the hearers." Thus, "what is essential is not that everyone shall speak, but that everything worth saying shall be said." With the focus on the listeners rather than the speakers, the state may play a moderating role to ensure that ideas essential to decision making are brought forward and redundancies limited.[26]

New York Times adopted the citizen-critic thrust of Meiklejohn; *Red Lion* adopted his town-meeting and informed-decision-making thrust. "The people as a whole retain their interest in free speech by radio and their collective right to have the medium function consistently with the ends and purposes of the First Amendment."[27] First Amendment scholars would expect at this point a reference to Justice Brandeis's famous recitation in *Whitney v. California*[28] of the myriad purposes the framers of that amendment had for the protection of freedom of speech. Instead, the Court followed with a statement which, to someone unfamiliar with Meiklejohn, would be startling: "It is the right of the viewers and listeners, not the right of the broadcasters, which is paramount."

With this positioning of the listeners' right above the broadcasters', new light is shed on the previous sentence about ends and purposes of the First Amendment. Instead of the usual First Amendment concern with governmental interference in the marketplace (or with individual liberty), the marketplace metaphor was taken in a different direction. *Red Lion* focused on what happens when the market malfunctions and some ideas are wholly or partially blocked from entry. The answer suggested was that government might selectively intervene to remove entry barriers, thereby promoting efficiency. Therefore, instead of being a negative force in the marketplace, the government had a positive role to play.[29]

The affirmative role of government seemed to be a response to the hard problem posed by the contention that "broadcasters will be irresistibly forced to self-censorship and their coverage of public issues will be eliminated or at least rendered wholly ineffective" by governmental supervision.[30] The broadcasters had mounted a strong chilling-effect argument. *New York Times* had held that the potential chilling effect of governmental regulation could render that regulation unconstitutional; it was very likely, in fact, that an attempt to impose a fairness doctrine on the print media would be unconstitutional because of its chilling effect on the decision to publish.[31] How, then, could such an effect be avoided in broadcasting? Justice White provided a direct answer: the government would be responsible for preventing any chilling effect. Should the government perceive that a licensee is too timid, the FCC would have the duty to strip the licensee of its right to broadcast. In the Court's view, the chilling effect would not exist, because the same mechanism that was thought to cause the chill would also serve to warm it up. In essence, the Court told its readers that broadcasters were a heartier breed than print journalists, an assertion that was as preposterous then as it is now. Nevertheless, the notion was essential to the new First Amendment theory offered by the Court to deal with what it believed were the new problems created by broadcasting.

The Court's conclusion that it must chuck its standard First Amendment treatment and develop an entirely new theory for broadcasting cases is a powerful testament to its belief either that standard First Amendment theory was generally inadequate or that radio was radically different from anything that had come before. Although one could argue for the former, it is more likely that the Court held the latter view. The justices deciding the case in 1969 were all raised during the era of the crystal set; many were born before the invention of the vacuum tube. For them, radio was as novel as Pac-Man was for many of us. Because radio was different, they created a new theory to comprehend its differences.

Red Lion dealt with the central problem of the First Amendment and broadcasting: how can the licensing process function consistently with the First Amendment? How can licensed media be "the press" as we understand the term? One answer, acceptable fifty years earlier, was that broadcasting wasn't the press and so would not be treated like the press. Indeed, Meiklejohn felt that answer to be good enough in the late 1940s.[32] But broadcast media had changed in the ensuing twenty years. Television journalism had greatly increased in prominence, with more and more Americans turning to it as their primary source of news.

The focus of legal disputes shifted also, from entertainment (as in *NBC*) to coverage of public issues and affairs (as in *Red Lion*). And so the easy answer from a simpler past yielded to a more sophisticated analysis, albeit one reaching many of the same conclusions.

The new analysis was based on a new set of assumptions about broadcasting. First, duties were owed to listeners, whose rights were paramount. Second, government supervision was necessary to enforce those duties. Third, government was the arbiter of a station's coverage of the issues, as to both sufficiency and balance of coverage. Fourth and finally, the licensed broadcasters were a durable lot and would be undaunted by the possibility of partisan decisions; even so active and judgmental a regulatory scheme as this one would not chill their willingness to air controversial issues.

Government licensing of broadcasting promises a lot. The remainder of this book will be directed to the question of whether government has kept the promise that Justice White believes was made. Does the faith in the Commission and government regulation expressed by the Supreme Court comport with how licensing actually works? Or have we created a system that, although it avoids the more obvious pitfalls of the English experience, nonetheless succumbs to partisanship and an occasional lashing censorship?

II
LICENSING

OVERVIEW

In Part I we saw the Supreme Court add its imprimatur to the conclusion, shared by the Congress, the Federal Communications Commission, and everyone else, that broadcasting was indeed different from print. In *NBC* the Court fully sustained government power over the industry in its infancy, and then in *Red Lion* reiterated its position vis-à-vis a mature industry. What were the consequences of excluding broadcasting from the print tradition? Foremost was the conclusion that broadcasting, unlike print, could be licensed. No one could occupy a frequency without the Commission's determination that the operation would be in "the public interest." Unlike all other resources in America, the electromagnetic spectrum was not for sale: it was too valuable. Instead, the Federal Radio Commission, and then the Federal Communications Commission, were directed to give it away, but for limited periods and on the condition that a station be operated in "the public interest"—a term left purposely undefined.

Chapter 4 tells the story of the adoption of the Radio Act of 1927 and then the Communications Act of 1934. Those statutes (the latter still in effect over fifty years later) reflect the initial and continuing decision that anyone wishing to broadcast must first come to the government to obtain permission.

Once the decision to license had been made, the obvious problem arises: who is to get a license and under what criteria? How does a regulatory agency decide what is in "the public interest"? Should licenses go only to friends of the licensors? Should they be passed around to various types of individuals to reflect the diversity of society? In the beginning there was no need for an answer (although the question concerning the propriety of partisan licensing would have been met with a resounding no), because it turned out that almost anyone willing to put up the money for a radio station could acquire a vacant AM frequency.

Newspapers had often sought to have radio stations in their communities. Following his landslide victory in 1936, however, President Roosevelt became unalterably opposed to the ownership of radio stations by newspapers. Perceiving newspaper publishers as solidly Republican allies of the hated economic royalists, FDR wished to block the creation of similarly uniform radio opposition to his administration. He thus made a major attempt to put partisan considerations into licensing, an attempt that ultimately failed.

The story of television acquisition during the golden giveaway of the 1950s provides a nice contrast to FDR's efforts to prevent opponents from obtaining broadcast licenses. Amazingly, VHF licensing in the 1950s would have brought a smile to FDR's face had he been able to watch as the Republicans, hardly sophisticated in comparison with FDR, pulled off with respect to television the partisan scheme that he had attempted with radio fifteen years earlier. Both FDR's efforts and the later developments in television are the main focus of chapter 5.

The story of licensing would not be complete without addressing the question of what happens when the license term expires. Unless the Commission rules have been flagrantly violated, renewal is typically automatic, and for a quarter of a century it appeared that stations could not lose their licenses. Indeed, Nicholas Johnson (without doubt the most interesting FCC commissioner of his era, 1966–73, and possibly of any era) all but flatly asserted that loss of a license was impossible. Yet broadcasters believed, and with good reason, that he was wrong. As the 1970s began, the Commission, with encouragement from the D.C. Circuit, had made what appeared to be a substantial shift. License renewal was no longer pro forma for those stations that strayed from the straight and narrow. Because the credibility of FCC actions ultimately turns on whether the licensees have any reason to worry about Commission sanctions, chapter 6 explores the issue of license renewal in an era of flux, the 1960s.

4

THE DEVELOPMENT OF
THE COMMUNICATIONS ACT

World War I had been good to Westinghouse Electric and Manufacturing Company, but peacetime ended the banquet at the public trough. And if that were not enough, everywhere Westinghouse turned it seemed to be stymied by its rival, General Electric. Perhaps the cruelest blow was its exclusion from the new alliance among GE, AT&T, and the Radio Corporation of America, which appeared to have a stranglehold on valuable patents relating to uses of the vacuum tube.[1]

But Westinghouse had an asset that would prove highly useful: blind luck. One of its talented employees was Frank Conrad, a genius at solving technical problems. For Conrad, work and play were the same thing. When weekends arrived, he would go into his garage and start tinkering with his amateur equipment, now upgraded by vacuum tubes thanks to his war work. By 1920, Conrad and interested friends were gathering in his garage to talk with other amateurs and play phonograph records over the air.[2] (In what was probably the first write-in request show, he even received letters requesting particular selections.) Although others in the country were doing the same thing, Conrad's transmissions were made unique by a fortuitous advertisement in the *Pittsburgh Sun*. The Joseph Horne Department

Store took note of Conrad in one of its advertisements, which informed readers: "Amateur Wireless Sets, made by the maker of the Set which is in operation in our store, are on sale here, $10.00 and up."[3]

One person who read the ad was Conrad's superior, Westinghouse Vice-President Harry P. Davis. As he later told the Harvard Graduate School of Business Administration in an address, "Here was an idea of limitless opportunity": create a mass market for receiving sets rather than cater to technology buffs. He wanted to know if Conrad could set up a stronger transmitter at the Westinghouse plant—say, by the time of the presidential election, November 2, 1920. Conrad said he could indeed. Westinghouse would supply the audience.[4]

With a hundred-watt transmitter going up, Westinghouse applied to the Department of Commerce for a license to launch a broadcast service. The department assigned the letters KDKA, which were commercial shore-station call letters, and authorized Westinghouse to use a channel away from the amateur frequencies and comparatively free of interference.[5]

Conrad was not present at Westinghouse on November 2. Westinghouse was sufficiently fearful the KDKA apparatus would fail that Conrad was ordered to stay by his garage to carry on should that unfortunate happenstance occur. It didn't, and by the time Westinghouse signed off on election night, Warren Harding had triumphed—and so had Westinghouse.

The Westinghouse coverage had not been the only election evening broadcast, but what distinguished it from others, such as the *Detroit News* on WWJ, was its promotional aspect. Westinghouse was publicizing itself and its crystal sets to millions of Americans, creating a new, universal need.[6] And success breeds success. Hopelessly outdistanced by its competitors at the beginning of 1920, Westinghouse was invited to join the GE–RCA–AT&T alliance in 1921. It was a just reward for a company that brought into being an industry so dynamic that, with but a momentary pause, it outstripped the applicable law overnight.

The "applicable law" was sparse. It consisted of two statutes, the Wireless Ship Act of 1910[7] and the Radio Act of 1912.[8] The Wireless Ship Act simply required that any steamer licensed to carry fifty or more people be equipped with an efficient apparatus for radio communication, with a competent operator in charge. The Radio Act, enacted to fulfill U.S. obligations under the first international radio treaty, forbade the operation of a radio apparatus without a license from the Secretary of Commerce and Labor and imposed some restrictions on the character of wave emissions, the transmission of distress signals, and the like. Because broadcasting as such did not exist in 1912, the statutes did not treat it. But lawyers are trained to use whatever law is at hand when a problem arises, and so, when broadcasting began, the Secretary of Commerce, Herbert Hoover, set aside 833 kilocycles and licensed all applying broadcast stations to operate on that frequency.

Despite the success of KDKA and WWJ, only 5 broadcasting licenses were issued in the following twelve months. Then in December 1921, 23 licenses were issued; in January 1922 the number dropped to 8, but in February it was back up to 24. Then the explosion hit. For the next five months the numbers of radio broadcast licenses issued were 77, 76, 97, 72, and 76. By the end of 1922, 670 stations had been licensed, of which 576 were still alive.[9]

In the absence of a legislative policy to deal with the exploding industry, some substitute was necessary. In search of one, President Harding instructed Hoover to call a conference of manufacturers and broadcasters. The first National Radio Conference was held in early March 1922. At the end of four days, the conferees unanimously agreed that the nation needed a radio policy. As Hoover noted, "This is one of the few instances where the country is unanimous in its desire for more regulation."[10]

Indeed, virtually any regulation would have alleviated broadcasting's most pressing problem, signal interference among broadcast stations, which had been a topic of editorials in both the October and the November issues of *Radio Broadcast*.[11] In November, the editor wrote:

> Every month sees a remarkable growth in the number of stations licensed for radio broadcasting. This might be taken as a sign of healthy growth of the new art, but a little reflection seems to point to the opposite conclusion. . . . It seems to us that a curb should be put upon the licensing of broadcasting stations or there will soon be country-wide troubles of the kinds which recently occurred in New York—conflicts between the various stations for the most desirable hours and the resulting interference of signals between the several stations, which made listening no pleasure.[12]

If the well-established larger concerns represented at the radio conference had their way, listening would soon become a pleasure. Westinghouse had candidly announced that it was in broadcasting to stimulate sales, and it could foresee no decrease in demand so long as broadcast quality was not reduced.[13] Something had to be done about the flood of stations.

The point man on radio legislation was a nondescript congressman from Maine, Wallace H. White, Jr. He was the first member of Congress to take radio seriously and, for years, the only one who understood the industry. His interest began immediately after the war, in reaction to the Navy Department's desire to maintain control over radio. Secretary of the Navy Daniels had announced that "having demonstrated during the war the excellent service and the necessity of unified ownership, we should not lose the advantage of it in peace."[14] Given a strong U.S. tradition of civilian control of the military, many congressmen disagreed with Secretary Daniels. One opponent was White, who began drafting bills to ensure that civilian communications remained under the jurisdiction of the Secretary of Commerce.[15]

By the time Hoover took over Commerce in 1921, White was ready to send him a draft of a new radio act.[16] Since White was the only congressman showing an interest, Hoover usually invited him to attend the National Radio Conferences. Always the team player, White would dutifully introduce the conference's product as legislation. Indeed, his ability to "go along" was the trait that, years later in the Eightieth Congress, won him the Senate Majority leadership. He was precisely what the Republicans wanted—someone who would defer to Vandenburg on foreign affairs and to Taft on domestic ones. His deference was well practiced in the radio arena: when Hoover said forward, White went forward; when Hoover said stop, White stopped.

The get-along-go-along representative from Maine stood in sharp contrast to his Senate counterpart, Washington's Clarence Dill. White was bland, Dill flashy; White lasted for thirty years, Dill but two Senate terms. By the age of thirty, Dill had been elected to Congress, in 1914, and reelected, in 1916—the first Democratic congressman from Washington. He voted against the draft and against entry into World War I. With the change in mood following U.S. entry into the war, the voters of his district sent him home to Spokane. But four years later he upset the incumbent Republican and became Washington's first-ever Democratic senator.[17]

Dill had acquired his radio expertise fortuitously. One day an old acquaintance who represented two western newspapers, one of which operated a radio station, asked him how he would like to have a story in the morning paper. Dill liked that idea very much; he constantly gave speeches in his home state with just that eventuality in mind. The only price for the free publicity was sponsorship of a little amendment to the Copyright Act, exempting musical broadcasts from any obligations under the copyright law. Dill was pleased to oblige and became an overnight celebrity with broadcasters, even though, as he admitted, he did not know what a wavelength was. But he learned quickly enough, and radio soon became his hobby. He accumulated a dozen receiving sets and kept one turned on in his Senate office at all times. With no one else in the Senate particularly interested in radio, he became its expert.

He would not have ascended to expert status quite so readily in the House, where White had manifested a long-standing interest in radio and was introducing radio legislation before Dill ever gained his Senate seat. Yet for White, the Radio Act of 1927 was a crowning achievement; his time in the House was otherwise burdened with persistent but mundane business from his home district, in particular, the construction and repair of lighthouses off the Maine coast. Dill, however, was more flamboyant than White, and his ambitions went beyond lighthouses. He was dreaming of a massive hydroelectric power project to be built in eastern Washington—which eventually won him the title that meant the most to him: Father of the Grand Coulee Dam.[18]

In September 1922, White introduced a House bill incorporating the radio conference's recommendations;[19] after redrafting, it passed the House in 1923 but then died in Senate committee. White persevered in introducing Hoover's radio bills, but the Senate was uninterested in radio and doubted the immediacy of the problems; some of its members, moreover, were potential presidential candidates unwilling to aggrandize a competitor like Hoover. The Senate passed no radio bills.

Stations in the same area were thus forced to attempt a form of self-regulation, that is, a voluntary division of broadcast hours. Although not an ideal situation, a mutual agreement was about the best that could be done, given the state of the art and the absence of legal control. Fortunately, however, the technology was improving, and by the end of 1922 it had become possible to broadcast on other frequencies besides 833 kilocycles, with the better receivers able to tune out any unwanted frequency.[20]

Early in 1923, though, Hoover concluded that the problem was "simply intolerable" and called a second radio conference. Realizing that congressional action would not be forthcoming, the conference went on record stating that Hoover had the authority "to regulate hours and wavelengths of operation of stations when such action is necessary to prevent interference detrimental to the public good."[21] A bold statement, especially considering that less than two months earlier the D.C. Circuit had decided that Hoover wholly lacked authority to refuse to license a station. The opinion held that the Radio Act of 1912 gave the Secretary of Commerce the discretion to select a wavelength for broadcasting, but thereafter his duty was to issue a license to all comers.[22]

Hoover preferred the conclusions of the radio conference. In the late spring of 1923 he reassigned all stations, using a large number of new frequencies. He further created several classes of stations with varying amounts of power to serve different-sized areas. If necessary, Hoover intended to force time-sharing on the stations, should more wish to go on the air than the newly expanded frequencies could hold.[23]

His approach worked for a time. The expanded radio band, along with the 1923 downturn in radio economics, allowed Hoover to give licenses to all who asked.[24] But by 1925 the band was filled again: in November there were 578 broadcasting stations, a third of which were using five hundred or more watts of power. Of greater concern were 175 pending applications for new stations.[25] The situation spelled trouble. In Cincinnati, two stations on the same frequency had been unable to reach any agreement on time-sharing and had simply broadcast simultaneously for weeks.[26] No listening pleasure there.

Hoover eventually abandoned his policy of not stepping in on local time-sharing disputes and imposed settlements in Cincinnati and elsewhere. Furthermore, he began taking strong actions against those who invaded wavelengths assigned to others. Some stations would wander deliberately in search of better (i.e., clearer) air; others simply lacked the equipment or technical competence to stay on their own frequency. One of the unintentional wanderers was the Los Angeles evangelist Aimee Semple McPherson. Her roaming, like that of others, caused interference and aroused bitter complaints. After repeated warnings, Hoover ordered her station shut down, which a local inspector did. The next day she telegraphed Hoover as follows: "Please order your minions of Satan to leave my station alone. You cannot expect the Almighty to abide by your wavelength nonsense. When I offer my prayers to Him I must fit into His wave reception. Open this station at once." Hoover compromised, and McPherson was persuaded to employ a competent manager to keep her station on its assigned frequency.[27]

Competence was not a problem for Zenith—its assigned wavelength was. Hoover had given Zenith the same frequency for broadcasting from Chicago as General Electric had for its Denver station. The only problem with the assignment was a limitation imposed on it: Zenith could broadcast Thursdays between 10:00 P.M. and midnight if, and only if, General Electric did not choose to broadcast then. Zenith viewed the arrangement as unsatisfactory, so it came up with a solution of its own: it jumped to a frequency ceded by treaty to Canada. This decidedly impermissible move left Hoover with little choice but to move against Zenith.[28] A federal district judge threw the case out in April 1926, finding that the Radio Act gave Hoover no power to impose restrictions on a station's frequency, power, or hours of operation. Thus, use of an unassigned frequency, even one ceded to Canada, did not violate the existing federal law. That was strike two for Hoover.[29]

The third strike came shortly thereafter. The House and Senate had finally passed nearly identical radio bills, but the legislative session had ended with the House and Senate conference committee unable to agree on where the authority to regulate radio should lie: with Hoover in the Commerce Department, as White's House bill provided, or with an independent commission of "men of big ability and big vision," as Senate sponsor Dill argued.[30] A few days after the conference committee reported lack of agreement and the session adjourned, Hoover precipitated the crisis himself by requesting an opinion on the issue from the Acting Attorney General. The solicited opinion agreed with the district judge's *Zenith* conclusions.[31] Hoover then issued an announcement that he was abandoning all efforts to regulate broadcasting.[32] The industry was left wholly on its own, with an admonition from Hoover urging it to undertake self-regulation. The situation was later described by Justice Frankfurter, in *NBC,* as follows:

> The plea of the Secretary went unheeded. From July, 1926, to February 23, 1927, when Congress enacted the Radio Act of 1927, 44 Stat. 1162, almost 200 new stations went on the air. These new stations used any frequencies they desired, regardless of the interference thereby caused to others. Existing stations changed to other frequencies and increased their power and hours of operation at will. The result was confusion and chaos. With everybody on the air, nobody could be heard.[33]

So, four and a half years after Congressman White introduced the first radio conference's bill, Congress was forced to act. The happy alternative of doing nothing and watching progress chart its own course was no longer viable.

The Radio Act of 1927 put first things first.[34] Who owned the airwaves? The public. Where would control lie? With the federal government. Those who wished to use the airwaves would have to ask permission from the government before receiving, at best, a limited right to use the air. Ownership would not, and could not, be transferred to the private sector. Furthermore, anyone wishing to use the air who doubted the government's claim was a sure loser. Licenses were granted only to those willing to sign a waiver "of any claim to the use of any particular frequency" against the United States. The act vested nothing except a license to use the airwaves for a limited term not to exceed three years. The license was free, but the public retained its right of reversion.

In support of the radio conference recommendations, White argued that

> in the present state of scientific development there must be a limitation upon the number of broadcasting stations and it [the radio conference] recommended that licenses should be issued only to those stations whose operation would render a benefit to the public, are necessary in the public interest, or would contribute to the development of the art. . . . We have written it into the bill. If enacted into law, the broadcasting privilege will not be a right of selfishness. It will rest upon an assurance of public interest to be served.[35]

The concept of rendering public service in exchange for the privilege of using the federally controlled spectrum was translated into the statute. In a fit of progressivism strangely out of place for the Coolidge era, Congress set forth virtually every power and duty in the Act with reference to a standard of the "public interest, convenience or necessity." The charm of the Act was its vagueness; in essence, it was an injunction to do good. As Dill noted, "It covers just about everything."[36]

Congress had enough historical wisdom to know it did

not want a National Board of Censors. Thus, section 29 made it plain that the licensing authority did not include the power of censorship and could not "interfere with the right of free speech by means of radio communications." How the injunction in section 29 not to censor would mesh with the equally strong injunction to award licenses with exclusive reference to the public interest was left for future resolution.

But the future was not long in coming. In its First Annual Report, the Federal Radio Commission perceived the tension and noted that although the law prohibited censorship, "the physical facts of radio transmission compel what is, in effect, a censorship of the most extraordinary kind. . . . There is a definite limit, and a very low one, to the number of broadcasting stations which can operate simultaneously." That conclusion meant that some applicants would be told, "There is no room for you." In making decisions among applicants, was the public-interest standard helpful? "How shall we measure the conflicting claims of grand opera and religious services, of market reports and direct advertising, of jazz orchestras and lectures on the diseases of hogs?"[37]

Who would make the decisions? It was, after all, this very point that had deadlocked the conference committee just eight months earlier. The Radio Act split the difference in the dispute between the Senate's desire to remove the Secretary of Commerce from the field and White's desire to leave Hoover supreme. For one year, a geographically balanced five-member commission was to exercise the government's licensing function; then the function would revert to the Secretary of Commerce. Dill liked the compromise, and he accurately predicted that "if we ever got a Commission we would never get rid of it."[38]

When would the decisions be made? Soon. Dill's and White's handiwork required considerable immediate action, since the Radio Act included a provision that licenses issued under the Radio Act of 1912 would expire in sixty days. By that point, the Federal Radio Commission was to be in existence and could begin to bring order to the chaos.

But several unforeseen obstacles littered the path. First, only three of the five nominees were confirmed before Congress adjourned, and two of them died almost immediately thereafter.[39] Second, no budget was passed. Thus the FRC began its life with but one confirmed member, no staff, and no appropriated funds; it lived on handouts from Hoover's Department of Commerce.[40] What to do? First the FRC extended all licenses temporarily; then it began the task of reallocating frequencies. Sixty-day licenses were issued to facilitate the revisions, but it was apparent that at least a hundred stations would have to be cut. Faced with that headache and needing time to think, the Commission, like much of the federal government, came to a virtual halt during the Washington summer. By late fall more commissioners had been added, and in March 1928 the FRC had for the first time a full complement of confirmed members.

But another headache faced the Commission in early 1928. Congress, convinced that the Commission had done too little to implement section 9 of the Act, which called for "fair, efficient, and equitable radio service" for each state, passed an amendment to the Act. Offered by E. L. Davis of Tennessee, it ordered the Commission to equalize broadcast allocations among the five geographic zones created by the Act.[41] These zones, however, ranged in size from 129,000 square miles to ten times that size. The four zones east of the Rockies were approximately equal in population, whereas the huge western zone comprised about half the number of people in any one eastern zone. The five zones were irregular in shape, different in size, and created solely for geographic balance on the Federal Radio Commission, yet they were now designated to be the procrustean bed for broadcast engineering. The Commission was faced first with the task of deleting upward of one hundred stations; it then would be faced with the even more arduous task of taking away from some areas to give to others. To top it all off, Congress put the Commission on a short leash: the commissioners would have to undergo reappointment and reconfirmation in eleven months.

Before turning its attention to the Davis Amendment, the Commission made one major effort to clarify the status of marginal stations. On May 25, 1928, FRC General Order No. 32 tersely informed 164 stations that "after an examination of the[ir] applications for renewal" the Commission "has not been satisfied that public interest, convenience, or necessity will be served" by renewal. The stations would be knocked off the air unless they prevailed at a hearing scheduled for July 9.[42]

On the appointed day, 110 stations were represented in the auditorium of the Interior Department Building. The Commission had no procedures and, indeed, had just two weeks earlier acquired its first General Counsel, the able Louis Caldwell. So it did the obvious thing—it let everyone say whatever they wished. Caldwell, too, did the obvious thing, which was to keep his eyes on the possibility of judicial review. Protecting the Commission from reversible errors was his job, and he concentrated his questions on technical matters, such as the timely announcement of call letters or the engineering ability to operate on the frequency allocated. When he strayed from technical questions, discussion became very general and very vague. Here he favored questions that carried a reference to the "public interest, convenience, or necessity [that] would be served" by nonrenewal.[43]

Two exhausting weeks later, everyone had been heard and it was time for decisions. Of the 164 stations cited by General Order No. 32, only 62 were deleted, most of whom voluntarily surrendered their licenses. Of those that fought, well over three-quarters escaped without even a reduction in power. The results were insufficient to have justified spending a hot July in an unairconditioned Washington, D.C.

In reallocating stations under the Davis Amendment, the Commission could not afford to be as lax. It moved to comply with the amendment in a two-step process. The first step was the issuance at the end of the summer of General Order No. 40, which enunciated the general principles to be followed in setting the allocations of frequencies and power for the country. In drawing up its allocations, the Commission refused to make the complete equalization called for by the Davis Amendment. Instead it endorsed a compromise between engineering and economics to prevent legal niceties such as mathematical compliance from laying waste to thousands of dollars of investment in broadcasting hardware. The Commission also granted stations the opportunity to comment on the proposal before it took effect. With the new allocations, the number of stations on the air would be reduced by about a hundred.

The second step was implementation, and on November 11, 1928, the Commission changed the assignments of 94 percent of all broadcasting stations.[44] There were, of course, winners and losers, and as one of the commissioners later reflected, "We had to make some moves in a rather high-handed way. . . . We took a lot of hearsay and I fear we did a lot of injustices."[45] But the Commission also brought the spectrum under control.

It remained to be seen whether the Commission would enjoy judicial approval of its actions, for many stations litigated their loss of licenses or their changed frequencies or hours. As it turned out, the Commission was a big judicial winner—and interestingly, it won two ways. Its choice against strict compliance with the Davis Amendment was sustained, with the D.C. Circuit fully agreeing that the Commission need not injure existing stations to equalize facilities. The "paramount consideration after all is the public interest," which would be ill served "by unnecessarily injuring stations already established which are rendering valuable service to their natural service areas."[46] Its action of taking from one area to give to another, in conformity with the Davis Amendment, was also sustained. Finally, the Commission prevailed on the issue of reassigning a frequency from one station to another in an adjacent state but within the same zone. The loss of Chicago's WIBO and WPCC to a Gary station provided the first full-fledged Supreme Court opinion on the Radio Act and began a long-term trend of Commission victories in the courts.[47] With the spectrum under control and judicial approval in hand, the Commission's most pressing task was completed. Now it only needed to act as ringmaster, occasionally bringing an unruly beast such as a Brinkley or a Shuler under control.

The shifts from the Republican era to the New Deal had no immediate significant effects. For one thing, of all the national problems, broadcasting was hardly high on anyone's list. For another, unlike many other regulatory moves, the federal action under Coolidge and Hoover had pretty much solved the problems. As it turned out, then, the only real issue for the New Deal in the early days was whether to allocate channels to "educational, religious, agricultural, labor, cooperative, and similar non-profitmaking associations," as senators Robert Wagner and Henry Hatfield wished.[48] FDR had no such wish. He simply wanted to remove regulatory power over AT&T from the Interstate Commerce Commission's fixation on railroads. He got his way by the simple expedient of adding a common-carrier section to the Radio Act and renaming it the Communications Act.[49] The substance of the Act was, in fact, barely touched in the name-change transition. Indeed, the only change of substance came two years later with the repeal in 1936 of the Davis Amendment, the bane of the Commission's early existence.[50] From the New Deal perspective, Hoover, White, and Dill had done a fine job. Their progressive impulse to license in the public interest was fully reaffirmed.

5

GIVING AWAY
THE POT OF GOLD

Neither Coolidge nor Hoover had had any interest in politicizing broadcasting. Hoover, moving from the Commerce Department to the presidency, once worried about the potential for commercialization of the infant industry but was unconcerned about who got on the air. His FRC had preferred certain types of radio programs, yet it was not aggressive in pursuing them. It would take a finely tuned politician to perceive the opportunities inherent in Commission licensing. Not surprisingly, the first president to comprehend its political potential was FDR, though his foray into the broadcast licensing arena was slow in coming. Whatever fears broadcasters, as businessmen, may have had about the activist Roosevelt, there was no evidence during his first or much of his second term that he considered the FRC or the FCC anything but a rest home. The bursts of energy that accompanied the first and second New Deals simply passed the sleeping Commission by. Its name was changed, but not its image.

The FCC had not inherited a distinguished tradition from its predecessor. One of FDR's early appointees, former Bull Mooser George Henry Payne, publicly referred to a belief (which he apparently held himself) that the FRC had been industry-dominated.[1] Supporting facts were not hard to find. As its final benefaction to broadcasters, the FRC in its last two weeks of existence granted almost 150 applications for power increases and changes of frequency, many with as little as twenty-four hours notice.[2] New and dramatic changes in staffing and policy would be required if that way of doing business were to be changed.

Many New Deal agencies were populated with, to use Senator Dill's phrase, "men of big abilities and big vision."[3] But FDR showed no immediate interest in changing the workings of the Commission. Former Mississippi Supreme Court Justice Eugene O. Sykes was carried over as chairman, and like his immediate successors (former congressman and close friend of FDR Anning Prall and the elderly ex–Federal Power Commission chairman Frank McNinch) he was hardly dynamic. Here it is important to remember how administrative agencies differ from courts: a chief justice is simply first among equals and can set an agenda only with help and by persuasion; an administrative agency, by contrast, takes its tone and character from its chairman. Without the chairman's support, no departure from the status quo is possible, and without active leadership there is little for the agency to do. The FCC had no programmatic agenda; indeed, there seemed to be little else to do but continue drawing paychecks.

Then came the 1936 election and the Court-packing plan. The election, of course, was a dramatic victory for the incredibly popular president. Despite the opposition of 95 percent of the nation's newspapers, FDR's chief tactician, Postmaster General James Farley, became a prophet by revising the slogan "As goes Maine, so goes the nation" (Maine then holding its general election a month before the rest of the country) to "As goes Maine, so goes Vermont."[4] Roosevelt carried the remaining forty-six states. His mandate to govern thus seemed assured.

This mandate in mind, then, Roosevelt turned on a recalcitrant Supreme Court with his February 5, 1937, message to Congress and his plan to pack the Court. The plan, which dominated the entire 1937 legislative session, went down to defeat in the Senate in June (after Owen Roberts pulled his famous switch and began voting in favor of the constitutionality of New Deal economic measures).[5] Roosevelt had suffered few legislative defeats, and he did not take this one well. But the defeat was both a harbinger of things to come and the continuation of a tradition: second-term presidents, no matter how good and no matter how popular, cannot repeat the successes of the first term. FDR, like Washington, Jefferson, Jackson, and Wilson before him, had spent his legislative force. The 1938 session of Congress confirmed this fact. The economy was still stagnant, and so was the legislative program of the New Deal (with the exception of the Fair Labor Standards Act). Increasingly frustrated, FDR turned on his critics—but his attempted purge of anti–New Deal congressmen in the 1938 elections wholly failed, in yet another defeat.

In the same vein, FDR had decided to retaliate against his critics from the press. It was galling enough to be opposed by an overwhelming number of newspapers in the United States, but did those same economic royalists have to be granted licenses to broadcast? Shouldn't—couldn't—something be done to prevent a replication of the newspaper industry in radio? To accomplish this, the FCC had to be changed: the lethargy of the past would not suffice.

What the FCC needed was a dynamic chairman—someone like Bill Douglas at the Securities and Exchange Commission—and excellent staffing, again like the SEC or like the "Happy Hot Dogs" distributed from the Harvard Law School by Professor Felix Frankfurter either directly or through Tommy ("the Cork") Corcoran. In the winter of 1939, Douglas, perhaps the New Deal's finest administrator, had accepted the deanship at Yale Law School. But he feared that FDR would attempt to delay his exit from government by switching him from the SEC to the FCC, where active chairmanship was needed. "That agency had been rocked, not with scandal, but with inefficiency, and I had heard the President say he would clean it up," Douglas noted.[6]

Douglas might well have been an apt point man in FDR's forthcoming effort to cut broadcasters down a notch, but FDR ultimately had other notions as to where Douglas could best serve the New Deal vision. The FCC job went instead to the tough, resourceful James Lawrence Fly, General Counsel of the Tennessee Valley Authority. Fly was sometimes Machiavellian, always energetic, and clearly able to stand up to industry giants. Hugh Johnson aptly captured Fly in this description: "The cockiest Fourth New Deal wight who ever figuratively and gleefully cut a tory's throat or scuttled an economic royalist's ship."[7]

Fly had a strong commitment to the importance of competition, and when he arrived in late summer 1939, embodying the supposed Brandeisian philosophy of the second New Deal—with its turn away from centralization toward renewed appreciation of pluralistic competition within a free market regulated principally by the antitrust laws—the FCC started to change.[8] For Fly did not come alone. As a condition of taking on the lackluster Commission, Fly extracted a promise that there would be enough new talent to make the necessary changes. "Talent" meant Harvard Law School, and the Frankfurter network instantly began producing lawyers. Telford Taylor, who at thirty-two had already spent time in the departments of Interior, Agriculture, and Justice as well as the Senate Commerce Committee, moved in as General Counsel of the Commission. Philip Elman, who would go on to be a two-term Frankfurter clerk, joined the office. Tommy the Cork, who appears to have been the implementing force in the staffing changes, then reassigned

Joseph Rauh, a former Cardozo and Frankfurter clerk, from his work with the Fair Labor Standards Act in the Labor Department to be Deputy General Counsel. Although Rauh was eager to participate in the preparation for war, he lasted with the FCC for more than a year before moving on to Lend-Lease. Suddenly the FCC had youth, boundless energy, and brains equal to those of any department of government—as well as a determination to start doing things.[9]

Whether Fly knew from the outset of FDR's specific desire to rid broadcasting of newspaper owners, he learned quickly enough, for that was FDR's number-one priority. A one-sentence memorandum from the president to Fly conveyed it all: "Will you let me know when you propose to have a hearing on newspaper ownership of radio stations."[10] Although the need to clear the Chain Broadcasting problem (discussed in chapter 3) from the FCC's docket caused a brief delay, the agency soon announced that it was undertaking an "immediate investigation to determine what statement of policy or rules, if any, should be issued concerning applications for high frequency broadcast stations (FM) with which are associated persons also associated with the publication of one or more newspapers [and also] concerning future acquisition of standard broadcast stations [AM] by newspapers."[11] A little over three months later, the Commission fueled the controversy further by issuing a notice that it was expanding the inquiry to the relation between newspapers and radio broadcasting in general.[12] The notice was accompanied by a subpoena to the publisher of the *Nashville Banner,* who was possibly the most active participant in the various committees concerned with the relationship between broadcasting and newspapers. On advice of counsel, he refused to appear, and the Commission was suddenly in litigation.

The newspaper-broadcasting interests argued before the courts that the Commission wholly lacked power to consider, much less adopt, general rules limiting newspaper ownership of broadcasting stations. Thus, if the Commission lacked power to adopt the rules, it could not then subpoena anyone to discover information to further the adoption of the rules. Although the Commission won the subpoena battle, and an order requiring testimony was affirmed, the D.C. Circuit dealt the Commission a major blow on the issue of its power:

> If in this case it had been made to appear . . . that the Commission's investigation was solely for the purpose of consideration or adoption of a hard and fast rule or policy, as the result of which newspaper owners may be placed in a proscribed class and thus made ineligible to apply for or receive broadcast licenses, we should be obliged to declare that such an investigation would be wholly outside of and beyond any of the powers with which Congress has clothed the Commission.[13]

The Commission was thus on notice that it could not adopt the blanket rules that FDR seemed to want.

It could, however, continue to conduct its inquiry. In what appears to have been an effort at compromise, the court stated that although the Commission could not go on a fishing expedition it might "without interference seek through an investigation of its own making information properly applicable to the legislative standards set up in the Act. We should not assume that the investigation will be conducted for any other purpose or in disregard of constitutional limits."[14] This statement followed an approving recitation of a number of questions the Commission proposed to investigate, including whether newspaper ownership of broadcasting stations restricted or distorted the news, unduly limited access to newsgathering sources, tended to prejudice free and fair discussion of issues, provided economic stability, and encouraged technological development.

These issues were "clearly within the inherent powers of the Commission."[15]

But despite FDR's continuing interest and the leeway granted by the court, the investigation was to founder on legal doubts created by the decision, the fact of war, and a congressional buffeting probably unmatched in the history of congressional dealings with administrative agencies. An administrator lacking Fly's toughness would have surrendered quickly once the big guns were out. But Fly did not back down, and he was forced to do battle on three different House committee fronts as well as to fight for the agency budget. Since he also served as the chairman of the newly created top-level Defense Communications Board, Fly's very survival is a tribute to the toughness and energy of this able Texan. But the newspaper-ownership battle could not be won.

In January 1944 the Commission abandoned its efforts, noting the "grave legal and policy questions involved."[16] It nevertheless reminded broadcasters that it would not "permit concentration of control in the hands of the few to the exclusion of the many who may be equally well qualified to render such public service as is required of a licensee."[17] The caveat was bravado, although perhaps necessary as a warning to newspaper-broadcasters that the Commission might still act, and as a palliative for FDR, who was never reconciled to his loss. Paul Porter, Fly's successor, was to note later that FDR "was constantly leaning on me to get the newspapers out of broadcasting."[18]

Where FDR failed in radio, the Republicans under Eisenhower succeeded in television. To be sure, the Republicans had advantages. First, the television licensing procedure was often comparative, following diverse criteria, and thus allowed the agency some choice among applicants. Furthermore, the TV allocation specified where stations would be located, rather than licensing according to demand, so all knew where stations were available. Second, the Republicans lacked FDR's objective of prohibiting newspaper ownership. Most newspapers were Republican-controlled, and it would have been folly to ban them from acquiring television licenses. All the Republicans wanted was a bit of fine tuning.

After World War II, the FCC began to hand out licenses for the new television technology, granting 108 by 1948. Becoming aware that it was moving haphazardly into a new era and a new field, however, the Commission in 1948 froze all applications in order to study the situation. At the end of four years of study, the Commission rejected the fortuitous-growth model of radio regulation (by which the Commission put stations where there was demand for them) and instead introduced a master plan (with emphasis on *plan*) for the entire United States. Stations, either VHF or UHF, were to be allocated to communities by a set of priorities created to ensure "a fair and equitable" distribution.[19]

The lack of sufficient people in some areas, and hence a lack of possibilities for profit, did not occur to the Commission. More important, the Commission did not realize until later that mixing UHF and VHF stations in the same market wasn't going to work for very long. Everyone wanted the V. Licensing of the VHF stations became the primary occupation of the Commission for the decade of the 1950s and was the greatest public giveaway in almost a century. It thus carried a strong potential for scandal.

By the time of Eisenhower's election in 1952, not a single Republican senator had ever voted on an appointment made by a Republican president. After twenty years of famine, the party pros were hungry. At that time, the composition of the FCC was four Democrats and three non-Democrats, thanks to Truman's superb ability to find independents and tame Republicans for service on the regulatory agencies. Yet within less than two years three highly partisan Republican appointments swiftly transformed the Commission into an agency ready to satisfy the longings for the perquisites of power sorely missed for so long.

Eisenhower himself seems to have been unconcerned with the FCC and television. Staffing the agency thus fell to his top assistant, the crusty, hard-driving former governor of New Hampshire, Sherman Adams. And pressure from the old-guard GOP senators, such as Styles Bridges and John Bricker, produced a Commission in which the Republicans needed to add but a single vote to control decisions.[20]

At its best, the Eisenhower-Adams goal was not simply to find real Republicans for the FCC, but rather to find appointees who had already demonstrated their talents. Thus, service on state regulatory agencies coupled with the appropriate political backing became an important ingredient in selection. Two of the first Republican appointees to the Commission, George McConnaughey and John Doerfer, and the first nominal Democrat, Richard A. Mack, had such experience and support.

McConnaughey had met John W. Bricker in officer training camp during World War I, and they had remained fast friends. As Bricker's political career had advanced, so had McConnaughey's public one, and the powerful Ohio senator, then chairman of the Commerce Committee, boosted McConnaughey's career once again in 1954 by having him designated chairman of the Commission.[21]

Doerfer had the benefit of the active endorsement of an early Eisenhower supporter, Wisconsin Governor Walter Kohler, which advanced his appointment, despite the fact that Doerfer was from Joseph McCarthy's home state.[22] Although McCarthy approved the nomination, he provided no active backing. Nonetheless, Doerfer quickly began to act like a McCarthy protégé. His target was Edward Lamb, a highly successful capitalist with numerous broadcast properties who had supported liberal candidates of both parties. By the summer of 1953, all of Lamb's applications, routine or otherwise, were being delayed because of Doerfer's concerns about unspecified charges against Lamb. The issue may have been fellow-traveling, but at one point, according to Lamb, Doerfer had said, "It would be better if you were still a Republican." In true McCarthyite form, the Commission withheld from Lamb the specifics of the accusations against him as well as the identities of his accusers.[23]

If Doerfer was not a McCarthy man in fact, there was little doubt that Robert E. Lee, who had the enthusiastic and tireless support of Styles Bridges, was. Lee had begun his career with the FBI and then, under J. Edgar Hoover's sponsorship, had moved to the House Appropriations Committee, where in 1947 he compiled a list of 108 cases of alleged disloyalty in the Truman State Department. This stale and inaccurate list became the basis for McCarthy's Wheeling, West Virginia, speech in February 1950. Later that year, Lee assisted McCarthy in his successful campaign to purge Maryland Senator Millard Tydings. Lee had never made a secret of his close association and friendship with the Wisconsin senator.[24]

These three partisan Republicans joined with the four remaining commissioners: Richard Mack of Florida, pliable and corrupt; conservative Democrat T. M. Craven, from the Storer Broadcasting group; House Speaker Sam Rayburn's nephew, Robert A. Bartley; and lifetime FCC employee Rosel Hyde. These seven did not need to attack anyone—all they had to do was grant favors. They stood as temporary custodians to a huge pot of gold, and it was their decision who would get their hands into the pot.[25]

Applications were to be granted using the criteria developed in more than two decades of radio licensing. The public interest was, of course, paramount, and the statutory language of public interest, convenience, or necessity re-

mained unamended. An uncontested application was a
fairly straightforward procedure. The Commission looked
at whether the applicant's programming proposals were acceptable and likely to be implemented. In the case of competing applications—and with the stakes high, there would
be many—the criteria were more diverse. Commissioner
Doerfer summed them up as follows:

> (1) Proposed programming and policies, (2) local ownership,
> (3) integration of ownership and management, (4) participa-
> tion in civic activities, (5) record of past broadcast perfor-
> mance, (6) broadcast experience, (7) relative likelihood of ef-
> fectuation of proposals as shown by the contacts made with
> local groups and similar efforts, (8) carefulness of operational
> planning for television, (9) staffing, (10) diversification of the
> background of the persons controlling, (11) diversification of
> control of the mediums of communication.[26]

At best, the standards were uneven. As Henry Friendly
aptly noted, they mingled "matters of high policy," such as
diversification of control of the mediums of communication, "with mere pieces of evidence," such as carefulness of
operational planning.[27]

Taken as a whole, the criteria meant that the Commission
was searching for a winner who presented a prospect of varied service to the community; a past record of broadcast service, if any, would of course be a most salient factor. Local
residents were preferred to outsiders, and active ownership
was favored over absentee; these reiterative points both assumed that local citizens better understand and therefore
would better serve the community. Although the foregoing
criteria apply largely to service, local ownership, integrated
into station management, also implies the possibility that
the station will not have other media ties. This last point is,
of course, a separate criterion and has at times been seen
as the most important in licensing decisions. Ironically, it

clearly conflicts with giving credit for experience in the broadcasting field; the only way to create a performance record is through other media ties, as no one abandons one media outlet simply to apply for a different one.

Probably no one could have allocated licenses based on these criteria in a way that would have satisfied everyone. The issue at hand, however, is not whether the Commission satisfied everyone, but whether it did a difficult job tolerably well and avoided the "capricious" decisions that Justice Frankfurter put outside the bounds of propriety in the Court's *NBC* decision.

Not all the applications posed problems. Take, for example, the uncontested application for an Austin VHF station filed by Claudia Taylor Johnson of Stonewall, a small hamlet in the Hill Country some sixty miles west of Austin. Already the licensee of an Austin AM station, Mrs. Johnson filed an application with the Commission in March 1952 to operate Channel 7 in Austin. Her application was certainly prescient. The freeze was still on (albeit about to be removed), and the allocation plan for the United States had not been published. Thus it was not officially known whether Austin would get Channel 7 (or any other VHF station). A month later, when the allocation plan was published, Austin not only got Channel 7, but it also became one of the three largest areas in the United States to be allocated but a single VHF station. Channel 7 was thus an especially lucrative prize. Even so, no other applicants had emerged when the deadline for filing closed three months later. In the first batch of decisions handed down after the freeze, Mrs. Johnson—who was also known as Lady Bird—was awarded Channel 7. Oddly enough, there were applications for the worthless UHF stations in Austin, which were sure to go dark (and did). Why, then, did anyone waste time applying for UHF when VHF was available for a comparative hearing? The "successful" applicant for one of the Austin

UHF stations summed it up perfectly: "Lyndon was in a favorable position to get that station even if someone else had contested it. Politics is politics."[28]

When the time came to evaluate competing applications, however, decision making was distinctly problematical; as noted, there is more than a little tension between the Commission's two operative policies, and in many cases they flatly conflict. The Commission's handling of these conflicts is best illustrated by an examination of specific licensing decisions. I shall explore those affecting Sacramento, Madison, Tampa, Boston, and Miami.

The Sacramento facts brought the two policies into relatively sharp conflict. One applicant, McClatchy Broadcasting, owned an AM radio station and one of the two dailies in Sacramento, as well as other newspapers and radio stations in central California. The opposing group, Sacramento Telecasters, was locally controlled and without media holdings. The hearing examiner found McClatchy superior in every area of comparison except diversification and so awarded it the license. The Commission reversed the hearing examiner's decision, and the D.C. Circuit agreed that the Commission "may attach decisive significance to the fact that the one applicant is dissociated from existing media of mass communications while the other applicant owns radio stations and newspapers in the area."[29] An easy case.

The situation in Madison was more complex. One applicant owned two Madison newspapers and a local AM station. The opposing applicant, Radio Wisconsin, owned a Madison radio station as well as five other AM, three FM, and three television stations in the region. In addition, the principal stockholder of Radio Wisconsin had controlling interests in four Wisconsin newspapers. How to weigh local concentration against regional concentration? The Commission decided, not unrealistically, that the greater concern was with local rather than regional concentration and held for Radio Wisconsin.[30]

In the battle for Miami's Channel 7, three of the concerns submitting applications were owned entirely by local residents who lacked any other mass media holdings. These were ideal, but the fourth was not. Biscayne Television Corporation was owned by two main shareholders, each of whom controlled one of Miami's two daily newspapers. Additionally, each owned an AM and an FM station in Miami, as well as newspaper and broadcast interests elsewhere. Even more clearly than in Sacramento, this case should have gone against the newspapers. But instead, Biscayne's past broadcast experience got it the license.[31]

In Boston, a similar situation unfolded. Two of the four applicants were ideally constructed to meet most of the comparative criteria and had no outside media interests; a third was an outsider group with other TV interests; and the fourth was Greater Boston Television, owned by the *Boston Herald-Traveler,* the largest morning and evening newspaper in Boston and the owner of a local AM and FM station. Not only did the *Herald-Traveler* prevail, but the FCC also refused to reopen the case in the face of allegations by the *Boston Globe,* the other daily newspaper, that the *Herald* had repeatedly attempted to force a merger, later threatening to use the TV channel, if acquired, to drive the *Globe* out of business if it refused to merge.[32]

The 1952 allocation plan gave Tampa two VHF frequencies. In the early 1950s, Tampa was a two-newspaper town, with each of the two owning a local AM station. Like most newspapers that owned local AM stations, the two Tampa papers determined to expand into television. The morning *Tribune,* with a circulation of 110,000, applied for one of the frequencies, and the afternoon *Times,* with a circulation of slightly less than half the *Tribune's,* applied for the other.

The *Times* was opposed by applicants with no communications interests in the Tampa area. The *Tribune* was opposed by two applicants, one with no communications interests and one with communications interests in the nearby St. Petersburg area.

The *Tribune* won its competitive hearing.[33] Although it lacked integration of ownership and management and was not even owned by Tampa residents, whereas its opposition was locally based, and despite its diversification problem, it prevailed, based on its past broadcast record. The Commission chose to downplay integration and local ownership in favor of past broadcast record, even though that record was equaled by one of its competitors. Diversification was not significant "when there is a variety of diversely owned stations and newspapers in the community":[34] thus did the Commission note the thirteen newspapers in the larger community, including two Spanish-language papers and two, with circulations of about seventy thousand, in nearby St. Petersburg.

The *Times* was in better shape than the *Tribune,* for it was owned almost entirely by local residents, promised considerable integration, and had a superior past broadcast record. Given the de-emphasis on diversity in the *Tribune* case, the *Times* looked like a sure winner. But it lost.[35] Four weeks after the *Tribune* decision, the Commission handed down its *Times* decision with emphasis on—you guessed it—diversification. No mention was made of either the two Spanish papers or most of the other papers in the region. The focus was instead on the *Times,* "one of the two daily newspapers (and the only evening newspaper) in Tampa," which had "the largest circulation of any afternoon newspaper on the Florida west coast."[36]

Each of the Tampa decisions is perfectly plausible, and we need not conclude which is correct—but one is clearly wrong. As long as the two decisions are not read together, each can stand, but the conjunction of the two is unsettling. It is hard to believe the same city is being discussed; and unless one knew better one would conclude that the *Times*, not the *Tribune*, was the dominant newspaper in the area.

VHF licensing during the 1950s was a "scandal," as Professor Louis Jaffe of Harvard put it in an article in *Harper's* magazine.[37] Viewed objectively, it was a crazy quilt where diversification played a dominant role in some cases and was inexplicably ignored in others. Even the favorite shibboleth of administrative law scholars, "expertise," decidedly fails to explain what was happening. Jaffe's article suggests that the FCC had been applying "spurious" criteria. Jaffe probably knew what those "spurious" criteria were but did not think he could support his hypothesis. Later, Bernard Schwartz, a young law professor on leave from New York University to conduct a study of the Big Six administrative agencies, was able to explain the situation.

Schwartz's conclusions, published in his book *The Professor and the Commissions* and in a tightly reasoned article in the *Georgetown Law Journal,* make sobering reading. First, why did the McClatchy and the Madison newspapers and the *Tampa Times* lose? The McClatchy newspapers were strong opponents of Richard M. Nixon and had been the first to publish the facts about his slush fund, a scandal that led to the "Checkers speech," which saved his spot on Eisenhower's winning ticket. The *Madison Capital Times* had opposed Senator Joseph McCarthy more vigorously than had any other Wisconsin paper, and he had written several letters to the Commission opposing any grant to it. As one commissioner, Robert E. Lee, owed his appointment to Senator McCarthy, and another, John Doerfer, was a Wisconsin Republican, the senator's comments likely had effect. The *Tampa Times* simply had the misfortune of being one of those rare newspapers that supported the Democratic party.

And what about the license winners? They liked Ike. Es-

pecially the *Boston Herald,* which was the leading Republican
newspaper north of New York City. Only one Democratic
newspaper was a winner, the *Miami Daily News,* and it had
had the good sense to join forces with the Republican *Miami
Herald.*

According to Schwartz's study of the nine newspaper applicants that won comparative hearings, not a single one
had supported Adlai Stevenson in 1952, and only the *Miami
Daily News* was a Democratic newspaper. If the Republicans
were big winners, Democrats were big losers. Of the fourteen losing newspapers, nine were supporters of the Democratic Party. Two of the losers had supported Eisenhower
but were in a contest with another newspaper that had also
supported Eisenhower. Three others, although also Eisenhower supporters, classified themselves as politically independent.[38]

The Eisenhower FCC managed what Roosevelt and later
Nixon only dreamed of doing. Friends were brought to
the public trough and given both an outlet to the voters and
an opportunity for enormous profits. The participation
of opponents was essentially limited to transferring money
from themselves to their lawyers. And the system worked
smoothly, without the nasty judicial review that deterred
FDR's proposed newspaper bar and always hovered as a
threat to Nixon's hopes to purge the *Washington Post.*

Justice Frankfurter and the Court had promised better in
NBC. The judiciary was to prevent the use of the licensing
power to give or take away on the basis of "political, economic or social views." But, at least with regard to the grants
and denials of licenses to a substantial number of VHF
money machines in the 1950s, Justice Frankfurter's promise
was hollow. Licensing carries the potential to be used politically, and the temptation to do so was irresistible.

6
THE NONRENEWAL THREAT

Testifying before Congress in 1970 (against a bill that would have made the broadcast license virtually unchallengeable), maverick FCC Commissioner Nicholas Johnson concluded with a neat climax: "The broadcaster in America today is, without question, the single most powerful man civilization has ever permitted to roam wild. We have used a very long thread to tether a dinosaur. He finds it restricting and asks that it be removed." The idea that broadcasters could do anything without fear was thus succinctly and memorably set forth. Of course there is licensing, but—ran Johnson's implication—it is a mere formality required every third (now fifth) year, and a small price to pay for access to America's mint. Any FCC threat of nonrenewal of the license has no credibility[1]—and credibility is necessary for an even minimally effective system.

The Commission had once had credibility. The stations deleted under General Order No. 32 knew what the Commission could do. So, too, did those that lost under the Davis Amendment reallocations. And then of course there was WIBO, Chicago, a station with $350,000 of equipment and profits of $9,000 a month. But the Commission looked at WIBO and saw two problems. First, it saw a station in Illinois, a state with too many stations, that could easily be in Indiana, a state with too few. Second, it saw a station that was simply retransmitting network programming, in unfavorable contrast to WJKS, which catered to the foreign population of Gary, Indiana, with "educational" programs that emphasized "loyalty to the community and the Nation." The Commission acted on what it saw, and WIBO was deleted.

The Supreme Court unanimously agreed with the Commission's decision: "Those who operated broadcasting stations had no right superior to the exercise of this [congressionally delegated] power of regulation. They necessarily made their investments and their contracts in the light of, and subject to, this paramount authority." The Commission's power to remove stations was "not open to question." Credibility? You bet. No broadcaster operating during the Roosevelt administration doubted for a second that the threat of nonrenewal was real. The broadcasters' conviction did not depend on a memory from the mythical past: they were seeing it happen before their very eyes.[2]

Had Nicholas Johnson made his dinosaur analogy in the late 1930s, when FDR decided to knock newspapers out of broadcasting, he would have persuaded no one. Johnson of course knew that. His point was not that the threat of nonrenewal was illusory during the early days. He was speaking rather to 1970, not to 1930 or 1940, or even to 1950. Had he addressed the point, he would have argued that the threat had slowly lost its credibility through disuse. During the 1950s, with the handing out of the lucrative VHF licenses, the FCC gave; it did not take away. And although the giving had dried up considerably by the 1960s, the Commission had not begun to take away. If broadcasters had the brains of a dinosaur, they would know the tethering thread imposed no restraints. The credibility of license nonrenewal, according to Johnson, had evaporated.

Broadcasters had difficulty seeing it that way. Whether one believed the broadcasters' view or Johnson's depended on how one evaluated the broadcasting landscape—a landscape that was perceptibly changing.

A major shift in FCC procedures came with the Commission's heightened interest in the fairness doctrine, resulting largely from a change in its procedural course. Until the early sixties, any fairness complaint against a station went into the station's file to be evaluated at renewal time. This method produced neither fairness adjudications nor opportunities for response to presentations found to be unbalanced; licenses simply were not denied on the basis of fairness complaints.

On the recommendation of Henry Geller, a young Commission attorney, the Commission changed this rather feckless procedure. The new method required that the Commission deal with fairness complaints as they occurred; a timely Commission response, of course, better served the purpose of the fairness doctrine by imposing balance during the period when the controversial issue was under discussion.

As every lawyer knows, procedure affects substance. When the FCC began to review fairness complaints, it became more involved with the doctrine itself. The famous *Cullman* rule, requiring a licensee to present the opposing view free of charge if no paid sponsor was forthcoming, was an outgrowth of the Commission's newfound interest in fairness.[3] And then Fred Cook's complaint to the Commission against Red Lion Broadcasting began a complex series of events that led not only to a Supreme Court decision four years later but also to the codification of the Commission's personal-attack rules in the interim. As I noted in chapter 3, *Red Lion* was an open-and-shut case, and the Commission members were therefore delighted when the station decided to appeal the Commission's order to the D.C. Circuit. They knew the time had come, after years of broadcaster speeches on the unconstitutionality of the fairness doctrine, for the judicial seal of approval on the FCC position.

The decision to appeal was made by the owner of Red Lion against overwhelming advice to the contrary. The step taken by Red Lion appalled the broadcast establishment, whose members had been patiently waiting for the "right" case with which to assault the fairness doctrine. Instead, they were now watching a right-winger bring a case that the FCC saw as "a thing of beauty" and intended to take "all the way." Nevertheless, when Red Lion could not be dissuaded, the National Association of Broadcasters chipped in with assistance.[4]

Just as the broadcast establishment feared, Red Lion was smashed in the D.C. Circuit. The Commission had also anticipated the result and had meanwhile been working on a highly explicit set of rules covering personal attacks and editorials. Three weeks after the happy day of victory in the D.C. Circuit, the Commission confidently issued its new rules.[5]

Surprisingly, the Commission action gave the broadcast establishment a new avenue of hope. They could now jettison Red Lion and all the discomfort surrounding the defense of an ignorant right-winger and file their own suit attacking the FCC's rules. The Radio Television News Directors Association went to court, hoping that the new rules and a better litigant would alter the posture of the fairness doctrine problem. The "real" broadcast establishment also jumped—CBS and NBC, not wanting to be left behind, also attacked the FCC's overzealous new rules. The Commission quickly backtracked and exempted bona fide newscasts from the personal-attack rules.[6] But the broadcasters, unmollified, pressed on with their attack. CBS attempted to set a high-minded tone by distinguishing itself and its traditions from "the station involved in *Red Lion* [which] has made no effort to comply with the general fairness doctrine."[7] The FCC, retreating still further, exempted from its new rules bona fide news interviews and commentary or analysis in the course of bona fide newscasts.[8] Eric Sevareid was now in the clear; the Reverend Billy James Hargis was not. But still the establishment hammered on, and while the Supreme Court was delaying action on *Red Lion,* the Court of Appeals for the Seventh Circuit in Chicago gave the broadcasters a stunning victory:[9] they would be allowed to appear at the Supreme Court alongside the disreputable Red Lion. What the broadcasters did not foresee was that they would all go down together.

The Supreme Court found the personal-attack and editorial rules to be as valid as the adjudication against Red Lion. Justice White didn't even pause over the Commission's pattern of retreat when faced with the CBS charges of overreaching; he simply noted that the rules had been "twice amended." The Commission itself could not have scripted a more complete victory—the judicial seal of approval came, not from the D.C. Circuit as expected, but from the highest court in the land.[10]

While raking in its chips from *Red Lion* and the broadcast establishment, the Commission had not been idle. In its most innovative and intriguing initiative of the 1960s, the Commission joined the Surgeon General's crusade against cigarettes by ruling that the standard cigarette advertisement urging Americans to smoke Marlboros was not simply one cigarette company hawking its wares but rather a presentation of one side of a controversial issue of public importance. The issue? The view that smoking is "socially acceptable and desirable, manly and a necessary part of a rich, full life." Not bad. Judicial approval was easily garnered from the D.C. Circuit, and broadcasters and the tobacco industry were unable to convince the Supreme Court to touch the case.[11]

What next with respect to fairness? Who could know? But it was clear to even the most casual observer that the fairness doctrine was enjoying a more varied and active life in 1969 than it had been just a few years earlier. If credibility of enforcement had been weak before the 1962 procedural change, it made a strong comeback after the cigarette ruling, the personal-attack and editorial rules, and the stunning judicial affirmance of the Commission actions.

It is, of course, a long road from finding and correcting fairness violations to stripping an offending station of its right to broadcast because of them. The Commission fully understood this, and, however cocky it may have been over its triumphs, it nonetheless shrank from announcing the final solution to fairness misconduct—"capital punishment" for a licensee. The saga of Lamar Broadcasting's WLBT in Jackson, Mississippi, illustrates this fact only too well.

As anyone might guess, a station in Jackson, Mississippi, was not going to be partial to the civil rights movement. WLBT played the role of southern racist to the hilt. As early as 1955, the station deliberately cut off a network program on race relations on which Thurgood Marshall was speaking and in its stead flashed, "Sorry. Cable Trouble." Two years later, the station put on a program urging the maintenance of segregation and then refused eleven requests to present opposing views. The station wished there were no opposition and acted on the wish. The Commission noted complaints regarding these actions when reviewing the station's file at the time of its 1958 renewal and initially deferred the renewal. But it subsequently granted a full renewal, finding that, although fairness violations existed, they were isolated instances of improper behavior and did not merit denial of the application.[12]

In the fall of 1962, James Meredith's entry into Ole Miss generated a new round of fairness complaints based on WLBT's unwillingness to present any view but the anti-integration case. The station's general manager blithely announced his own views: "The word of the hour, of the day, of the year, is 'never.'"[13] The Commission began its investigation, and in the interim WLBT's license again came up for renewal. Despite the charges of racism and fairness violations indicating that WLBT was not operating in the public interest (and was certainly doing nothing for the blacks who made up 45 percent of its audience), the station responded that it "had always fully performed its public obligations." This claim may have applied to Jackson's segregationists but hardly to its black community, which took the unprecedented step of requesting that the FCC allow them to intervene in opposition to WLBT.

The Commission, always reluctant to allow intervention (originally even by affected broadcasters), turned the community down, stating that it accepted the proposed intervenors' allegations as true. Nevertheless, it went on to grant WLBT a limited one-year renewal, largely on the theory that Jackson was so in need of a properly performing station that it was best to hope that this time WLBT would conform to Commission rules. Although arguably a surprising conclusion, it was predictable by prior standards. Licensees didn't lose, even in 1965.[14]

The United Church of Christ, for itself and the would-be intervenors, appealed to the D.C. Circuit and won a stunning administrative law victory granting them "standing"—the right to intervene and be heard—which set administrative law off on the new course of public participation with which we are familiar today. More relevant, the opinion, written by then Circuit Judge Warren Burger, a ten-year Eisenhower appointee, blasted the Commission, ordered a hearing, and hinted that since "past performance is [the] best criterion," WLBT was in a lot of trouble. Judge Burger's treatment of the Commission's rationale for the renewal was especially caustic:

> It would perhaps not go too far to say it elected to post the Wolf to guard the Sheep in the hope that the Wolf would mend its

ways because some protection was needed at once and none but the Wolf was handy. This is not a case, however, where the Wolf had either promised or demonstrated any capacity and willingness to change.[15]

Back at the Commission, the intervenors were begrudgingly allowed to present their case. ("Intervenors" was the judicial name; "intermeddlers" was the Commission attitude.) The hearing was conducted as if the intervenors were pitted against both WLBT and the Commission. The hearing examiner ruled against the intervenors in a manner sometimes bordering on the absurd, as he placed the burden of proof on the intervenors and then threw out their evidence. The Commission followed up by granting the full three-year license, despite its earlier conclusion that this very same conduct precluded a three-year renewal. The D.C. Circuit, again through Judge Burger, was astounded. It not only reversed the Commission's grant of renewal, but, finding the "administrative conduct reflected in the record . . . beyond repair," in an unprecedented step it also ordered the Commission to throw open the channel and let all comers apply. The Commission efforts to protect a horrible licensee had thus proved unavailing, and Lamar Broadcasting was out by court order.[16]

Judge Burger's opinions for the D.C. Circuit took licensing and its premises very seriously. A licensee is a public trustee. It has duties that must be performed. If it does not wish to perform those duties, then it must be replaced. The case illustrates clearly the pervasiveness of the belief in the distinction between broadcasting and print. No government action was ever taken against the *Jackson Daily News*. No matter how supportive of segregation, southern newspapers could publish whatever they chose. In other words, we may not like it, but we can't do anything about it.

Almost immediately after the D.C. Circuit ruling on

WLBT, the Commission turned to the Reverend Carl McIntire's WXUR in Media, Pennsylvania (a Philadelphia suburb), and demonstrated that it had learned its lesson. McIntire had been the producer of a program called the "20th Century Reformation Hour," which had reached Philadelphia through a Chester station; in 1964 the station chose to terminate the program. At the same time, however, the licensee of WXUR in Media put the AM-FM combination on the market (during that era, the FM would typically just broadcast the AM's programming), and McIntire moved to fill his Philadelphia loss by purchasing WXUR.

Purchase of a license is normally followed by a pro forma petition to reassign the license, but in this case various civic and religious leaders petitioned the FCC against the transfer, characterizing the right-wing McIntire as "partisan and extreme" on public issues and as a "divisive" force who helped create a "climate of fear, prejudice and distrust of democratic institutions." Somewhat perplexed, the Commission granted the transfer but took the unusual step of warning McIntire about the obligations of the fairness doctrine (which his statement of programming policy had of course promised to satisfy). McIntire took over at the end of April 1965; fifteen months later, WXUR's three-year license was up for renewal, and the same opponents were back at the Commission, this time shouting "we told you so." As indeed they had.[17]

The Commission opinion, issued after the renewal hearing, noted that "at the heart" of the proceeding was the question of compliance with the fairness doctrine. It seemed that McIntire had violated the fairness doctrine and the personal-attack rules in the way other stations ran commercials or played Beatles records—as a matter of course and without thinking about it. The Commission's broadcast bureau had monitored WXUR's programming for at least eleven consecutive hours on each of eight consecutive days,

and the intervenors had done their own monitoring, all
with the same incredible results: during these periods, only
one side of a series of controversial issues was presented in
every case but one. Such behavior from a station that concentrated on controversial-issue programming might well be
seen as approaching total violation. On the rare occasions
when the station presented an opposing view, it was done
under the least auspicious circumstances. For example, an
uninterrupted program blasted the civil rights movement;
a spokesman on a countering program faced a badgering
host who asked such questions as "Do you think you acted
like an American when you led a group of people and broke
all the windows in the school?" or "Getting back to South
Media, basically what do you people want? A handout?"[18]

This show, disingenuously entitled "Freedom of Speech,"
was hosted by Tom Livezey, a man the hearing examiner described as "still swinging a stone age ax." Former CBS News
President Fred Friendly noted that Livezey possessed "a
special talent for attracting those citizens of the City of
Brotherly Love who stayed up late worrying about Jews,
blacks, radicals, and Billy Graham." An exchange with one
such listener went as follows:

> *Listener:* About this B'nai B'rith Anti-Defamation league . . .
> why don't they get upset at all this smut and filth
> that's going through the mails?
>
> *Host:* And who do you think is behind all this obscenity
> that daily floods our mails, my dear?
>
> *Listener:* Well, frankly, Tom, I think it is the Jewish people.
>
> *Host:* You bet your life it is.[19]

Despite the fairness violations and the attacks, the Commission's hearing examiner ruled that McIntire's license
should be renewed. The examiner condoned the violations
in part on the grounds that the station was so short-staffed

that it was impossible for McIntire to keep up with all the violations. That conclusion was a little short on logic. The examiner's other conclusion, however, was more interesting. He found, as indeed was true, that WXUR was meeting one of the asserted purposes of the fairness doctrine: the presentation of controversial issues. Few stations in the nation— and none owned by the likes of CBS, NBC, ABC, or the *Washington Post*—came even close to offering as much controversial programming as did WXUR. So far so good, but what about balance? The answer here was ingenious: anyone wishing to hear the other side of the issues presented on WXUR could do so with ease. All viewpoints were present in the Philadelphia area, and no listener need be uninformed. Denying WXUR its license would thus serve none of the affirmative purposes of the fairness doctrine and would in fact undercut the fairness doctrine by reducing the amount of controversial programming in the area.[20]

Nice but irrelevant, answered both the Commission and the D.C. Circuit. Once it became clear that McIntire was violating the fairness doctrine to such an extent, the excuses given by the hearing examiner could carry no weight. The station was a rogue, and its behavior was inexcusable. The only appropriate sanction was death: McIntire's license was not to be renewed, and WXUR was off the air.[21]

By sheer luck, McIntire drew on appeal the most favorable panel of the D.C. Circuit possible, one consisting of both Chief Judge Bazelon and Judge Skelly Wright, the two most liberal members of the court—but to no avail. The third member, Judge Tamm, agreed with everything the Commission said. He was joined in the result by Judge Wright, who ignored what the Commission said was the "heart" of the matter but nevertheless voted for the Commission by relying instead on an alternative but secondary ground offered by the Commission: McIntire's broken promise to obey the fairness doctrine. Wright did not inquire whether the promise could be validly required. Chief Judge Bazelon wrote a rare dissent, but it was just that, a dissent—nice for the broadcasting casebooks, but of no use to McIntire or others worried about fairness enforcement. Nor was it enough to convince the necessary four members of the Supreme Court to grant review of the case. Justice Douglas wished to, but no other member did.[22]

The demises of WLBT and WXUR were indeed surprising, given the Commission's previous record on fairness violations. But they were nothing as compared to the sixteen-year saga that eventually led to the demise of Boston's Channel 5, WHDH.

The FCC began its hearings on applications for Channel 5 in 1954. In 1957 the *Boston Herald-Traveler,* the largest morning and afternoon newspaper, was selected for the license through a wholly owned subsidiary, Greater Boston Television. The *Herald* was the most influential Republican newspaper north of New York City, and, as suggested in chapter 5, its acquisition of the license was probably Republican favoritism: no other explanation seems plausible.

Naturally, the losers appealed. While the appeal was pending, potentially improper ex parte contacts between the *Herald*'s publisher, Robert Choate, and the FCC chairman were revealed. The court remanded the case to the FCC to hold a hearing concerning the contacts. The Commission determined that the contacts had been a subtle, but improper, attempt to influence the licensing, and it reopened the entire proceeding for a comparative hearing with all applicants, granting WHDH a temporary authorization to continue broadcasting in the meantime. At the hearing, WHDH was again awarded the channel, but, because of Choate's actions, it received only a limited four-month license. When WHDH applied for its renewal, the Commission took the unusual step of inviting competing applications. While the whole matter was on appeal, Choate died, and the court in 1964 remanded the case back to the Commission to consider the effect of Choate's death on the proceedings. The court also authorized the Commission to combine the renewal proceedings with those appealing the grant of the four-month license.[23]

Now intervening was the Commission's 1965 Policy Statement on Comparative Hearings, which attempted to clarify the standards (discussed in chapter 5) for determining how to pick and choose among competing applicants. The 1965 Policy Statement limited the criteria for choosing among competing applicants to diversification of ownership, past performance, integration of ownership and management, and program proposals.[24] Suffice it to say that a good lawyer can create a very good applicant on paper, and any applicant with outside media holdings is likely to be in trouble in a comparative hearing against the lawyer-constructed applicant.

That is, of course, just what happened to WHDH. Greater Boston Television could do nothing about its newspaper, and two of the competitors for Channel 5 carried no such liabilities. In a case that sent shock waves throughout the industry, Greater Boston, which had operated Channel 5 competently but not superbly since 1957, lost its license solely because it was owned by the *Herald-Traveler* newspaper. The 1969 decision was followed by a second opinion on reconsideration that attempted to pacify the industry with statements about the "unique events . . . [that] place WHDH in a substantially different posture from the conventional applicant for renewal of broadcast license."[25]

The D.C. Circuit, as usual, swallowed the Commission position, indeed with some relish, for it fostered the much-celebrated goal of diversification. The court found the Commission could appropriately prefer "those who would speak out with fresh voice." The difference between "fresh" and "polluted," as Judge Leventhal's opinion implies, was other media holdings in the area.[26]

Diversity was indeed an important objective, and replacement of WHDH with the new victor added one more media owner to Boston. The addition, however, was temporary. The *Herald-Traveler* had been supported on the profits of WHDH, and shortly after the station went off the air, the *Herald-Traveler* ceased publication. (And yes, a decade later the hearty, high-toned crew who ousted WHDH to bring a "fresh" voice to Boston sold out to the media conglomerate Metromedia for a mere $220 million.)[27]

In his concurring opinion in the *WHDH* case, Commissioner Johnson noted happily that stripping WHDH of its license was an "interesting experiment" in the implementation of a policy of locally owned and operated stations in major markets.[28] He, at least, gave every indication that he would like to see many more such interesting experiments. Thus although Johnson may have been technically correct in asserting that broadcasters had little to fear from the FCC, the broadcasters knew it was not for lack of effort on his part, and they would hardly have regarded him as a source of unbiased accuracy on their status. Furthermore, regardless of reality, broadcasters and others must base their actions on what they perceive to be the realities of the situation. And that perception changed radically in the late 1960s.

Even Professor Louis Jaffe of Harvard Law School, who had attacked the grant to WHDH in his 1957 *Harper's* article, characterized *WHDH* in the 1969 *Harvard Law Review* (the most prestigious journal in American law) as a "spasmodic lurch to 'the left'" and interpreted the decision as follows:

> The [Commission] . . . has apparently decided . . . that a broadcasting licensee applying for renewal has no advantage over rival applicants: the criteria applicable to an original grant are to be equally applicable on renewal. If so, this decision overrules an administrative practice of at least eighteen years standing . . . during which time enormous investments have been

made, apparently in reliance on that practice. The newly announced principle could mean that all licenses are now at hazard every three years, a proposition which would work a revolution in the industry.[29]

It is important to note that this new hazard was imposed independent of the Nixon administration's concentrated attack on the eastern media establishment. *Red Lion,* Jackson, and Boston were decisions with which Nixon commissioners and judges were not involved, and indeed, the same can be said about McIntire, a unanimous Commission decision, affirmed by a panel with the two most liberal judges on the nation's most liberal court of appeals.

The broadcasters' perceptions of reality begin to look at least as accurate as Johnson's, maybe more so. *Red Lion* demonstrated that fairness enforcement might be seriously undertaken. The Commission had acted swiftly and eagerly when given the chance to codify the personal-attack rules and showed a dogged determination to use the fairness doctrine aggressively in at least some circumstances. The D.C. Circuit had enthusiastically added its imprimatur to the Commission's cigarette ruling. The Supreme Court chose not to review the cigarette ruling, probably because it believed the ruling to be correct. And *Red Lion*'s unanimous opinion contained not a word of doubt. Indeed, as noted, the Supreme Court believed that it would be quite proper to strip a station of its license should it transgress the fairness doctrine, but left unspecified the amount of the necessary transgression.

Both *Lamar Broadcasting* and *WXUR* demonstrated that major fairness transgressions were reason enough to call the fiduciary duty violated and require forfeiture of the license. Judge Burger's opinion in *Lamar* had been adamant—so adamant that it ordered a reluctant Commission to kill WLBT. *WXUR* was technically a Nixon case, as the actions

all occurred during his administration. But it was not the
result of political paranoia, and if a right-wing station could
go, what about a station on the left, where the tension between administration and broadcasters was much greater?
One might indeed have expected a Nixon FCC to swing into
action against an offending foe without the prodding of the
D.C. Circuit or the massive violations of Lamar or WXUR.
Given the risks of a wrong judgment, a licensee would have
been foolish and reckless to assume otherwise. To be sure,
the courts were not an arm of the Nixon administration and
could be looked to for protection, but from *Shuler* to *WIBO*
to *Lamar* to *Red Lion,* the idea of judicial protection of
broadcasters offered no great comfort. On the contrary,
with the one small exception of the D.C. Circuit's negative
opinion in the case of the subpoena to the publisher of the
Nashville Banner, the courts had operated as all administrative law textbooks said they should: as an approving arm of
the governing agency. Why should the FCC be different,
when, as *NBC* had demonstrated for twenty-five years, the
First Amendment was not a relevant constraint?

More ominous than any of the previous three cases was
WHDH and the D.C. Circuit's approval of the FCC actions.
For WHDH, if not a perfect role model, had done nothing
wrong. It lost simply and solely because it was owned by a
newspaper and its challengers were not. Nor were the implications of the decision restricted to Boston and people
such as Choate. As Professor Jaffe noted, the Communications Act does not distinguish between original licensing
and relicensing. Thus, either Commission or court would
have to create such a distinction to limit the reach of *WHDH.*
The Commission, of course, promised that it would. But was
the promise good? And, if good, would the D.C. Circuit
give its endorsement? After all, the Commission also promised Lamar another chance, and the D.C. Circuit instead
gave all concerned a civics lecture.

Furthermore, there is no apparent distinction between newspapers and other broadcast properties, whether VHF, UHF, AM, or FM. If diversification is a major goal—and both Commission and court fully agreed that it was most significant—then all multimedia owners were put on notice. Another limiting device would therefore be necessary to restrict the *WHDH* decision to a Boston newspaper alone, and whatever device was seized upon might well find the D.C. Circuit less than enthusiastic. Until limitations were announced and approved, broadcasters that were co-owned with other media outlets anywhere could not sleep securely.

Commissioner Johnson thus is not totally, or even mostly, correct if one takes an objective look at the situation at the end of the decade. Broadcasters, however, were not taking a perfectly objective look. Their glasses had the rose tint of self-interest, of high-dollar involvement, that precluded objectivity. If they failed to show concern about their investment, who would? The threat of extinction was credible, as even a dinosaur should have understood, and broadcasters had to be at least modestly aware of it. Furthermore, threats of extinction are decidedly more credible in a hostile environment. As chapter 8 will document, at the time Johnson testified, the horizon was darkening and would continue to do so for several more years. If licensing needs credibility to work, then in 1970 it could work, for credibility it had.

III
SUPERVISION

OVERVIEW

In Part I we saw that radio was perceived, virtually unanimously, to be outside the sphere of the press. Accordingly, the First Amendment protections to which it could lay claim proved to be minimal at best, although over time, and especially within the past two decades, broadcasting unavoidably has come to be seen as part of the press but not quite entitled to all the First Amendment protections that are available to print. Even though the First Amendment as tailored for broadcasting differs from the traditional one, a core belief that no governmental censorship or excessive supervision would chill the discussions available to the American people has been asserted as a central commonality.

Part II dealt with the decision to license broadcasting and with the selection process for licensees. Occasionally the contested case cried out that the licensing process was based on criteria that could not withstand the light of day. The criteria did not have to. Finally, Part II discussed a major claim that once a license was issued, renewal was virtually automatic. This was not, however, the case in the 1930s, and it proved not to be the case as the 1960s came to a close. Thus, for two important periods—at least—the threat of license loss has been a credible one. Ominously, the second period coincided with the coming of the presidency of Richard Nixon.

With this as background, Part III takes up FCC supervision of its licensees. In what ways, if any, did the Commission become involved with the programming decisions of those it chose to license in the public interest? Did the Commission attempt to impose its own politics or cultural values on broadcasting? And when it did, with what success? Part III examines four topics: the fairness doctrine, the Nixon administration attacks on the networks, the problems confronting the FCC generally by presidential (and to a lesser extent, congressional) interest in Commission decisions affecting incumbents, and programming that transgresses mainstream boundaries.

Chapter 7 traces the fairness doctrine from the efforts in the late 1920s in *Great Lakes Broadcasting* to muzzle broadcasters perceived to be mouthpieces for labor or socialist policies, through *Mayflower Broadcasting* and the coercion of the anti-Roosevelt Sheppard stations, to, once again, *Red Lion*. The book at this point reviews the facts of *Red Lion* in a new light: the Kennedy-Johnson effort to restrain right-wing broadcasting.

Chapter 8 focuses on Richard Nixon's vendetta against the eastern establishment press, and in particular on the variety of his attacks on the three networks. More than a decade after his resignation, his systematic attack on the networks and the *Washington Post* still makes sobering reading. How much of an aberration is a paranoid administration? The laws of broadcasting have not changed in the years since Nixon's exile. Are we thus in any better position to fight off another president with an inclination to threaten his foes with financial devastation?

Chapter 9 looks at three legal areas: the fairness doctrine and the access it provides to nonbroadcasters; equal time; and candidate access. From the elasticity of the fairness doctrine to the precision of the equal-time provision, Commission decisions favor, first, the president over all others and, second, incumbents over challengers. It is as if the Commission had learned from former Texas Longhorn football coach Darrell Royal, who, explaining his bowl game plans, would state: "You dance with who brung you." The commissioners always knew who brought them.

Chapter 10 details the two-decade effort by the Commission to ban certain programming from the air, especially those forms offensive to middle-class values. To some extent it is a chapter about cultural folly. Was it really appropriate for the Commission to concern itself with whether an announcer used the phrase "let it all hang out" with some frequency? If so, to what effect? When the Commission determined to eradicate from the air songs promoting or glorifying the use of drugs, wasn't it really attacking the music of a generation it did not understand and barely tolerated? Can such a spree of censorship avoid excesses? This one did not. Songs that were violently antidrug, as well as songs having nothing to do with the drug scene, were censored by broadcasters as fear demanded caution and distance from Commission sanctions. Finally, the Commission's all-out assault on four-letter words and talk shows concerning sexual matters on the radio again highlights the differing treatments of the print media and broadcasting. It also demonstrates the central theme of this book: if we allow licensing, the licensing body is likely to condemn to silence that which it fears, hates, or cannot understand.

7

USING AND ABUSING
THE FAIRNESS DOCTRINE

Main Street doesn't include unions or socialists, and as WIBO's cancellation had shown, the FRC liked good old-fashioned Main Street Americanism. The continued operation of the Socialist Party's New York station, WEVD (with call letters celebrating the noted labor leader and socialist candidate for president, Eugene Victor Debs), was thus in jeopardy. In equal trouble was Chicago's WCFL, owned by the American Federation of Labor. These stations were what the Commission called "propaganda" stations, those that strayed from the norm and spoke to a particular audience. In reaction to both spectrum scarcity and its hostility to these stations, the Commission lashed out at them. In 1929 in *Great Lakes Broadcasting,* the Commission had noted that there was "not room in the broadcast band for every school of thought, religious, political, social, and economic, each to have its separate broadcasting station, its mouthpiece in the ether. If franchises are extended to some it gives them an unfair advantage over others, and results in a corresponding cutting down of general public service stations."[1] This attitude boded ill for WEVD and WCFL.

WCFL had applied for an increase in power and in hours of operation on the grounds that it broadcast programs of particular interest to organized labor and that the large membership of the national labor organization justified a station "to be used for the exclusive benefit of organized labor." The Commission refused the request, declaring that "there is no place for a station catering to any group. . . . All stations should cater to the general public and serve public interest as against group or class interest."[2] Nevertheless, WCFL was not deleted; neither was WEVD, which also escaped with a warning to operate with "due regard for the opinions of others."[3]

These cases, plus the almost simultaneous decision in *Great Lakes,* form the beginnings of the fairness doctrine. But it took until just before World War II for the Commission to articulate successfully what it was looking for from its licensees, should they stray from Main Street. A licensee who "believe[d] in the American form of government" provided the occasion.[4] It is thus fitting that this doctrine carries a genuinely American name: the *Mayflower* doctrine.

In 1939 Mayflower Broadcasting applied for a frequency already being used by one of the two Boston stations of John Sheppard III, the owner of a group of New England stations forming the Yankee Network. Sheppard was the president of a family corporation that had moved from department stores into radio, and the Yankee Network, centered in Boston, was by the standards of the day a fair-sized regional network.

The United States had been good to the Sheppards, and the Sheppards were the kind to reciprocate. As a small gesture of their belief in our form of government, when CBS gave fifteen minutes of airtime to Earl Browder, the Communist Party leader, the Yankee Network refused to carry the program but did run the reply the next night. Sheppard took his news from the Hearsts and his commentary from, among others, Father Coughlin, who by the mid-1930s had moved from the left to the far right, persistently attacking FDR—"Franklin Doublecrossing Roosevelt"—along the way. In addition to partisan commentary, a Sheppard station would take partisan editorial positions.

With war approaching in Europe, the National Association of Broadcasters, attempting in part to pre-empt the FCC, had announced that paid sponsorship of programs dealing with controversial issues was inappropriate.[5] The NAB then ruled, over Sheppard's objections, that Father Coughlin could not be carried on a sponsored basis. Some stations got the message and dropped him altogether; even Sheppard acquiesced by accepting only enough revenue to cover line costs and overhead for the controversial priest.[6]

If Sheppard avoided trouble with the NAB, he found it with the FCC over editorializing. When the Mayflower Broadcasting Corporation filed its competing application to operate on the same frequency as one of the Sheppards' Boston stations, the FCC set that application, along with the Yankee Network's application for renewal, for a comparative hearing. Even though Mayflower was soon disqualified for making misrepresentations to the Commission,[7] the Commission nonetheless proceeded to scrutinize the Yankee Network's qualifications. The licensee was found to be deficient by virtue of its "serious misconception of its duties and functions under the law."[8]

> It is clear that with the limitations in frequencies inherent in the nature of radio, the public interest can *never* be served by a dedication of any broadcast facility to the support of [the licensee's] own partisan ends. Radio can serve as an instrument of democracy *only* when devoted to the communication of information and exchange of ideas fairly and objectively presented. . . . It cannot be devoted to the support of principles he happens to regard most favorably. . . .
>
> The licensee has assumed the obligation of presenting all sides of important public questions, fairly, objectively and without bias. . . . These requirements are inherent in the conception of the public interest.[9]

The Commission had grounds for denying Yankee a renewal, but Sheppard had prudently ordered the editorials to stop when the Commission had requested details about station programming. And he promised never to editorialize again: "Since September 1938 'no attempt has ever been or will ever be made to color or editorialize the news received' from usual sources."[10] Since the licensee had gotten the message—very clearly—it was allowed to continue. Furthermore, by granting the renewal, the Commission had immunized itself from judicial review. The Yankee Network, having gotten all it could want, would not complain. Nor would others—most broadcasters didn't care, because they never editorialized.[11] It was a painless trade: the Yankee Network kept its Boston stations; broadcasters kept away from partisan politics.

No more editorials. No more attacks on policies with which the broadcaster disagreed. It was an interim solution, the best available until the ban on newspaper ownership of licenses could be adopted and broadcasting be rid of the opponents of FDR. Whether intentionally or not, the timing of *Mayflower,* the selection of an anti-FDR station, and the ingenious action of the Commission in foreclosing an appeal suggest that the decision was a New Deal initiative to cope with what seemed to be an increasingly hostile communications empire.

After the war, however, everything changed. In 1949, while the Commission staff worked over the various possibilities for television allocation, the Commission held eight days of hearings on *Mayflower,* abandoned that doctrine, and instead clarified the duties of a station under the fairness doctrine: to present controversial programming and to maintain an overall balance in the programming. Broadcasters could return to editorializing, but they must be fair.[12]

As noted in chapter 6, the Commission's initial procedure handled fairness complaints so as to all but relegate them to the circular file. The 1962 procedural change not only brought fairness complaints to the Commission's immediate attention, but it also marked a genuine Commission interest in the doctrine. The change occurred shortly before the events in *Red Lion* began. I have portrayed *Red Lion* in earlier chapters as a sitting duck for the FCC; the facts of the case, however, are decidedly more complex than that formulation suggests, and they deserve a full airing.

The Reverend John M. Norris had been a member of the United Presbyterian Church but left it, "not exactly defrocked." After some circuit riding in South Dakota, he returned to his native Pennsylvania and in 1950 decided to preach the gospel from a radio station. He applied for and obtained a license for a daylight-only station in Red Lion, Pennsylvania, a small hamlet near York that by the 1960s had twelve-channel cable and could pick up seven over-the-air television stations as well as twenty other AM and about a dozen FM stations.[13]

Although the station did not thrive financially—its top rate was twenty-five dollars for an *hour* of prime time—it filled a niche: right-wing Christian broadcasting. Like Carl McIntire's WXUR, the gospel it aired advocated a mix of getting the United States out of the UN, abolishing foreign aid, abolishing Social Security and unemployment compensation, promoting right-to-work laws, selling the TVA, impeaching Earl Warren, and fighting integration and medicare. Among the regulars who bought time on "the World for God, Christ and the Bible in Red Lion, Pennsylvania," were McIntire (who was a Norris discovery), Dan Smoot, Dean Manion, H. L. Hunt's "Life Line," and the Reverend Billy James Hargis's "Christian Crusade."[14]

It was two minutes of a Hargis program that brought Norris more contact with the federal government than he ever wanted. Of course, Hargis was capable of drawing fire. A man whose heroes were Senator Joe McCarthy and General Edwin A. Walker (who led the 1962 racist charge at Ole Miss) and who blamed liberals, agnostics, and "all men who reject the Second Coming of Christ" for a "destroyed church and enslaved America" stood out in any era. Before turning to an examination of how Hargis and Norris set the stage for a classic freedom of the press confrontation, we must first look at the White House and the Democratic National Committee under presidents Kennedy and Johnson. Our starting point is the battle over ratification of the Nuclear Test Ban Treaty in the summer of 1963.[15]

The predominant protreaty committee SANE (National Committee for a Sane Nuclear Policy) was so identified with world federalism and comprehensive disarmament as to be a potential target for a right-wing fear campaign. At President Kennedy's behest, a new committee was formed to assist ratification. That committee, the Citizens' Committee for a Nuclear Test Ban Treaty, took as one of its functions the need to counter attacks on radio by the ultra right wing, using as its vehicle the FCC's fairness doctrine, which required that if a station presented one side of a controversial issue of public importance it also must present the other side.[16]

During the treaty debate, the Commission had expanded the fairness doctrine by adding the *Cullman* doctrine[17] (named after Cullman Broadcasting), which required that if only one side was presented during a sponsored program— as the right-wing attacks typically were—the other side must be presented, even if no one would pay. With this ruling, the new treaty committee was ready to respond to Hargis, McIntire, and other right-wing commentators. Henceforth, virtually every time a well-known commentator attacked the treaty, the committee requested response time. The tactic worked—and the Kennedy administration learned an important lesson.

Less than a month after the treaty was ratified, Kennedy's appointment secretary and trusted friend Kenneth O'Donnell requested a meeting with former *New York Times* reporter Wayne Phillips, then a special assistant to the head of the Housing Administration. O'Donnell instructed Phillips to meet with Nicholas Zapple, counsel to the Senate Communications Subcommittee, who later recalled that Phillips represented the Democratic National Committee, which was "determined to use the Fairness Doctrine to counter the radical right."[18]

The briefings Phillips received left him with no doubt that the DNC expected him to see if the fairness doctrine "could be used to provide support for the President's [now LBJ's] programs." Upon learning just how extensive right-wing radio was, Phillips realized that monitoring it would be a huge task, and he gave Wesley McCune, a Democratic Party aide who operated a service that researched the right wing, "a large bundle, about ten thousand dollars," to buy equipment and keep track of radio transmissions for the Democrats. Additionally, the DNC prepared a do-it-yourself kit to enable friends of the DNC to use the fairness doctrine against offending stations. Finally, Phillips enlisted the aid of a friend from New York newspaper days, Fred Cook.[19]

What Phillips wanted from Cook was a nice campaign "biography" of the probable Republican presidential candidate, Barry Goldwater. While Cook was working on the Goldwater hatchet job, Phillips suggested that he write an article for *The Nation,* his usual employer, on the right-wing radio stations. (McCune had already given Phillips material for such an article.)[20] "Hate Clubs of the Air" was published by *The Nation* in late May.[21] It described various right-wing broadcasters—many of whose programs appeared on the Red Lion station—labeling them John Birchers and informing the "liberal forces" that one remedy against the rightists' "wild-swinging charges" was to demand "equal time" under the fairness doctrine. Interestingly, and accurately, the article noted that aides of the DNC were monitoring the stations. Phillips subsequently recalled that "thousands of copies of Cook's article were sent to state Democratic leaders and to every radio station in the country known to carry right-wing broadcasts together with a letter from Sam Brightman of the DNC pointing out that claims for time would be made in the event of attacks on Democratic candidates or their programs."[22]

After Goldwater's nomination, the DNC stepped up its efforts. According to Bill Ruder, an Assistant Secretary of Commerce under Kennedy, "Our massive strategy was to use the Fairness Doctrine to challenge and harass right-wing broadcasters and hope that the challenges would be so costly to them that they would be inhibited and decide it was too expensive to continue." In a summary written near the end of the campaign, a memo noted that Democratic requests had produced almost seventeen hundred hours of free airtime. And, as Phillips himself added, "even more important than the free radio time was the effectiveness of this operation in inhibiting the political activity of these right-wing broadcasts."[23]

In the interim, Cook produced his book, *Goldwater: Extremist on the Right.* No major publisher was interested, but the Democrats promised to buy fifty thousand copies at twelve cents each. Grove Press printed the book and sold forty-four thousand copies in addition to seventy-two thousand taken by the Democrats.[24]

One of the readers, or at least scanners, of the book was the Reverend Billy James Hargis, whom Cook had already blasted in "Hate Clubs of the Air." Hargis responded somewhat in kind, although he debased the tone of the exchange several notches. In a taped program, he attacked Cook as a "professional mudslinger" and went on to accuse Cook of dishonesty, falsifying stories, attacking J. Edgar Hoover, and defending Alger Hiss. For good measure, he took a swing at *The Nation,* "one of the most scurrilous publications of the left which has championed many communist causes over many years." The tape was sent to stations airing "Christian Crusade." On November 25, the two-minute attack in the fifteen-minute program aired over Red Lion. One of the listeners was the DNC, still cheerfully monitoring its hard opposition three weeks after the election.[25]

The DNC had supplied Cook with a list of stations that normally carried "Christian Crusade" and advised him on requesting reply time on the stations and on petitioning the FCC. Red Lion was only one of the stations from which Cook demanded time. Some stations complied, others did not, and still others offered time for sale at the same rate that Hargis paid. Red Lion was in the third class. Norris's response was blunt: "Our rate card is enclosed. Your prompt reply will enable us to arrange for the time you may wish to purchase." He also enclosed letters he had written to the DNC and the ACLU when they had requested airtime to respond to a Dan Smoot program. Indeed, although the eighty-two-year-old Norris may not have realized the Democrats were monitoring him, he did believe he was being "harassed." His conclusion: "I have never before been subjected to such religious and political persecution."[26]

Unsatisfied with Norris's offer to sell him time, Cook, with some help from the DNC, moved to the friendlier territory of the FCC. Virtually all of the next year was spent in an exchange of letters, bolstering both Norris's belief that he was being harassed and the Commission's equally solid belief that Cook had been attacked and was entitled to reply time. The station's offer to grant a free reply only if Cook could not afford to pay the $7.50 for fifteen minutes was inadequate—the licensee had a duty to air the opposition even if no one would sponsor it. The fact that Hargis was responding to an attack by *The Nation* that Cook had instigated was irrelevant. A broadcaster has the duty to be fair; *The Nation* does not.

When the Supreme Court affirmed the FCC position in June 1969, the Court was unaware of these facts, as were the lawyers. The facts came out only some years later, and they cast doubt on the easy confidence with which Justice White's opinion for a unanimous Court dismissed any concerns about a chilling effect flowing from fairness doctrine enforcement.

Although *Mayflower,* likely, and *Red Lion,* certainly, constitute open uses of the licensing procedure to silence political opposition, for the most part no one knew that licensing was being put to political use. It would be a mistake to believe that such uses were the rule rather than exceptions. It is too difficult to conceal partisan uses of FCC power, and it is too much to ask the courts, even those as compliant as the D.C. Circuit traditionally has been, not to notice such uses when they are occurring. The enforcement powers of the Commission and the courts must be kept in the background. If anything but occasional resort to them is necessary, the system will not work. The threat to chill partisan programming can be blunt and crude so long as no enforcement is on the horizon.

If the legal process is to be called into play, however, then a degree of subtlety is necessary, as *Red Lion* and, to a lesser extent, *Mayflower* demonstrate. For this reason, as chapter 8 will show, the Nixon administration attacks on the media were designed to work directly on broadcasters without legal enforcement. Spiro Agnew's famous crusade required no action from the FCC, and indeed, when an administration supporter in Houston picked up what she thought was the Agnew cue and requested the FCC to develop guidelines for network analysis of a presidential speech, the Commission quickly and unanimously declined. Such regulation would have been too bald an act of censorship.[27]

All this should have been, but was not, obvious. Thus, in a fit of euphoria, an exceptionally hawkish group decided to charge CBS News with massive fairness violations—shades of McIntire—on the issue of national security. The group based its actions on a study by Ernest Lefever, which had declared that "CBS News shortchanged the American people and thus compromised its public trust." The complaint filed by the American Security Council Education Foundation (a successor group to the one sponsoring Lefever's study) charged CBS with "virtually boycotting views suggesting that the U.S. is losing or has lost military superiority to the Soviet Union and that a greater effort should be made to strengthen American defenses."[28] A massive fairness violation of the magnitude charged would indeed have been a breach of public trust and probably a prime candidate for "capital punishment." At a minimum, CBS News could have been ordered to remedy its fairness violations with massive presentations of the other side; at a maximum, it could have lost its five VHF money machines, some of the very best in the United States.

The Lefever study had used four subtopics—Vietnam, U.S. military and foreign affairs, Soviet military and foreign policy, and Chinese military and foreign policy—as the cornerstones of an overarching national-security structure. The study charged that CBS had violated the fairness doctrine by presenting stories that either supported the then-current perception that the Soviet military threat was well met by U.S. military preparations or suggested that the Soviet threat was less serious than the Nixon administration believed and that national security efforts should thus be decreased. All but ignored, the study charged, was information suggesting that the Soviet threat was consistently greater than perceived and should be countered by an increase in military spending.

The study contained massive methodological flaws, but these were either unseen or ignored in the initial rash of publicity. For example, a statement by the Secretary of Defense that "the thing to do if you go the $30 billion route [of budget cuts as proposed by George McGovern] is to direct the Department of Defense to spend at least a billion dollars on white flags so that it can run them up all over, because it means surrender" was classified as a run-of-the-mill administration defense statement, whereas a statement by Senator Proxmire, also opposing the McGovern proposal, was placed in the category of decreasing our national security. As Fred Friendly was to demonstrate in 1975, the study had such gaping holes that it bordered on the ludicrous—except to those who were convinced that it was right without even reading it.[29]

For well over a year after it was released, the study effected no more than exchanges between its proponents and CBS News. Then the front shifted as the American Security Council Education Foundation took the action that was implicit in the study. It headed for the FCC, charging that on the most important issue of the time—war and peace—the major television news organization and network was systematically feeding its viewers a distorted and unfair picture over the range of issues encompassing national security.

But the fairness complaint was doomed from the start. First, the study was, as noted, methodologically flawed. Second, it asked the Commission to push CBS News to a position significantly to the right of either the Nixon or the Ford administration. Although a constituency for the hard right doubtless existed, it was waiting for Ronald Reagan in 1980 and was not represented on either the Ford or the Carter Federal Communications Commission.

The Commission in 1977, wanting nothing to do with the complaint, simply tossed it out without bothering to hold a hearing. It concluded that the complaint had failed to meet the fairness doctrine requirement that it present a particular, well-defined issue. National security as an umbrella over four subissues was simply too amorphous (probably mean-

ing that it was too big). On appeal, the D.C. Circuit, as it always seemed to, agreed with the Commission. Even if the
complaint were correct, the duty of the complainant was to
present a manageable issue to the Commission for determination. Here, a majority of the court concluded, the complainant had not. Ridiculous, replied the dissent; the issue
"was plain as day: whether this Nation should do more, less,
or the same about the perceived threats to national security." Thus, if the charges by ASCEF were accurate—and a
hearing would be necessary to make that determination—
CBS's dovish position constituted a massive fairness violation. Yet the majority of the court, the dissent charged,
ducked the hard questions, "instead carving an ill-defined
safe harbor into which the commission may sail when the
waters are rough."[30]

But the dissenters, like ASCEF, failed to understand that
ordering CBS News to present stories one way—even as a
correction—is too openly an act of censorship. Obvious censorship still retains a bad name in our society. If we are to
have government censorship, it must not be aboveboard: it's
got to be out of sight. That is how we accommodate our traditions. That is how *Mayflower* and *Red Lion* work: not by
Commission action or judicial review, but by threat, pure
and simple. Nixon's head of the Office of Telecommunications Policy, T. Clay Whitehead, put it best: "The value of
the sword of Damocles is that it hangs, not falls."[31]

8

THE NIXON ASSAULT
ON THE NETWORKS

November 13, 1969, was an amazing night. When the millions of viewers of the networks' nightly news turned on their sets at 7:00 P.M. in the eastern time zone to see their favorite anchors, they got instead, regardless of the network selected, live coverage of a speech from Des Moines, Iowa, by the vice-president of the United States. Although the buildup to the speech and network coverage had begun with the election of Richard Nixon a year earlier, events had gained an incredible momentum within the preceding month.[1]

The Nixon administration's campaign against the "liberal eastern" media is well known, but this book would omit a crucial chapter if it did not reiterate at least that part of the story involving the attacks against network television and the *Washington Post*'s broadcast holdings. This is a part of a larger topic—but a highly important part—constituting the essence of the administration attacks. Although other presidents have assailed the media, pressured the media, and used the federal government in attempts at censorship, no other American president understood so well that broadcast properties were valuable *and licensed*. This understanding, coupled with a militant drive to make the airways conform to Richard Nixon's views of what America should be, led to unprecedented efforts to force network television to tone down criticism of Nixon and to better present his views. The efforts began in the latter half of his first year in office and died only when Watergate crushed everything in its path. They were enacted on a wide variety of fronts, but all shared an underlying theme: financial incentive. The government, if it is willing to be consistent and thorough, can have a major impact in determining whether certain operations are profitable and whether certain people will have the right to acquire a fortune through television.

The catalyst of Agnew's speech, as of virtually everything during that period, was Vietnam. Two days before the scheduled October 15 antiwar demonstrations in Washington, the president's press secretary, Ron Ziegler, announced that the president would soon be making a major speech on Vietnam. In the three weeks between the announcement and the speech, excited speculation abounded: what would the president say?

The November 3 speech in fact contained nothing new; it simply reiterated the president's determination to stay the course. In his memoirs, however, Nixon states that this talk, which came to be known as the "silent majority" speech because of the president's call at the end for the support of "the great silent majority" of Americans, was one of those rare speeches that "influence the course of history."[2]

Others were less sure of its greatness. As was customary, each network, having been given a copy of the speech and a briefing by Henry Kissinger well in advance, provided commentary after the speech. Instead of praising it—or, as Nixon put it in his memoirs, "presenting impartial summaries of what I had said"—the network correspondents focused on what he might have said, while pronouncing the substance as nothing new. Nixon, his immediate family, and the White House staff were incensed.[3]

Among the most enraged of the staffers was Patrick Buchanan, a conservative ideologue who saw liberals behind every typewriter and microphone.[4] A few days after the speech, he sent Nixon a memorandum suggesting a direct attack on network commentators. To Buchanan, the First Amendment presented no obstacle to silencing liberals who criticized the president's necessary attempts to explain the appropriateness of his policies to the American people. Buchanan implemented his view in a follow-up speech drafted for Vice-President Agnew, who was just coming off a shrill rhetorical blast at the antiwar movement and the "effete corps of impudent snobs who characterize themselves as intellectuals." Nixon himself edited the Buchanan draft, toughening its already strident language. When the president was done, he commended his own work with his usual flair: "This really flicks the scab off, doesn't it?" That it did. And more.[5]

Agnew's Des Moines speech began with an assertion of the vast power of television and the absence of checks on that power. Coupled with complaints about "instant analysis and querulous criticism," the theme was reiterated again and again.

The purpose of my remarks tonight is to focus your attention on this little group of men who not only enjoy a right of instant rebuttal to every Presidential address, but, more importantly, wield a free hand in selecting, presenting, and interpreting the great issues of our nation. . . .

Nor is their power confined to the substantive. A raised eyebrow, an inflection of the voice, a caustic remark dropped in the middle of a broadcast can raise doubts in a million minds about the veracity of a public official or the wisdom of a government policy. . . .

The American people would rightly not tolerate this concentration of power in government. . . .

Is it not fair and relevant to question its concentration in the hands of a tiny, enclosed fraternity of privileged men elected by no one and enjoying a monopoly sanctioned and licensed by government? . . .

As with other American institutions, perhaps it is time that the networks were made more responsive to the views of the nation and more responsible to the people they serve. . . .

The great networks have dominated America's airwaves for decades. The people are entitled to a full accounting of their stewardship.[6]

The networks had decided to air the speech live because, given Agnew's performance a month earlier and the rhetoric in the advance copy of this speech, it was likely to be newsworthy. Yet, in contrast to the network response to Nixon's "silent majority" speech, only CBS immediately followed Agnew's speech with its own rebuttal. CBS President Frank Stanton accurately concluded that the speech was an "unprecedented attempt by the Vice President of the United States to intimidate a news medium which depends for its existence upon government licenses."[7] Agnew's pro forma and disingenuous platitudes denying an intent to cause government censorship only underscored the point.

The White House, of course, was aware that its threat had teeth. Television was a licensed medium that was forced to deal with government on a regular basis, and now the licensing agency was falling into the hands of Nixon appointees. Credible threats, whether veiled or overt, could make the networks tone down opposition. This indeed was the gist of an amazing memorandum sent by Jeb Magruder to White House Chief of Staff H. R. Haldeman during the hectic month prior to the Des Moines speech.

The Magruder memo, entitled "The Shotgun versus the Rifle," was in response to a Haldeman request for a "talking" paper "on specific problems we've had in shot-gunning the media and anti-Administration spokesmen on unfair coverage." Magruder argued that individual complaints about specific programs were "very unfruitful and wasteful of our time." Continual calls to the networks from Buchanan and Herb Klein (apparently the two charged by the administration with making such complaints) had been unproductive. Magruder proposed to replace the complaints with methods that might have a "major impact" on news organizations, that might cause them to "begin to look at things somewhat differently." His proposal for "concentrated efforts" to coerce the change included five policies, three of which are relevant here. The suggestions would, he maintained, "do more good in the long run."[8]

The first proposal related to the new chairman of the FCC, Dean Burch, who would be sworn in before the month was over: "Begin an official monitoring system through the FCC" as soon as Burch took over. The monitoring system would point up the legal basis of the administration's position, and it would route the complaints through the FCC rather than Buchanan and Klein.[9]

Second, Magruder proposed using the Anti-Trust Division of the Justice Department to investigate possible media antitrust violations. "Even the possible threat of anti-trust action I think would be effective in changing their views in the above matter." Third, he wanted to deploy the Internal Revenue Service against "the various organizations we are most concerned about."[10]

Although it is tempting to dismiss this memo as a subaltern's attempt to look important in the eyes of his boss, such a conclusion would be inappropriate for several reasons. For one thing, the boss had specifically requested the memo. For another, attached to the memo were twenty-one requests, made within the previous thirty days, from the president to White House aides requesting specific actions on perceived unfair coverage. Finally, and most important, much of what Magruder suggested was implemented. The memorandum was thus clearly part of what William Safire, a Nixon speechwriter at the time, later acknowledged to be an "anti-media campaign" to "discredit and malign the press" that was "encouraged, directed, and urged on by the President himself."[11]

Burch took office just before the "silent majority" speech was delivered and quickly broke all FCC precedents by demanding from the networks transcripts of the commentary that had followed the speech.[12] It is worth pausing to consider the implications of this action. Just why did Burch want the transcripts? Was it out of an intellectual curiosity heretofore undisplayed? Or did he think that what was said on a network news program was related to the FCC's functions? Was he planning a change in FCC procedures whereby the Commission, rather than a listener, would initiate complaints against offending licensees? Did he think that the FCC's job was to monitor the networks? The networks took the understandable position that Burch's request was not friendly and that a Nixon FCC might well move against them.

This wholly logical interpretation was soon reinforced by a series of related actions by administration officials. Herb Klein and Ron Ziegler called broadcasters to request that copies of commentaries made following future presidential speeches be forwarded to the White House. Paul O'Neil, who was enjoying a sinecure appointment to the Subversive Activities Control Board—an agency without functions since the Supreme Court decisions in the 1960s—also called asking about plans for editorial coverage of presidential addresses. So did his wife.[13]

Although additional emphasis was hardly necessary, Herb Klein brought the point home—just in case anyone had failed to get it. Appearing on CBS's "Face the Nation" three days after the Des Moines speech, Klein told the panel of reporters that if the press did not take steps to correct its shortcomings, "you do invite the government to come in." [14]

Whether the networks believed they had invited the government in or not, it was apparent by the end of the first year of the Nixon administration that the White House was indeed "in" and was planning to use its powers to move the press—and not just the networks—into more favorable coverage of the administration. A week after his Des Moines speech, Agnew went before the Chamber of Commerce in Montgomery, Alabama, and widened his attack to include the *Washington Post* and the *New York Times*. He noted that "the day when the network commentators and even the gentlemen from the *New York Times* enjoyed a form of diplomatic immunity from comment and criticism of what they said—that day is over." But after this blast, the administration stopped its highly public jawboning. It was time to see how the message was taking. [15]

In fact, the Agnew-style bullying never recurred. This is not to say the networks were not criticized, for Agnew went on the stump again immediately after CBS aired its controversial "Selling of the Pentagon" in early 1971. Rather, the administration used other means to accomplish the same objectives, such as the meetings held in the summer of 1970 between White House special counsel (and political thug) Charles Colson and the heads of the three networks. [16]

Colson's memorandum to Haldeman indicates that the thrust of his three meetings was constant: the president must have access to network television, and responses to him should be as limited as possible. Because CBS was the network perceived as most anti-administration, the majority of the memo deals with Colson's meeting with CBS owner William Paley and the network's president, Frank Stanton.

The most remarkable notation in Colson's memo is his assertion that the networks were "startled by how thoroughly we were doing our homework." If there had been any doubt before, all three networks were now on notice that their news programs were being monitored and analyzed, and with real seriousness. The factual predicate from which Colson spoke and his aggressive presentation of the administration's position appear to have made the network executives nervous, accommodating, and "almost apologetic." [17]

In his meetings with network heads, Colson was able to satisfy himself that the president would have the necessary access to television, but he was less successful on the second front, that anti-administration people or network commentators should not be allowed to weaken the president's message. Nevertheless, one statement elicited by Colson from both CBS and ABC was astounding: both said that "most" speeches made by the president in his official capacity created no obligation for the networks to provide opposing viewpoints. If the networks meant that on most occasions the president did not address controversial issues, or if they meant quid pro quo response, then they were correct; but given what Nixon was really saying—that he wanted as much airtime as possible for himself with as little as possible for his opponents—Colson is correct in noting in the memo that this "is not the law." NBC took the more accurate position that not all presidential speeches were controversial, and thus replies would not always be mandated. [18]

On the issue of who responds, the administration scored considerable, but not complete, success. "ABC will do anything we want." That network's position was that time could regularly be granted to members of Congress—Republicans as well as Democrats—to respond to the president. NBC's view was similar. But CBS maintained its position that the Democratic leadership had to be given some time to respond to the president. [19] Colson's conclusion may thus have overstated the networks' capitulation, but it indicates the

substance of his memo: "These meetings had a very salu-
tary effect in letting them know that we are determined
to protect the President's position, that we know precisely
what is going on from the standpoint of both law and policy and that we are not going to permit them to get away
with anything that interferes with the President's ability to
communicate."[20]

Although not dealing specifically with the networks, a
brief recitation of the administration's actions with respect
to public broadcasting is in order here. The administration
was determined that public broadcasting should not be allowed to develop into a fourth network producing public-
affairs programming similar to or, worse, even more liberal
than the others'. According to a 1979 interview with T. Clay
Whitehead, an otherwise obscure bureaucrat who for a
brief period became the point man for the attacks on PBS,
there were two schools of thought within the administration
with regard to public broadcasting. One held that public
broadcasting should be done away with, the other merely
that it should be kept away from public-affairs programming. The key to each side was money. The administration
was very successful in applying financial pressure,[21] the outstanding example being Nixon's veto of a two-year $155 mil-
lion funding bill.

As described by Buchanan on the "Dick Cavett Show," the
bill was voted out of the Senate eighty-two to one, with the
idea that Nixon would be forced to sign it. "And Mr. Nixon,
I'm delighted to say, hit that ball about 450 feet down the
right foul line into the stands—and now you've got a different situation in public television." Privately, Buchanan was
more blunt: he told a public television executive at a cocktail
party, "If you don't do the kind of programming we want,
you won't get a f——ing dime."[22]

This aggressive stance was supplemented by warnings

from Whitehead that public broadcasting must be different
from CBS and NBC; by attacks on the salaries of former network correspondents Sander Vanocur and Robert MacNeil,
who had moved to PBS; and by appropriate appointments
to the dispersing agency, the Corporation for Public Broadcasting.[23] The attacks delayed, but could not halt, the growth
of public-affairs programming on PBS. They also sent Vanocur back to commercial television. And, probably most important, they stood as a constant reminder of the administration's extreme distaste for any evidence of liberals on a
television screen.

Of course, all the bullying in the world will get an administration nowhere if it can't be backed up with a credible
threat. Vetoing public-television funding and forcing settlement at a much lower amount demonstrated full credibility
in the PBS dispute. A like showing of credible threat to the
networks emerged on many different fronts. The first and
potentially most powerful threat lay in licensing, and the administration's bête noire, the *Washington Post,* bore its brunt.

The *Washington Post* Company, it should be noted—as
Agnew did in his Montgomery speech—is more than a
newspaper. It owns *Newsweek* and, more to the point, VHF
stations in Miami, Jacksonville, and Washington, D.C. Both
Florida stations were met by challengers at license renewal
time, the Miami station twice.

A word is in order about challenges to incumbents. Despite the stripping of WHDH's license in 1969, the FCC
has traditionally been loath to take a license away from its
holder and give it to a challenger. The times it had done so
are so rare as to belong in a museum. Generally, for a challenger to have any hope of success, the incumbent must be
part of a media family, thereby presenting diversification
problems, *and* must also be the worst station in the market.
Although the latter point is very subjective and always de-

batable, it essentially means the station that is most cavalier about the presentation of news, public affairs, and locally oriented programming. Furthermore, with chances of success so dim, challengers would want to be sure of their positions—there is no point in burning legal fees without an outstanding claim on the merits. What makes the challenges to the *Post* stations so striking is that the *Post* stations were the best, not the worst, in their markets. Indeed, the case could be made—and Commissioner Nicholas Johnson made it—that they were the best stations in the United States.[24]

During the 1970 battle over G. Harold Carswell's nomination to the Supreme Court, the Jacksonville station had uncovered his 1948 speech praising segregation[25]—which demonstrates both the station's quality and a reason for threatening it. Although a 1970 challenge to Jacksonville (headed by the man who would be appointed finance chairman of the 1972 Nixon campaign in Florida) went nowhere, almost simultaneously a group of Miami businessmen, including former partners of Nixon's friend Bebe Rebozo, challenged the *Post's* Miami station. Seven and a half months later they withdrew their challenge in an agreement requiring the *Post* to pay their legal fees (a compromise that Joseph Alsop referred to as paying the wolf's dental bill after he bites you).[26]

Next came the famous September 15, 1972, meeting in the Oval Office between Nixon, Haldeman, and John Dean, presidential counsel and architect of the Watergate cover-up. The following is the transcript of part of that meeting:

> *President:* The main thing is the *Post* is going to have damnable, damnable problems out of this one. They have a television station . . . and they're going to have to get it renewed.
>
> *Haldeman:* They've got a radio station, too.

President: Does that come up, too? The point is, when does it come up?

Dean: I don't know. But the practice of non-licensees filing on top of licensees has certainly gotten more . . . active in . . . this area.

President: And it's going to be Goddamn active here.

Dean: (Laughter) (Silence)

President: Well, the game has to be played awfully rough.[27]

Following Nixon's reelection, *Post* reporter Carl Bernstein was told by a friend who worked for the *Washington Star* that Colson had asserted in early November that "as soon as the election is behind us, we're going to really shove it to the *Post*. All the details haven't been worked out yet, but the basic decisions have been made—at a meeting with the President."[28] Indeed, before the year was out, the Miami station was challenged by a group including two law partners of former Senator George Smathers, a close friend of Nixon's.

The *Post* had been going it alone during most of 1972. But just before the election, CBS aired two substantial segments on Watergate. The White House was furious. Colson called CBS owner William Paley and blasted him at length. After the election Colson informed Stanton that CBS would pay the price for not playing ball during Nixon's first term. The price? "We'll bring you to your knees in Wall Street and Madison Avenue. . . . We'll break your network." What he meant was that the five CBS-owned and -operated stations would be taken away.[29]

Of course, none of this happened. But there is no doubt that the White House was very serious about what it intended to do to the *Post* and CBS. Watergate prevented a titanic test of strength.

Bullying and vengeance were not the only techniques practiced. The White House also had an arsenal of tactics aimed directly at the bottom line of the networks' financial statements, regardless of any challenges to specific stations. Two such strategies involved legal action, and one carried with it a little more bullying but with a promise of legal changes.

Nothing so focuses attention as discussions affecting the financial end of a network's prime-time programming. In September 1971 the president himself entered this fray by offering his support to the head of the Screen Actors Guild for a request the union had made to the FCC. The union's concern was reruns. As costs of producing prime-time programming had mounted, the networks had increasingly turned to reruns to flesh out their schedules. Where once a thirty-nine-week series had been the norm, the number had steadily dropped as more and more reruns appeared on the screen. Because no additional costs are associated with reruns, they fit the network needs perfectly (assuming viewers will watch). But they also put actors out of work. At a time of unemployment in Hollywood, reruns were bad news. The union requested an FCC rule limiting the networks to a maximum of thirteen weeks a year of reruns. CBS estimated that such a rule would cost it $150 million a year. Even assuming this figure to be outrageously exaggerated, the proposal was clearly expensive. The president wrote a letter to the Screen Actors Guild, backing their position and stating that if reruns were not voluntarily limited, "we will explore whatever regulatory recommendations are in order." Whitehead quickly picked up the theme in a speech that referred to the "spreading blight of re-runs."[30]

The timing of the rerun proposal hurt; the networks had just begun making painful programming adjustments in response to two new FCC rules. One of these rules limited the networks' ability to have any financial interest in the syndication of programs following their first network run. The other limited the amount of its own programming a network could provide for prime time. The impact of these rules on network finances was unclear, but the assumption was that it would be adverse. Topping off this problem with a limit on reruns would have been a very expensive dose of regulatory activism. Indeed, the Commission itself made no move on reruns and appeared to consider its new prime-time policy experimental.[31]

At about this point, the Justice Department stepped in and filed suit against all three networks, alleging (on the basis of data five years old) that the networks were monopolizing the ownership of prime-time programming. The lawsuit had in fact been kicking around the antitrust division for a decade and a half, but the division, averse to losing causes, had looked but never pushed. Now, caught in the whirl of the government's pervasive anti-network campaign, it filed. The *New York Times* was not alone in its editorial handwringing: "There are elements in the background of the present Federal action against the broadcasters which engender doubt whether its origins may not lie as much in politics as in zeal for law enforcement." Not surprisingly, the networks saw the suits as yet another example of political harassment—this time with a potent financial punch.[32]

The administration's approach crystalized in a luncheon address Whitehead made in December 1972 to the Indianapolis chapter of Sigma Delta Chi, the Society of Professional Journalists. The location had been chosen quite deliberately. The speech was a direct attack on the eastern media, and the White House wanted it delivered in middle America to continue the symbolism of Agnew's Des Moines speech. The text, which was released in Washington but a few hours before the luncheon was scheduled to begin, was so electrifying that by the end of the opening speeches the meeting was jammed with representatives from television stations from a wide area.[33]

Although most of the immediate attention focused on Whitehead's call for more active participation of managers in determining what is programmed—an idea that harkened back to the Chain Broadcasting Rules—other parts of his speech were reminiscent of Newton Minow's famous 1961 speech castigating the owners of American television for tolerating the creation of a "vast wasteland" in their programming. Minow, appointed by President Kennedy as FCC chairman, was one of the New Frontier's most noted regulators, and his speech had created a firestorm among broadcasters, with its implicit threat of government monitoring to adjudge quality programming. However, in the halcyon days of the early 1960s such criticisms were more than offset by the applause of liberals eager to support government in its efforts to reform popular culture.[34]

But, like most of the New Frontier, Minow was more rhetoric than reality. His Commission's signal achievement was pushing passage by Congress of the All-Channel Television Receiver Act, a piece of legislation mandating that new television sets be equipped to receive UHF stations, thus laying the ground for a massive increase in UHF broadcasting, a change that increased options if not quality.[35]

Whitehead's speech, although it was milder than Minow's, met with indignation from both broadcasters and liberals. Stashed between its blander elements were several paragraphs designed to make the hair on network executives' heads stand on end. And in contrast to the New Frontier, there was little confusion between rhetoric and reality in the Nixon administration.

More active decision making on programming meant licensee responsibility for "*all* programming, including the programs that come from the network." In fact, this had long been FCC doctrine, but, like most FCC doctrine, it had also been long ignored. Whitehead's suggestion that some

network programming might be unsuitable locally was un-
mistakably clear from the most quoted paragraph in his
speech.[36]

> There is no area where management responsibility is more im-
> portant than news. The station owners and managers cannot
> abdicate responsibility for news judgments. When a reporter
> or disc jockey slips in or passes over information in order to
> line his pocket, that's plugola, and management would take
> quick corrective action. But men also stress or suppress infor-
> mation in accordance with their beliefs. Will station licensees
> or network executives also take action against this ideological
> plugola?[37]

Shortly thereafter, Whitehead rammed the point home
again by asking, "Who else but management can or should
correct so-called professionals who confuse sensationalism
with sense and who dispense elitist gossip in the guise of
news analysis?" Thus the administration was making clear
that the policing of networks should be done in the first instance by local stations (who were thought to be so separated
geographically and intellectually from the networks that
the policing would be genuine). But what motive would the
local stations have for carrying out the policing function?
Again, Whitehead was leaving nothing to the imagination—
the administration had a new amendment to the Communications Act ready to go. The bill carried one of the elements
nearest and dearest to a broadcaster's heart: a longer term
on the license. A nice tasty carrot. But it also carried a stick
large enough to be fairly labeled a club. Broadcasters must
demonstrate that they have been substantially attuned to
the needs and interests of the communities they serve (thus,
by implication, not the eastern establishment) and must
show they have "afforded reasonable, realistic and practical
opportunities for the presentation and discussion of conflicting views on controversial issues." This latter require-

ment was not entirely new, nor was it even Whitehead's, but this new context gave it a significance it had previously lacked.[38]

Although the Whitehead speech is superficially comparable to Agnew's Des Moines speech, in fact it went considerably further, for it looked to the creation of over six hundred censors of network programming: all the affiliates. On the assumption that they might have a differing perspective from that of their networks, the administration was offering the affiliates great rewards to demonstrate the fact. It was an almost perfect economic reward to encourage what was already in their ideological self-interest.

It is only fair to note that many of the administration tactics discussed in this chapter were threats of legal action rather than affirmative steps toward that action, and indeed the few attempted steps toward legal action failed. What then was the real effect of the campaign against the media? Before attempting an answer, reference should be made to the broader context surrounding the attacks on television stations and networks that have been the subject of this chapter. This context included the unprecedented (an overworked but often accurate word when applied to the Nixon years) attempt to enjoin the *Times* and the *Post* in their publication of the Pentagon Papers, the use of subpoenas to harass reporters, and the even more intimidating uses of the FBI and IRS against journalists. I have discussed a portion of the administration's assault on the media: those on both the giving and receiving ends knew it was part of a larger picture. In some of these other areas, the attack was more successful than what has been described here.

William Safire's memoir states that in early 1973 the administration had its bootheel on the "liberal establishment press's neck."[39] Ben Bradlee, executive editor of the *Washington Post*, expressed the view that the First Amendment was in greater danger then than at any time that he had witnessed, and James Reston believed that Nixon had "won the battle . . . at least in the public's mind."[40] It is hard to know. The *Post* continues to be published, and the networks hardly became pro-administration. But Nixon's victory over McGovern was staggering, and the reality of the campaign's promise of "four more years" could only have been ominous to the broadcast establishment. Furthermore, there is evidence that the administration's campaign to rid the air of opposition had a certain amount of success.

On November 15, 1969, two days after Agnew's Des Moines speech, Washington, D.C., was the site of one of the largest antiwar demonstrations in the nation's history. It might have provided an opportunity for the networks to demonstrate that they were not intimidated by the administration. Instead, the demonstration by five hundred thousand Americans against their government was all but ignored by the networks. If a contrast was necessary, it came the following July 4, when Bob Hope came to Washington as the leader of "Honor America Day," a celebration of what Nicholas Johnson accurately labeled as "the apple pie view of America." All three networks lavished hours of coverage on the event. This is not to say that the decision to provide extended coverage of "Honor America Day" was unsound, but the contrast to the virtual exclusion of the massive demonstration in November makes no journalistic sense. It is explicable only as a capitulation to White House wishes.[41]

Similarly, the administration almost escaped discussion of Watergate on network television during the 1972 campaign. The total time devoted on the news to all Watergate coverage on NBC was slightly over forty-one minutes; ABC had sixty-five seconds more. ABC gave only twelve seconds on its news to the *Washington Post* headline story that H. R. Haldeman was involved in Watergate.[42]

Only CBS attempted any in-depth coverage of Watergate. It ran a two-part series on Friday, October 27, and Tuesday,

October 31. The Friday program was fourteen minutes long and covered the break-in and campaign espionage activities. It ended with Cronkite's promise of a second part the following week. Over the weekend, Charles Colson was on the phone threatening William Paley. Paley in turn summoned CBS executives, shared his doubts about the Friday segment, and "strongly hinted" that part two should be stillborn. The news division resisted, and a compromise was reached limiting part two to eight minutes. The happiest viewers in the nation were at the *Washington Post,* which had been virtually alone in its coverage of the scandal. Bradlee stated that "editors throughout the country really downplayed the Watergate story and dismissed it as a vagary of the *Washington Post.* The editors began to move these stories up only after Cronkite did the two segments on Watergate—they were blessed by the great White Father."[43] Maybe editors moved the stories up, but the network brass at NBC and ABC did not.

CBS may have helped the *Washington Post,* but it was *not* the *Post.* The *Post* remained the vanguard, risking its reputation and its three VHF stations; CBS simply aired two segments of responsible journalism, something possibly overdone but also overdue. Then, despite the growing problems with Watergate—or maybe because of them—CBS yielded in June to the long-standing administration desire that it abandon instant analysis. Roger Mudd wrote a balanced but ultimately critical commentary on the network's decision, scheduled for CBS Radio a day later, but it too was eliminated. Only when Colson's memo concerning his meeting with Paley and Stanton (and with the executives of the other networks) was leaked four and a half months later did CBS return to its former practice. A respectable argument against instant analysis existed, and Paley was indignant at suggestions that he caved in to pressure (a position fortified by CBS's refusal to reassign Dan Rather from his White House beat despite administration efforts to get rid of him). Still, there is reason to doubt Paley's resistance, and the moves along the way demonstrate that even the boldest of the networks was no *Washington Post* or *New York Times*.[44]

Even without Whitehead's carrot-and-stick speech, the administration's bullying had produced some success in inducing affiliates to question the policies of their networks. In a greeting to broadcasters delivered by Herb Klein, Nixon had early on made a pointed distinction between the news performance of local stations and that of the networks. Taking this cue, and being sympathetic with at least some of the views expressed, affiliates turned their annual meetings with the networks into forums for serious questioning of news performance. Indeed, after "Selling of the Pentagon" one disgusted CBS affiliate reportedly attempted to start a clandestine movement to get stations to leave CBS for another network. Since affiliates are the lifeblood of a network, this was a serious concern.[45]

In an interview with ACLU researcher Fred Powledge, CBS News President Richard Salant noted the problems with affiliates and how these problems had grown following the Agnew speech. According to Salant, affiliates read the situation, especially after the first challenge, "to mean that if they didn't make the networks behave themselves, and if they didn't appeal more to middle America, they were going to be faced with this kind of thing. And a license contest is a very difficult and very expensive thing. It's capital punishment. So these guys decided to play it safe."[46]

As Salant saw it, "journalism" meant to the affiliates putting what the mayor said on the six o'clock news; it did not include evaluating his comments. Why so much Vietnam? And why present it in a way that discredits the national establishment? A number of the members of the CBS affiliates' advisory committee even vowed to go to Vietnam to let CBS reporters know how unhappy they were with the network coverage. The network dissuaded them. But the underlying problem persisted. Salant continued: "We have two very soft underbellies. One is the affiliates, who have the perfect right under the law, and the obligation, to turn down everything from the network that they don't want. They can put us in news completely out of business by simply turning off the faucet. Our second soft underbelly is our licensing. There's no solution to either problem."[47]

The administration saw these weaknesses. The campaign to use affiliates as administration censors may well have been the most intelligent and potentially successful idea the paranoid White House came up with. Its effect cannot be measured in hindsight, for Vietnam was already passing from the scene, and with it much of the contentiousness of the era. But with the landslide of the 1972 election and with efforts to intimidate television advancing on so many fronts, one of the administration's strategies—probably the carrot-and-stick approach—might have been successful. If it had, television journalism could have been reduced to the level of rip-and-read news (much as radio had been). But, like so many other initiatives of the Nixon administration, the war against the networks ended in 1973 with the Watergate debacle.

9

HELPING THE PRESIDENT

"President Eisenhower turned the other cheek today, and Senator Joseph R. McCarthy, always an obliging fellow, struck him about as hard as the position of the President will allow," James Reston commented in early 1954. The Democrats witnessed the affront with trepidation; as they saw it, Eisenhower would ignore the cancerous growth of McCarthyism—to oppose it might imperil GOP successes in the fall elections. Adlai Stevenson, in a nationally televised speech in Miami, hit the point hard: "A group of political plungers had persuaded the President that McCarthyism is the best Republican formula for political success." The Republican Party, "half McCarthy and half Eisenhower," had embarked on a campaign to win in the fall by "slander, dissension, and deception."[1]

Both McCarthy and the Republican National Committee demanded that the networks grant them equal time to respond. Interestingly, the networks were under no legal obligation to provide either with equal time. The equal-time provision, section 315(a), simply required (and continues to simply require) that when a legally qualified candidate uses broadcast facilities, all other legally qualified candidates for the same office must be accorded equal access to the same facilities. Because Stevenson was not a legally qualified candidate for anything, section 315(a) did not apply to the televising of his speech.

The fairness doctrine, of course, would have been applicable to the telecast. However, the built-in discretion of the fairness doctrine allowed the networks to determine whether the Stevenson speech changed the balance of existing programming sufficiently to require redress and, if so, who should respond to Stevenson, how and when the response would air, and how much time should be allotted. In other words, even though both the Republican National Committee and McCarthy demanded equal time, neither was entitled to any time as a right under section 315(a), nor were the networks under any obligation to accord whomever they chose to respond a like amount of time.[2]

The niceties of FCC doctrine were not of primary interest at the Eisenhower White House. At his Monday meeting with the Republican leadership immediately after McCarthy's request for equal time, the president announced that it was time to "stop this nonsense." The Republican leadership agreed, and the national chairman was instructed to call the networks and request equal time. He was also informed that, should there be any resistance, Eisenhower would personally call the network presidents. Furthermore, when the networks did agree and McCarthy threatened to go to the FCC, White House Press Secretary James Hagerty noted in his diary that Sherman Adams would "call [the] FCC chairman and get that nailed down." This was probably overkill, given the law's abundant provision of discretion for the networks, but the White House took no chances. Richard Nixon was selected to respond, and McCarthy received no airtime.[3]

For Eisenhower it was a happy coincidence that Commission doctrine provided just the result he wished. But those holding high federal office, especially the presidency, find a similar happy coincidence most of the time; they will always do well when dealing with the licensors of the broadcast press.

Several reasons account for this fact. First, laws are written by people who hold office and expect to continue doing so. It is thus quite unlikely that laws will be enacted that disadvantage officeholders vis-à-vis their opposition. Second, the Commission will have continuing relations with those who hold power. Each year, at a minimum, oversight and budget committee hearings will bring the commissioners to Capitol Hill. Third, when the president is involved, a majority of the commissioners will be of his political party; several, indeed in all probability a majority, may have been selected by the incumbent. Under these circumstances, the dynamics of agency decision making will favor the president over all others, and in other circumstances, incumbents over challengers. I would like to illustrate this point by using examples from a variety of doctrinal areas: the fairness doctrine and access efforts, section 315; and section 312(a)(7), which gives candidates for federal office the right to purchase airtime.

The bluntest use of the Commission occurred eighteen months into the Nixon administration. It began, as did so much, with Vietnam. President Nixon's November 1969 "silent majority" speech had begun a seven-month presidential blitz to amass support for his so-called Vietnamization policy. By June 3, he had presented to the nation five uninterrupted prime-time presidential speeches on Vietnam. Antiwar spokesmen had appeared on all three networks with frequency, but of course none was in a position to claim all three simultaneously for uninterrupted prime time. Nevertheless, overall, the Vietnam programming each of the three networks presented would have met any standards the fairness doctrine, as it then stood, demanded.

This situation set the stage for a number of fairness challenges. The antiwar opposition challenges were essentially geared to gaining more access to the airwaves, which seemed

Helping the President

to be dominated by the face of Richard Nixon. The initial goal of the antiwar forces was thus to respond to the unprecedented use of presidential prime time on a single issue.[4]

In cases presenting a variety of attacks on the issue, the Commission generally rejected claims that would change the fairness balance, although in two instances they did accept the claims, one of which had potentially far-reaching consequences adverse to the Democratic Party. The most wide-ranging argument of the antiwar groups was the idea that a new "equal opportunities" doctrine should be created. The Commission had already taken a step in this direction in its 1970 response to a letter from the Senate Communications Subcommittee Counsel Nicholas Zapple, in which it concluded that the fairness doctrine required something like equal opportunities in election circumstances where a spokesman for one candidate is given or purchases airtime. *Zapple* made considerable sense in addressing a situation that, despite the similarities in policy considerations, section 315 had missed. Nevertheless, section 315 had proven to be a procrustean bed, and the Commission was not eager to expand it further than its *Zapple* corollary. It did not make much sense to hold that every time a president speaks to the nation on a controversial issue a rebuttal of equal time must follow. If the networks wished to offer the time (and they most certainly did not), then they could do so, but the Commission was not about to require it.[5]

In a like vein, the Commission also rejected the arguments of certain members of the Senate (each of whom under the age of sixty believed that he ought to be the next president) that U.S. senators were automatically the appropriate spokesmen to oppose the president. Hubris was not in short supply in the Senate Office Buildings, but in a country the size of the United States individuals who had

d to the Senate might also have something to
ng for the senators would provide a reason
ness doctrine to exclude others.[6]

rtant, the Commission declined to extend the
irt's theory of *Red Lion*. When the Court had
'it is the right of the viewers and listeners, not
the right oi the broadcasters, which is paramount," youthful
law professors and "public interest" lawyers the nation over
began to salivate. The Supreme Court had announced that
viewers' rights were paramount; now all that remained was
the implementation. That, too, would be easy, as a flood
of law review articles set out to demonstrate. Broadcasters
should be required to provide "access" to the public air for
those ideas and opinions insufficiently heard. Whether access should be provided gratis or only to those who could
pay might have been a tough legal issue, but it was largely
assumed that free access was necessary. As to paid access,
that followed a fortiori.[7]

Broadcasters disagreed. Any toothpaste commercial or
used-car ad could air for the appropriate fee, but when the
issue became public affairs, only broadcasters could participate directly or through chosen spokesmen. It was an article
of faith that accepting money for issue-oriented advertising
("advertorials") was bad business and bad journalism. Thus,
when the claim was raised that broadcasters must accept
some form of paid access, they balked. The antiwar group
Business Executives' Move for Vietnam Peace presented the
issue of paid access to the Commission, and, in what may
have been the major Commission decision of the era, it flatly
rejected BEM's claim. If the broadcasters did not want BEM's
money (or ideas), they did not have to accept it. It was as
easy as that. And no antiwar ads would sully the airwaves.[8]

On one of the antiwar issues before the Commission, the
complainants scored a victory. The Commission agreed that
five prime-time presidential speeches were too many and

were not easily countered. As Commissioner Johnson's concurring opinion put it, "The unusually strong impact of Presidential messages is increased when, as here, those messages are delivered in a series, in prime-time, simultaneously on all three networks, without interruptions by commercials or questions, and with the dramatic urgency that a 'live' presentation—coupled with vigorous advance publicity—can create."[9] The Commission decision phrased the issue similarly and ruled that even though overall programming had been fair, network efforts on Vietnam had been insufficient. Fairness under these unusual circumstances required giving a network-selected opposition spokesman an undetermined amount of uninterrupted time.[10] To that extent, the president lost—he could not monopolize the air, and thus the debate, during prime time. If he wished to continue a prime-time blitz he must do so with the understanding that some opposition would appear as well (although clearly not with anything like equal time).

Nevertheless, all in all it was a pretty fair victory both for the president and for the broadcasters who had taken similar legal positions. They had won on their strongest issues, especially that of paid access, which had posed a substantial threat not only to Nixon's Vietnam and other policies but also to the networks' position that professional journalists should control the presentation of controversy on the networks. The only loss had come with regard to the claim that the president need not be countered when he took to the air, time after time after time, on the same topic. And even that loss, from the president's point of view, was completely overshadowed by his victory on the related issues raised by CBS's "Loyal Opposition" series.[11]

As the White House documents quoted in chapter 8 demonstrate, the Nixon administration was exceptionally concerned about the role of television in shaping the picture of Nixon's America. The president believed television was an essential vehicle for direct communication—over the heads of Congress and the establishment (read "liberal") press—with his "silent majority." The five Vietnam speeches were only a part of this effort. During his first eighteen months in office, Nixon took to television twice as often as presidents Eisenhower, Kennedy, and Johnson combined in their first eighteen months of office.[12] The media had wrecked the Johnson presidency—or so the White House thought—and it wasn't getting another shot. Two weeks after his fifth Vietnam speech, Nixon was back on the air again. This time he spent twenty-two minutes of prime time discussing domestic issues, concentrating on inflation and unemployment.

At this point, CBS decided to offer the Democratic National Chairman, Lawrence O'Brien, twenty-five minutes of airtime for a "Loyal Opposition" response. So far during the Nixon administration CBS had aired its "Loyal Opposition" series only twice, each time as the traditional opposition response to the president's State of the Union message. On July 7, the O'Brien broadcast aired. It consisted of excerpts of previously broadcast presidential statements on a variety of issues, followed by acid commentary by O'Brien. Vietnam, but one of the seven issues touched on, was presented at the end. The broadcast was hard hitting and very partisan.

As the Colson memo on his meetings with CBS's Paley and Stanton noted, Colson focused the discussion on the implacable hostility of the White House to such a broadcast. Colson made similar points to the other two networks: if presidential airtime were to be followed by programs like O'Brien's, then Nixon's use of the air had to be reconsidered. The meetings were designed to ensure that this eventuality would not arise.

Meanwhile, the Republican National Committee was pursuing an identical point in a different forum—the FCC. In what looks like a laughable legal position, the RNC argued to the Commission that it should have equal time to respond to the Democratic National Committee. Essentially, the Republicans wanted a second bite of the apple: the president had munched for a while, and if the Democrats were to be allowed their morsel, further Republican chewing would certainly be in order. Or so the argument went. Although the position taken was frivolous on its face, the allure of two chances at the apple had previously captured the Democrats' imagination. In 1968 they had requested from the Commission an opportunity to respond to the Republican response to President Johnson's State of the Union message. In a letter to Wayne Hays, the Commission had told them they were dreaming.[13] But now the Republicans dreamed the same dream, and this time they won. In a case that the D.C. Circuit would later characterize with perfect accuracy as "not the Commission's finest hour," the FCC in a pair of votes upheld the frivolous arguments of the RNC.[14]

The initial argument of the RNC was somewhat incoherent. That the RNC was angry was obvious; that it was serious was much less so. In substance, the RNC argued that a national committee was an "inappropriate" spokesman "to discuss specific political, economic and social issues—the gut issues." Since the DNC was an inappropriate spokesman for those issues, the RNC wished to make an equally inappropriate response. The DNC had made a political attack on the president and his party—rather than "an issue-oriented response"—thus injecting a "fresh issue not specially treated by any Presidential speech: *which political party should hold power.*" The "new issue" necessitated equal time. Ordinarily, a hanging curve ball such as the RNC lobbed up would have been slammed out of the ball park. Instead, the FCC responded like a nervous minor-leaguer and took the strike.[15]

The Commission first patted CBS on the head, acknowledging the network's bona fides and commending it for its "concern." CBS had, however, erred in not following through on "fulfillment of *its* purpose": it should have ensured that O'Brien did not stray from Vietnam. The O'Brien broadcast was unresponsive to the five presidential speeches on Vietnam; it therefore fell within the ambit of the Commission's newly created *Zapple* rule. Because time was given to one party, it was only appropriate—indeed it was required—that time be given to the other. Amazingly, the Commission forgot its 1968 *Hays* ruling and nowhere explained why the party in power had not been allowed two bites of the apple following a State of the Union speech but was allowed the extra chance now.[16]

CBS and the DNC could not believe it. Both quickly petitioned for reconsideration, challenging the Commission's factual predicate. Neither CBS nor the DNC had viewed the "Loyal Opposition" program as limited to Vietnam, and both noted that President Nixon had hardly limited his discussions to any single issue. The DNC also correctly pointed out that the Commission's ruling would inhibit future broadcasts by the opposition party, because the networks would be concerned about avoiding the effects of the Commission's ruling. CBS, beyond noting the gross unfairness of the "two bites of the apple" theory, asserted flatly that the situation was indistinguishable from that involved in the *Hays* ruling.

The Commission denied reconsideration but, finding that the parties had apparently "misconstrued" its earlier opinion, issued a new one setting out its "reasoning" at greater length. Its "reasoning" was modified to fit the new factual predicate that CBS had not necessarily expected O'Brien to deal exclusively (or extensively) with Vietnam. Instead of faulting CBS for not limiting O'Brien to the agreed subject, the Commission now faulted it for not having initially set Vietnam as the topic of discussion. Having made this error and opened up all issues for discussion, CBS could not "avoid the consequences of the 'political party' doctrine" that the Commission fashioned out of its *Zapple* holding. As for the CBS argument that the *Hays* situation was indistinguishable, the Commission apparently disagreed. However, although it cited *Hays* favorably in a footnote, it offered no explanation of how the circumstances or the ruling differed.[17]

The D.C. Circuit crushed the Commission on appeal, as well it should have. Moving from the assertion that the case was not the Commission's "finest hour," the court expressed its utter disbelief that the Commission could assert that the time frame was limited to the period from November 3, 1969, to June 3, 1970 (the period of the five Vietnam speeches), especially when CBS had offered the time on June 22—five days after Nixon had given a speech on economic issues. Noting that one of the Commission statements "blinked reality," the court had no trouble reversing the decision on the basis of administrative arbitrariness.[18]

Indeed, the Commission ruling may be as bad an example of administrative decision making as can be found, and it demands an explanation. How could the FCC wholly ignore a recent precedent that all but compelled the opposite decision? How could it misconceive the facts so badly? And then, after having had the facts corrected by the losing parties, how could it have ignored every event prior to November 3 and after June 3, when the O'Brien commentary was the first Democratic response during the entire administration? Finally, how could it have come up with a "two bites of the apple" conclusion, when the likely effect would have been the death of the "Loyal Opposition" type of broadcast?

Vietnam is probably the best starting point for an answer. Initially, it is easy to understand why O'Brien relegated the topic to the end of his speech. During the early part of the Nixon administration, the Democratic Party was hopelessly split on the war issue; it could not "yet" foist the war off on the Republicans, and pointing fingers thus had little appeal. Indeed, communicating as a "party" was all but impossible, given the range of views. O'Brien had no desire to respond to Nixon's five prime-time Vietnam speeches because the Democrats, institutionally, had nothing to say on the subject. That fact should have been obvious to the Commission.

There is, nonetheless, an explanation for the Commission's fixation on Vietnam. Quite simply, the issue dominated everything, the Commission docket included. In addition to the O'Brien speech, there was *BEM*, the related demands to respond to each presidential speech, and the attempts by antiwar groups to use the fairness doctrine to extract additional airtime. Everywhere the Commission turned, the issue was Vietnam. The "Loyal Opposition" controversy came at the same time and was grouped with these other cases; it is conceivable that the Commission saw them all as a package of Vietnam cases presenting only slightly different legal issues for resolution.

This attitude would help explain the vote of Commissioner Cox, an able Democrat appointed by Kennedy who went along with the Commission decision. A second Democrat, maverick liberal Nicholas Johnson, also went along with the Commission decision, but begrudgingly, noting that he thought the RNC was entitled to about five minutes of response time.[19] Since Johnson was devoting his considerable talents to expanding access requirements, fairness violations here and there were useful things; violations required additional access, and access per se was good. But the Commission majority was rejecting access at every turn, as *BEM* best demonstrates, and the majority did not vote for the RNC in order to increase access.

Furthermore, the failure to discuss *Hays* either initially or on reconsideration remains unexplained. It is conceivable that *Hays* was simply forgotten initially, but it was clearly not overlooked on reconsideration. It was cited in a footnote, even though it was asserted to be indistinguishable (a point on which the Republicans implicitly agreed by asking for its overruling). Nor does an explanation for ignoring all presidential speeches prior to November 3, 1969, immediately arise, although it is arguable that the issues discussed then had grown too stale. But the speech of June 17? That address can be ignored only by closing the books earlier—on June 3, as the Commission did. And a rationale for that action can come only from the dominance of Vietnam. Indeed, the charm of the Vietnam limitation is that it is the only way to avoid concluding that the Commission's decision making was intolerable. But it *was* intolerable: the Commission's outrageous decision all but assured that the networks would deny time to the Democrats, which was precisely the legal conclusion so devoutly desired in the White House, as well as being a political body-blow to the president's opponents.

Some fourteen months after the Commission's decision on reconsideration, the D.C. Circuit excoriated the Commission by affirming the legal position taken by CBS and the DNC throughout. And the "Loyal Opposition"? It was dead: dead during the pendency of the appeal, dead after the appellate victory. Sometimes even the most outrageous and unsupportable rulings do have their intended consequences. The Nixon administration's plan to have the air largely for its own once it got its Commission on board, if not perfect, did not work out badly.

In 1971 Nixon again went on a television blitz on each of the networks. This time, only ABC granted time to the Democrats. The RNC challenged ABC, and the DNC went after CBS and NBC, but on this occasion the Commission held that all the networks had behaved reasonably, and it left the two national committees where it found them—a position consonant with the elasticity of the fairness doctrine and fully approved by the D.C. Circuit.[20]

The fairness doctrine's elasticity makes it attractive to any who desire to challenge what is aired and allows leeway for the commissioners to lean toward their favorites. With a little imagination, almost anything—or nothing—can be a fairness violation. Not so with section 315: the equal-time provision, on the contrary, is known for its precision. It is triggered only when a formally announced candidate (who is legally qualified to hold the office) appears on radio or television, except, after 1959, as part of a "bona fide newscast."

As written, section 315 has an incumbent-politician bias, for by delaying an announcement for reelection an incumbent can appear on the air without triggering the equal-time doctrine. More interestingly, when it has come time to interpret section 315, the Commission and courts have virtually always—the *Lar Daly* case excepted[21]—interpreted the statute, despite its precision, to assist those who hold power. Moreover, when it has come time to legislate, the Congress has blatantly used section 315 to bolster the position of those already holding political office. This interaction between statute, Commission, president, and Congress can be quickly described.

Obviously, section 315 did not apply to Stevenson's Miami speech or to the various Vietnam speeches Richard Nixon gave before he announced his candidacy for reelection. We must go back in time to 1956, when, just as the presidential election campaign was reaching its climax, the Suez Crisis broke out. President Eisenhower took to the network airwaves on October 31 to report to the nation on the crisis and the American position. An immediate section 315 conflict arose: were there any exceptions to the section's blanket language? Could a president report to the American people on an international crisis without triggering time for an opponent—or, as the case typically is, for all the minor opponents across the nation as well? The networks needed an answer in order to comply with the law, whatever it was.

Although the issue was about as straightforward as could be, the FCC initially denied the networks' request for a ruling on the ground that any judgment would be "dependent on such an involved and complicated legal interpretation" that it could not be quickly made.[22] The networks responded by granting time to the Democratic challenger, Adlai Stevenson—not, it seems, what the FCC had assumed the networks would do. Suddenly the FCC sprang into action and resolved the alleged "involved and complicated legal interpretation": President Eisenhower's address was exempt from the equal-time requirement because Congress had not intended "to grant equal time to all presidential candidates when the President uses the air lanes in reporting to the Nation on an international crisis." The president had spoken in his capacity as "chief executive" of the nation, not that of Republican candidate for president. His speech was thus not a "use" within the meaning of section 315.[23] And Stevenson's speech? Well, that *was* a "use," and as a "use" requires a response, the networks were obligated to grant equal time to President Eisenhower. Not bad.

The FCC's determination would seem to be unquestionably correct. No Congress could intend that the president, in reporting to the nation on an international crisis the magnitude of Suez, should be forced to weigh into the need to speak the question of granting free airtime to a challenger. (Indeed, applying section 315 in its usual fashion would have forced the networks to choose between, on the one hand, allowing the president the air and then granting almost two dozen others like time and, on the other, excluding the president no matter how serious the crisis, because excluding the others is the only decision that makes sense.) In any case, just because its decision was correct does not mean that the Commission covered itself with glory in the process. The Commission had been unwilling to do the obvious until the networks made their decision to allow Stevenson airtime. The Commission then could have chosen to do nothing until after the election, a course consistent with its initial conclusion that the issue needed more study. But when a challenger to the incumbent gets a break, the Commission swings into action to protect the party with the appointing majority. Eisenhower, however, declined the airtime the Commission had so graciously awarded him.[24]

The sensible conclusion that not all appearances on the air were "uses" under section 315 lasted but three years. In 1959, Mayor Richard Daley of Chicago appeared on the local evening news smiling at the president of Argentina, who had just landed at the Chicago airport. Lar Daly, a perennial Chicago candidate (and this was election time) best known for dressing in an Uncle Sam costume while campaigning, demanded equal time. Not surprisingly, the station refused. But at the FCC, literalism became a high art form as the Commission surprisingly ruled that any appearance under any circumstances constituted a "use."

Congress could not believe it. Did the FCC seriously think that a news shot of a congressman deplaning must be excised lest any challenger demand and get equal time? A stream of outrage was heaped on the Commission. Even Clarence Dill flew east to explain that this was not what the drafters of the equal-time provision had intended. Congress speedily overturned the ruling and exempted "bona fide newscasts" from the requirements of section 315. Ignored in the posturing that led to the modification of the provision was that a like amendment, pushed by CBS three years earlier, had failed to win congressional approval.[25]

Although Congress did not turn specifically to Eisenhower's Suez speech in its *Lar Daly* debates, the substantive decision of the Commission was so eminently correct that it is doubtful it needed subsequent congressional approval to stand firm. Commissioner Ford, who represented the Commission at the hearings, had fully supported the Suez decision and used both the language of "international crisis" and "unusual significance of an official character involving the safety or welfare of the nation" to describe the Suez ruling. The extent of the ruling was tested in October 1964 when President Johnson took to the air to discuss the changes in leadership of the Soviet Union and the United Kingdom and the Chinese explosion of a nuclear bomb, all of which had occurred the previous week. A day later each network turned down a request for equal time from Republican candidate Barry Goldwater.[26]

It may have been important for President Johnson to have addressed the nation, but it was no international crisis, much less one the magnitude of Suez. The best the Commission could do was characterize it as involving "specific, current and extraordinary international events."[27] And that was enough for the Commission to bring it within the exceptions to "use" created in the Suez decision. Goldwater was a challenger, not an incumbent, and thus he was a loser. In his report to the nation, President Johnson had been nonpartisan. A president can afford to be, needing only to be presidential, and a nonpartisan report to the nation on foreign events two weeks before an election is the perfect showcase. Maybe the decision was correct, but if so, it simply underscores the advantages an incumbent enjoys.

Every challenger soon learns these advantages. A president can always find a way to the national news. A challenger to the presidency, however, must plan an early declaration of candidacy. All nonincumbents are thus automatically put under section 315, whereas the president (or any incumbent officeholder) is left outside the strictures of the Act until formally declaring candidacy. In December 1967, the networks simultaneously broadcast "A Conversation with Presi-

dent Johnson" as challenger Eugene McCarthy watched
helplessly. A quick trip to the D.C. Circuit was to no avail.
The Democratic National Committee received a like rebuff
in 1972 when a similar interview with Richard Nixon aired.
President Carter was the last of the fourteen candidates for
president in 1980 to formally announce his candidacy, as
was Ronald Reagan four years later.[28]

Until recently, even the possibilities of presidential debates worked wholly to the advantage of the incumbent.
Nothing in section 315 prohibits debates between presidential candidates, but in operation the provision once made it
impossible to hold them because of its failure to distinguish
between major and minor candidates. As a result, a debate
between the two real candidates required like amounts of
time for all the frivolous candidates whose combined votes
would not reach three digits. No station would present the
former if also required to air the latter. Nor was such re-
calcitrance a mystery—everyone understood.

Richard Nixon's kitchen debates with Nikita Khrushchev
had been a great asset. Theorizing that if Nixon could best
the tough Russian leader, he could best his Democratic opponent in a debate, the Republicans wanted to rid themselves of section 315 for the 1960 season. So, too, did the
Democrats, because John F. Kennedy was nowhere near as
well known as the vice-president. With similar incentives
to act, each party did so, and in August 1960 a one-season
suspension of section 315 at the presidential level sailed
through Congress. Millions of Americans then watched the
"great debates" between the two candidates, which were
later regarded as pivotal to Kennedy's subsequent election
victory.[29]

In the next session of Congress, Senator Warren Magnuson proposed legislation that would have made the 1960 suspension permanent,[30] but it went nowhere. Fear of broadcaster abuses was too prevalent. Furthermore, it was unclear

who would benefit from a repeal of section 315 with respect to the presidency. In 1963, repeal gained momentum in both houses of Congress, passing the House in June and the Senate in October. However, each passed a different version of the repeal, and a conference committee was required. By the time the committee reported back, Lyndon Johnson, not John Kennedy, was president, and Johnson had no desire at all to debate Republicans. He could win without debates. Taking its cue from the White House, the Democratic-controlled Senate tabled the measure it had previously approved. Despite the pious statements the previous year about how the repeal was designed to serve the public, not the candidates, Senator Norris Cotton put everything nicely in perspective during debate on the tabling by noting that the bill was to die because it no longer served the purposes of an influential candidate, indeed, *the* most influential candidate.[31]

No presidential debates were held in 1968 or in 1972. Johnson had announced his decision to withdraw too late for consideration of debates in 1968, even if Richard Nixon would have risked them again. Four years later, Nixon ignored George McGovern for the entire season: Nixon's campaign, and the electorate's response, indicated that he was running unopposed.

The Bicentennial election was different. Gerald Ford could hardly be classified as a legitimate incumbent, and no one could predict who would be tossed up by the Democrats. Responding to a request filed in 1975 by the Aspen Institute, the FCC ruled that broadcasters could telecast a debate that was a "bona fide news event." This meant that the networks could not arrange or stage debates but could cover them if someone else could get them going.[32] Enter the League of Women Voters and the 1976 debates. Finally, for the 1984 season the Commission removed the legal fiction that the League of Women Voters had anything to do with the bona fides of a debate, and broadcasters were allowed to air any presidential debate, even if they had set it up themselves. It made sense, and it worked. One legal advantage for the incumbent was lessened.[33]

Meanwhile, although section 315 problems were alleviated—debates were okay, and specially planted White House interviews with local stations running over several days were "bona fide news events," but reruns of Ronald Reagan movies were prohibited "uses" and thus blessedly knocked off the air for a campaign season—a different problem emerged. In 1972, Congress had decided that candidates for federal office had a right of access to the nation's airwaves at bargain basement prices.[34] But when did this right for presidential candidates attach? With announcements coming earlier and earlier, political commercials could conceivably begin airing as soon as the dust settled from the previous election. The networks, however, have a built-in hostility to such commercials: not only are the cheapest possible rates mandated for the commercials, but also, to the extent that they need substantial airtime, these commercials interfere with network "flow" and potentially jeopardize ratings. Therein lies a lot of money.

Thus, when Jimmy Carter requested a half hour of prime time to announce his candidacy for reelection in December 1979, the networks were aghast—not simply because they doubted that he had enough accomplishments to fill half an hour or that anyone in the viewing audience was wondering if he intended to keep his job; rather, the networks simply felt that eleven months prior to the election was too soon to open up the season to political preemptions. The three Republicans on the Commission agreed with the networks; the four Democrats did not. Carter thus won, although his Rose Garden policy, with which he planned to wait out the Iranian hostage crisis and wage his campaign, caused him to forego using the time the Commission had ordered the networks to sell him.[35] One can only speculate as to whether Senator Edward Kennedy would have received such a favorable ruling from the Commission.

Incumbents, of course, do not always win. Even Richard Nixon was handed minor defeats by the Commission. But a perfect winning percentage is not the issue. What is at stake is whether a government agency, the majority of which is composed almost always of members of the president's political party, can be expected to remain neutral in its decision making. Although as a practical matter FCC appointments represent the end rather than the beginning of a government career, the patterns of decision making suggest that appointees favor the president and the party who had the wisdom to select them in the first place. In some instances, such as the O'Brien decision, the Commission has reached so far to help its partisan sponsors that the outcome would have been laughable were it not real.

None of this is particularly surprising. The fact of licensing gives power to the licensors, and there will be occasions for this power to be used. Commissioners are not federal judges, appointed for life and enjoying independence (both in reality and in theory) once they ascend the bench. Commissioners are appointed for a term, and the appointment is often a political payoff. Administering laws enacted by incumbents, commissioners will inevitably protect the ins from the outs. Even if at times the Commission does not stray from the straight and narrow—President Truman's Commission and that of President Reagan under Chairman Mark Fowler are two notable examples—such orthodoxy cannot be guaranteed. Furthermore, as not only this chapter but the entire book details, licensing will always be used to further impermissible agendas. If we had a similar licensing of the printed word, like results would occur there.

10
MAINTAINING CULTURAL MORALITY

One of ABC's principal entries in the November 1974 Nielsen sweeps was the critically acclaimed movie *Midnight Cowboy*, with Dustin Hoffman and Jon Voight. Dealing with male prostitution, drugs, and a whiff of homosexuality, the movie merited the network's disclaimer concerning "mature subject matter."

Those who had seen *Midnight Cowboy* at a theater were probably amazed. Joe Buck accepting a marijuana cigarette at a party vanished. So did the boast, essential to his character, "I ain't a real cowboy, but I'm one helluva stud." Gone too was his crack about New York men: "I hear all the men are tutti-fruttis." At a low point, Joe participates in a homosexual act; that scene too had vanished. As an ABC censor explained, even a hint of a homosexual act was "unsuitable to a home audience." Fortunately, Joe's expectation of payment for having sex with women survived—the movie would have lost all sense without it. Nevertheless, even that point is reduced largely to innuendo. Quite a job of editing. A full one-fifth of the movie was left on the cutting-room floor by ABC's censors. *Midnight Cowboy* may have contained "mature subject matter," but no one seeing the ABC version was likely to notice it, absent the network's so informing them at the beginning of the broadcast.[1]

The annual autumnal denunciation of sex and violence on network television has been a ritual for a decade and a half. Those who do not participate can be excused for noting a major gap in the ritual's premise: the lack of sex on network television. For the true believer, however, it *is* there. After all, R-rated movies have been a staple since the networks broke away from PG ratings in the early 1970s, and if one ignores the lavish editing that eliminates the reason for the R, the R itself remains to offend. But as those who watch, rather than merely complain about, network television know, ABC's editing of *Midnight Cowboy* was not unusual at all.

The reason for the editing is not dread of the beast at the FCC. Although the FCC might conceivably care what types of entertainment the networks offer, fear of bringing the Commission down on their collective heads is not what motivates network programmers in this case. Rather, the motivating force is the marketplace. Television is a mass medium, and its entertainment programs need mass audiences to justify the billings to advertisers. As virtually all critics of television have noted, programming quality aims for a low enough common denominator to draw millions of sets to the same channel. This commercial need has always been perceived as a significant limit on how far ahead of popular culture television can afford to go. There seems to be little doubt that television could, if it wished, lead the advance guard, but network programmers are rightly reluctant to lead by too much. Fewer followers mean lower ratings and diminished corporate profits. For the 1970s, the sex that was appearing in R-rated movies was too much. Had the networks not exercised their powers to censor, they would have risked an intensely hostile reaction by organized groups who already believed that sex was overemphasized on television. "Real" sex, even in the R amount, might well have left the audiences watching the real violence on the next channel.

Unlike sex, violence in one form or another has been a staple of network television. From the highly rated "Untouchables" in the early 1960s to the ultimate violence of "The Day After" in 1983, viewers have had no difficulty finding an abundance of programs portraying aggression against people and property. And even before there were cries about "sex" on television, there were Senate hearings condemning TV violence for contributing to the rise of juvenile delinquency in the United States.[2] Yet despite a quarter century of hearings and complaints, violence remains a network staple. Why?

The answer is in the numbers: television violence is a national recreation. Viewers watch it by the millions; many may even like it, and virtually no one objects to it. To be sure, the college professor in the Volvo station wagon decries the violence and demands more British fare à la PBS. Other academics seeking government dollars and professional advancement practice grantsmanship through the violence game. An occasional Thomas Dodd or John Pastore in the U.S. Senate uses hearings to posture and look for convenient scapegoats for society's ills. When all is said and done, though, no genuine constituency cares about removing violent programming from the air. Simply put, liberals along the banks of the Charles River may be a majority in Cambridge, but the national following dwindles by the time one reaches Route 128. Without a substantial constituency somewhere out there, neither Congress nor the Commission, and certainly not the networks, will take action to restrict televised violence.

The Commission has heard the complaints against sex and against violence. Members, especially Chairman Richard Wiley, have made pronouncements, but the Commission has rarely acted, because with regard to sex the complaints have been without foundation, and with regard to violence the complainants have been insufficient in number. The commercial demand to track mainstream kitsch has proved to be a highly effective censor. More has not been needed, although in some quarters more has surely been desired.

With radio the situation has been different—much different. The dominance of television and the number of AM and FM stations in each market have allowed radio to evolve into a diversity of formats over the past twenty-five years. Stations do not attempt to reach every audience. Rather, they attempt to find their niche and program to a limited group. As a result, it is radio, not television, that reflects the diversity of American society.

Because radio is not pictorial, graphic portrayals of sex and violence are impossible. But because of its diversity, radio is vastly more likely to vary its programming from any mainstream norm. Thus, while the complaints about "sex" on television have been a joke, charges that four-letter words not heard in polite WASP society or rock songs extolling drugs were aired over the radio have found genuine targets.

When the issue has been "offensive" programming, radio, not television, has been the action arena, with the Commission a key player. Furthermore, because of the great diversity of radio, any attempt to restrict its programming raises squarely the issue of whether the Commission is promoting a basic moral, intellectual, or social viewpoint. As noted earlier, the economics of television largely eliminate the need for Commission action to maintain a homogeneous standard. The economics of radio, however, push exactly the other way. Because of this, for over twenty years the Commission has been faced with the issue of how much deviation from consensus morality would be tolerated in radio broadcasts. Although the course of Commission decision making has not been perfectly consistent, the general approach has been to give the diversity of radio a short rein, lest it offend mainstream Americans, whether they actually listened to the offending station or, as is more likely, did not.

In September 1959, two listeners of KIMN in Denver wrote letters complaining that offensive remarks had been broadcast over the station for a period of several months. Typical of the remarks was this comment by the announcer to a girl who identified herself as a college student: "No, kissing is another game. I'll teach you how to play that." Another such remark was a response to a caller who said she took KIMN with her everywhere: "I wonder where she puts KIMN radio when she takes a bath—I may peek—watch yourself, Charlotte."[3]

These incidents were of the "utmost concern" to the Commission. The owner of the station, Cecil L. Heftel, agreed. Not only was the language offensive—indeed, "inexcusable," in his words—but it was also used for what the Commission considered the basest of motives, "for the purpose of attracting a larger listening audience, with no discernible regard as to the propriety of the means employed." The Commission's Broadcast Bureau was so outraged by the language that it concluded only one sanction was appropriate: yanking the license. Heftel pleaded with the Commission, pointing out that he had been away from Denver during the time in question, that the station had lacked a program manager, and that as soon as he had heard of the complaint—from the FCC—he had fired the offending announcer because "the staff had been instructed to avoid broadcast of any offensive material." Desperate to retain his station, he "pledged to devote more personal attention in the area of programming" and offered to forego any appeal in exchange for a cease and desist order. The Broadcast Bureau and the chairman objected to the leniency, but a majority of the Commission, while finding the broadcasts to be outside the public interest, convenience, or necessity, consented to issue the cease and desist order.

The owner of Palmetto Broadcasting, E. G. Robinson of Kingstree, South Carolina, wasn't so lucky. At about the same time that the Commission was giving a relieved Heftel his cease and desist order, it was writing to Robinson about Palmetto's "Charlie Walker Show," alleging that the material aired was "coarse, vulgar, suggestive, and susceptible of indecent double meaning." After his reply to the complaint, Robinson received a second fateful notice: the Commission had designated the case for a hearing (the necessary prelude to a nonrenewal determination).[4]

The hearing focused on two issues: what Charlie Walker said during his occupancy of 25 percent of Palmetto's airtime, and what Robinson knew and did about it. "Uncle Charlie," as he referred to himself, was really "Vulgar Charlie." He had nicknames for the surrounding communities: Greeleyville was "Greasy Thrill"; Andrews, "Ann's Drawers"; Bloomville, "Bloomersville." He liked the suggestive phrase "let it all hang out." He hinted at sex: "Betsy, you're not producing, you're not. Betsy says give her time, she's not married yet. Now you know what I'm talking about." When not "suggestive," Charlie was worse: "He says: 'I believe that old dog of mine is a Baptist.' I asked him why he thought his old dog was a Baptist and he says, 'You know, Uncle Charlie, it is that he's done baptized every hubcap around Ann's Drawers.' 'You say it is all that all the hubcaps in Spring Gully is going to Heaven?'"

Robinson faced a dilemma. Should he argue ignorance of the conduct of a man who had been an employee for over six years and who occupied a quarter of the station's airtime? Or should he tackle a defense on the merits? Robinson took the first approach. Naturally, he fired his longtime employee in hopes of avoiding blame. But even with a human sacrifice, his claim of ignorance failed in two ways. First, it subjected him to the charge, taken from the Heftel decision, of "indifference tantamount in effect to abdication of control," which could easily cost him his license. Second, and far worse, his claim was not true. The hearing examiner found—and the Commission fully agreed—that Robinson knew what Uncle Charlie was saying and that he had thus misrepresented important information to the Commission. Such misrepresentation in and of itself had long been held a capital offense, and the Commission rested its denial of renewal in part on this ground.

A defense on the merits would have allowed Robinson to claim that Uncle Charlie had every right to say what he said because the Constitution protects expression, even when it is coarse, vulgar, and suggestive. But at the Commission, at least, this would have proved unavailing. The Commission had noted its patience, its unwillingness to endanger the First Amendment, and its determination that the public interest in "drastic or flagrant" cases such as this demanded silencing the offender. Charlie Walker's mouth constituted an abuse of the airwaves and subjected housewives, teenagers, and young children to "the great possibility" of hearing offensive and indecent programming. The Commission was convinced of its right and its duty to act. The facts "represent[ed] an intolerable waste of the only operating broadcast facilities in the community—facilities which were granted to this licensee to meet the needs and interests of the Kingstree area."[5] Nonetheless, planting his defense on the constitutional ground would likely have given Robinson a surer footing in his appeal.

Stripped of everything, Robinson appealed to the D.C. Circuit, this time fully resting his case on the claim of constitutional protection. But the three-judge panel quickly disposed of his claim on the misrepresentation ground, which was, even without other grounds, adequate to justify denial of a license. The majority opinion studiously avoided any reference to Robinson's First Amendment claims. Less circumspect was the concurring judge, who made it clear that nothing in the Constitution provided protection for the "obscenity" that Charlie Walker had consistently uttered.[6]

Kingstree, South Carolina, in 1960 was a long way, both geographically and culturally, from Berkeley, California, in 1964. Berkeley had then, as it has now, two of Pacifica Foundation's stations, a commercial AM and a noncommercial FM. Pacifica stations are not the standard top-forty type. They are listener- rather than advertiser-supported, and they cater to a left-to-radical, upper-middle-class adult audience. They would never win a ratings sweep.

In 1964, the Commission received complaints about some avant-garde drama and poetry as well as a discussion by eight homosexuals of their attitudes and problems. A pending application by Pacifica became the forum for airing the complaints. It was clear that the programs were atypical for Pacifica, and the Commission conceded that they were but a few isolated programs over a four-year period. Pacifica likewise conceded that some of the language aired by a poet reading from his works violated Pacifica's "own standards of good taste" but offered a credible explanation that the poet's flat, monotonous reading of eighteen poems prior to the offending one had so lulled the station's editor into inattention that he had not caught the offensive language.

The Commission used the occasion to distance itself from *Palmetto*. Here, the programs were serious and within "the very great discretion" vested in a licensee by the Communications Act. If Pacifica were sanctioned for these programs, then "only the wholly inoffensive, the bland could gain access to the radio microphone." Such a limitation could not be countenanced, and the Commission wished to make this fact clear.[7]

Commissioner Robert E. Lee reluctantly concurred. The

discussion by the eight homosexuals had upset him, though. He was

> convinced that the program was designed to be, and succeeded in being, contributory to nothing but sensationalism. The airing of a program dealing with sexual aberrations is not to my mind per se a violation of good taste nor contrary to the public interest. When these subjects are discussed by physicians and sociologists it is conceivable that the public could benefit. But a panel of eight homosexuals discussing their experiences and past history does not approach the treatment of a delicate subject one could expect by a responsible broadcaster.[8]

A reluctant concurring opinion, especially in the face of a sturdy declaration against blandness over the air, would normally have been of no moment. But now the Commission seemed determined to beat a hasty retreat. Just one year later, it handed Pacifica's West Coast stations a limited one-year license renewal. The Berkeley station had tried to soothe the Commission as best it could by concessions of "isolated errors," but these apparently became magnified in the Commission's eyes: the limited-renewal decision referred to the station's admitted failure to conform to Pacifica's own policies. "At the expiration of this [one-year] period you will be afforded the further opportunity to demonstrate adherence to your program supervisory representations." The Commission made no attempt to reiterate the necessity, noted only a year before, of freeing radio from the constraints of bland neutrality; that the decision of the Commission was four to three made it no less palatable.[9]

Controversy followed Pacifica throughout the decade as it applied for open frequencies in Washington and Houston. Its Los Angeles station was the precipitating factor. Two instructors at Los Angeles Valley College, one of whom was a local poet, had been fired for using a spectacularly offensive poem, "Jehovah's Child," in an adult-education English class. Four-letter words abounded and were used to "ascribe sexual acts to God." The incident prompted Pacifica to present a panel discussion on the issue of academic freedom. On the day of the discussion, Pacifica informed listeners that the program would air at 10:30 P.M., that the poem would be read and discussed, and that many listeners would find the poem offensive. Pacifica also informed listeners that the poem had been published in an issue of the *Los Angeles Free Press* a month earlier. "Jehovah's Child" was read at the beginning of the Pacifica program in order to make the academic freedom controversy comprehensible.

The issue of academic freedom for the college instructors turned into a question of broadcaster freedom when Commissioner Robert E. Lee attempted to use it as the reason to deny Pacifica its construction permit in Houston. From Lee's perspective, the poem was obscene—it lacked any redeeming social value—and Pacifica had finally gone too far. He was tired of hearing complaints about Pacifica's programming and believed the time had come to draw the line. Apparently without irony, he printed the poem as part of his dissent.[10]

Pacifica, as should be clear by now, was a rather unusual broadcaster. Its audience-supported concept and willingness to tackle issues were not the way most radio broadcasters, blissfully playing the top forty, wanted to go. Furthermore, the fact that Pacifica had survived and had once been lauded by the Commission did not mitigate the fact that it had more recently been handed a limited renewal (possibly for the same programming the Commission had been lauding a year earlier). Although the limited renewal had been spruced up in the garb of Pacifica's failure to implement its own policies, the substance was perfectly clear. Had the station avoided controversial programming and language—which also would have deviated from Pacifica's programming policies—no one would have cared. Pacifica courted controversy, and controversy leads to trouble. Lest this be doubted, the demise of Palmetto Broadcasting was a useful reminder. Every broadcaster now knew that the Commission was concerned about language. Whether or not the broadcasters believed they would prevail in court, litigation to preserve a license was not a favored approach; self-censorship was preferable to coercion by the powerful.

By the end of the decade, only Palmetto had been stripped of its license for offensive programming. KIMN had narrowly escaped serious sanction, and Pacifica, swatted hard once, remained on the air. The Commission's institutional positions were somewhat ambiguous and so, too, was its legal ability to curtail offensive programming. *Palmetto* was the only case in which the sanction had resulted in a trip to court, and the D.C. Circuit had sustained the Commission without reaching any of the serious questions about censorship. The Commission's own ability to turn an issue of censorship into something murkier had been highlighted in *Pacifica,* where the Commission managed to profess a desire for diversity while at the same time rebuking the licensee for its failure to conform its programming to internal standards. Commissioner Robert E. Lee had taken yet another tack in his proposal to deny the Houston construction permit: now he was questioning Pacifica's financial qualifications. Amorphous "public interest" ideas might well beguile the courts away from the volatile issue of censorship, but broadcasters knew the score.

The confusion of position and issues came to a head in 1970, when the countercultural explosion in American society started bearing down on the seven white males at the FCC, who now included some of Richard Nixon's appointees. Some stations had begun behaving as if they had little to lose from tweaking the Commission's nose on issues of freedom to broadcast. Their impudence set the stage for major clashes and gave the D.C. Circuit the opportunity to exercise its views on the Commission's power over cultural and moral standards.

The case that provided the transition from the 1960s to the 1970s came from Seattle. KRAB supplied the area with, in the words of the Commission, "unusual, stimulating and extraordinary programs. KRAB's programming is meritorious and the station does render an outstanding broadcast service to the area which it serves." Then came a weekend when the station aired an "autobiographical novel for tape" by the Reverend Paul Sawyer of the Lake Forest Park Unitarian Church, located in a northern suburb of Seattle. The president of KRAB auditioned parts of the thirty-hour tape and heard nothing objectionable and much that was interesting. The station decided to air the tape beginning on a Saturday morning, when no supervisory employees were at the station. Upon twice hearing objectionable material while listening at home, KRAB's president himself went to the station and terminated the program after two and a half hours of airtime. A single complaint was sent to the FCC—the *sole* offending-program complaint in the station's file. Yet the result was a limited one-year renewal.[11]

Again, as in *Pacifica*, the Commission did not directly face the issue of whether the words used, by themselves, would have justified the action (although statements by the new chairman, Dean Burch, suggested an affirmative response). Of course, the Commission did not officially embrace censorship; rather, it seized the course that the management itself offered up. KRAB had knocked its own program off the air for failure to comply with its standards, and the Commission relied on its 1965 *Pacifica* conclusion that the failure to exercise adequate supervision justified a Commission sanction. The Commission mentioned neither the specific offending words nor the context in which they were spoken. The decision thus carried a great potential impact, as broadcasters were on notice that at least some four-letter words would put them at risk—but just which words was not clear.

The "inadequate supervision" argument was a smoke-screen. To ensure that no one missed the point, Commissioner Johnson wrote it into his dissent, which contrasted *KRAB* with other Commission actions: KRAB was a listener-supported station.

> It devotes over 95 percent of its broadcast day to the performing arts, public affairs, news, and general educational programming. How many other stations can boast of such a record? Within recent years, this Commission has renewed the licenses of a station broadcasting 33 minutes of commercials an hour, a station that broadcast no news, and a station that defrauded advertisers out of thousands of dollars. Today the majority punishes a noncommercial station for a portion of a single broadcast in its attempt to provide its listeners with unconventional programming—and ignores one of the more outstanding broadcast records in the country.[12]

The Commission, its composition changed by Nixon appointees, was about to take a strong stand against any programming that offended its white middle-class values. KRAB had simply happened to be the first available station on the docket.

It was hardly the last. At 10:00 P.M. on January 4, 1970, a Sunday at the end of Christmas vacation, Eastern Education Radio in Philadelphia aired an interview with Jerry Garcia, the leader of a popular West Coast rock band. In the interview, which had been taped in New York a day earlier, Garcia had expressed his views on ecology, music, philosophy, and interpersonal relations. Garcia's discussion was couched in the slang of his generation; he had, for instance, used the word "like" in an improper and redundant way sixteen times in just the six paragraphs the Commission printed as an appendix to its decision. But Eastern Education Radio was not called before the Commission to compete in a grammar contest. Garcia had also used "shit" and "fuck" frequently, mostly either as adjectives or as substitutes for "et cetera," and occasionally as an introductory expletive. One of the examples cited: "Political change is so fucking slow." [13]

The case presented the Commission with the opportunity to strike frontally. Thus, unlike their reliance on the public-interest standard in *Palmetto* or on programming standards in *Pacifica* and *KRAB*, the Commission for the first time charged a station with violating section 1464 of the U.S. Criminal Code, which prohibits the broadcasting of "obscene, indecent, or profane" language. Garcia's language was not even close to "obscene" by court standards because it lacked appeal to the prurient interest. But the Commission, leaping on "indecency," concluded that the program was indecent because the language used was patently offensive and wholly without redeeming social value. The Commission also found that Garcia's use of the two words was completely gratuitous and that he could have expressed any of the ideas under discussion without resort to those words. The use of such language, the Commission concluded, "fosters no debate, serves no social purpose, and would drastically curtail the usefulness of radio for millions of people." [14]

The Commission postulated that if it did not crack down on Eastern Education's use of "indecent" language, other stations would follow suit. The result would be that "substantial numbers" of the listening population "would either curtail using radio or would restrict their use to but a few channels or frequencies, abandoning the present practice of turning the dial to find some appealing programming." The Commission also mentioned in passing the problem of children's access to such language. [15]

That the Commission took umbrage was obvious; that anyone else did was not. The Commission received not a single—that's right, not one—complaint about the program. Neither did Eastern Education until the Commission itself complained. The program came to the Commission's attention because the Commission staff happened to be monitoring it[16]—which may explain why the Commission did not bring up the patent offensiveness of the language used.

Commissioner Johnson once again hit the bull's-eye in his dissent: "What this Commission condemns today is not words, but a culture—a life-style it fears but does not understand. . . . What the Commission decides, after all, is that the swear words of the lily white middle class may be broadcast, but those of the young, the poor, or the blacks may not."[17] Radio had to remain in check. The availability of a diversity of frequencies in each community did not mean that a diversity of cultures could be represented on the air. Common middle-class morality demanded its due. It could be criticized, but not in the way that made criticism most effective: by the casual and calculated use of language designed to show disrespect for that culture.

Although the Commission might have pushed harder—and thus guaranteed a trip to the D.C. Circuit—it settled on a one-hundred-dollar fine and expressed the hope that Eastern Education would appeal. It made the perfect choice. Too little was at stake for the costs of the appeal, and every single licensee was put on further notice that the Commission would not tolerate this offensive language.

Having chastened one facet of the culture of the young, the Commission took on another: its music.[18] The lead had been taken by the administration's point man, Vice-President Spiro Agnew, who, speaking at a Nevada Republican dinner in September 1970, claimed that "in too many of the lyrics [of popular music], the message of the drug culture is purveyed. We should listen more carefully to popular music, because . . . at its worst it is blatant drug-culture propaganda."[19] Demonstrating that he (probably along with most of his generation) was incapable of listening more carefully, he cited as an example of such music "Acid Queen" by The Who, which contains lyrics that read in part:

> I'm the gypsy, the Acid Queen . . . pay before we start
> I'm the gypsy, the Acid Queen . . . I'll tear your soul apart
> My work is done now, look at him
> His head it shakes, his fingers clutch, watch his body writhe
> I'm guaranteed to break your little heart.[20]

How this blatant attack on the ravaging consequences of LSD "present[s] the use of drugs in such an attractive light that for the impressionable, 'turning on' becomes the natural and even the approved thing to do" is a bit of alchemy that the vice-president did not explain to his audience.[21]

Even though he picked an example directly counter to his point, the vice-president was at least modestly on target. A number of popular records were addressing drug use. Rock music was walking hand in hand with the cultural revolution that seemed to be occurring in American society—and part of that revolution was drug use, from marijuana to LSD. Causation is a more difficult point to prove, but the vice-president was in a solid American tradition in asserting that depictions of various social ills in the mass media were responsible for bringing such ills into existence in American culture. Similar assertions had been made about violence, first with respect to movies, then comic books, and finally television.[22] It was unlikely that an assertion linking popular music to countercultural behavior in the late 1960s and early 1970s would not be made in some quarter.

Less than six months after the Agnew speech, on March 5, 1971, the Commission moved into action in an attempt to ban "drug lyrics" from the air. Its opening shot was a terse notice professing to "point up" broadcasters' duties regarding drug lyrics, a topic "of current and pressing concern: the use of language tending to promote or glorify the use of illegal drugs [such] as marijuana, LSD, 'speed,' etc." Broadcasters were required to interpret the meaning of all song lyrics prior to broadcast to determine "whether a particular record depicts the dangers of drug abuse, or, to the contrary, promotes such illegal drug usage." The four-paragraph notice did not forbid stations to play these songs, and the word *censor* was never used. Rather, the Commission stated that a licensee's failure to review all songs before playing would "raise . . . serious questions as to whether continued operation of the station is in the public interest." With that said, it was unnecessary to add the obvious: songs that glorified drug use must not be played.[23]

Three equally short concurring statements were issued with the notice. Commissioner Robert E. Lee stated that he hoped the notice would "discourage, if not eliminate," such songs from the air. "I expect the Broadcast Industry to meet its responsibilities." Commissioner H. Rex Lee was rightly concerned that the Commission might appear to young people "as 'an ominous government agency' merely to stamp out *their* music." He would have preferred a slightly broader warning, aimed at the advertising of nonprescription drugs as well as youth culture music. Commissioner Houser agreed fully with Robert E. Lee and added that song lyrics were only part of a larger problem of a "pill-oriented society. . . . To the extent that broadcast media contributes, wittingly or unwittingly, to the drug problem, the Commission is charged with the responsibility of ensuring that the public interest will prevail through our recognition of the problem and the consideration of solutions." In dissent, Commissioner Johnson again accurately described the majority's action: "an unsuccessfully-disguised effort" to censor drug lyrics. He called on the industry "to respond to this brazen attack upon them with all the enthusiasm it calls for." But, he despaired, "given the power of this Commission, I am afraid they may not."[24]

Lee Loevinger, a former commissioner, had written in 1967 that "talk of 'responsibility' . . . is simply a euphemism for self-censorship."[25] He was right. The industry knew its "responsibility" and fell into line, some more quickly than others. A few were completely servile. WNTN in Newton, Massachusetts, simply eliminated all Bob Dylan songs "because management could not interpret the lyrics." Another station notified its employees of "an immediate ban on all music containing lyrics even remotely dealing with politics, sex, and to a minor degree ecology."[26]

Shortly after the notice, the Commission's Bureau of Complaints and Compliance took some of the mystery out of the reviewer's task when, borrowing from an existing U.S. Army list, it issued its own list of twenty-two songs containing "so-called drug-oriented lyrics." The list rapidly swept through the industry, and as a result, a number of very popular songs were effectively banned.[27] The Beatles lost "Lucy in the Sky with Diamonds" and "With a Little Help from My Friends." The Byrds lost "Eight Miles High" and "Mr. Tambourine Man" (a Dylan song). The official "do not play" list also included Arlo Guthrie's "Coming into Los Angeles," "White Rabbit" by the Jefferson Airplane, "Snowblind Friend" by Steppenwolf; even the Grateful Dead were hit with "Truckin'."[28] Naturally, there were some absurdities. "The Pusher" by Steppenwolf was included, although it was even more antidrug than "Acid Queen":

> I've seen a lot of people walkin' 'round
> with tombstones in their eyes,
> but the pusher don't care if you live or die.
> God damn the pusher, Goddamn I say, the pusher
> The pusher will ruin your body, Lord he will

lead your mind to sleep.
If I were the President of this land,
You know I would declare total war on the pusher man.[29]

Finally, on a personal note, the favorite song of both my children when they were young was "Puff, the Magic Dragon" by Peter, Paul, and Mary; this gentle song about growing up was misconstrued as an inducement to marijuana use. Thus its notes, too, were silenced in a season of panic.

The notice and the "do not play" list set the stage for a very probable visit to the D.C. Circuit. In a strategy apparently dictated by Commission lawyers, the Commission issued a second notice, designed to shift its position to a more defensible ground. The second notice stated in essence that the first notice should not be construed as a prohibition on drug lyrics and that no action would be taken against stations that did play such songs. The Commission then wrapped its first notice into its 1960 Statement on Programming Policy, asserting that it simply reiterated the obligation on the part of management to be aware of the programs they are airing. Who could object to that?[30]

But if the Commission had been merely reiterating its 1960 Policy Statement, what had been the purpose of the first notice? Why had there been assertions that the first notice should discourage and perhaps eliminate such songs? Where did the "do not play" list fit in, and why had the industry reacted so swiftly to comply with its "responsibilities"? When Chairman Burch testified before Senator Nelson in September 1971, he bluntly stated that Commissioner Johnson had been wrong and that the Commission "did not ban drug lyrics." Senator Nelson shortly thereafter asked Burch what he would do if a station continued to play songs promoting the use of drugs. Burch responded, "I know what I would do, I probably would vote to take the license away."[31] It was a neat trick. Drug lyrics were not banned, but should a station play such songs, it could lose its license. That, of course, has been the charm of licensing from its inception.

As Commissioner Johnson had anticipated, the big guns of the industry did not hasten to challenge the Commission. It fell instead to Yale Broadcasting to bring the case to the D.C. Circuit. The positions of Yale and the Commission were straightforward. Relying on the facts, Yale argued that the Commission was engaged in censorship and that it acted knowing full well how the industry would respond to such a notice as the Commission first issued. The Commission presented the case as if it had no facts and was instead simply reaffirming its 1960 Policy Statement that a licensee must be aware of the subject matter of its broadcasts. If the Commission's argument was accepted, Yale was behaving like a spoiled brat, contending that a station need not have the slightest idea of what it sends out.

As usual, the D.C. Circuit swallowed everything the Commission offered up. The opinion omitted discussion of the industry reaction and the reasons compelling such a reaction. Indeed, the court was mesmerized by the FCC's characterization and was moved to express its "astonishment that the licensee would argue that before the broadcast it has no knowledge, and cannot be required to have any knowledge, of material it puts out over the airwaves." In this context, Yale's argument was seen as a cautionary tale to the court, saying "a great deal about quality in this particular medium of our culture." The public interest demanded more. "Supposedly a radio licensee is performing a public service—that is the raison d'être of the license. If the licensee does not have specific knowledge of what it is broadcasting, how can it claim to be operating in the public interest?"[32]

These questions are good ones, and if the facts of the case were ignored, they would also be dispositive ones. But the facts were that the Commission was telling licensees to ban countercultural music or risk losing a license. And the court, part and parcel of the generation looking aghast at a culture in revolution, refused to see what could not have been clearer. The Commission's lawyers deserve credit for bailing it out, but only a willful neglect of the factual setting by the D.C. Circuit allowed the lawyers' version to prevail.

Amazingly, if the Commission thought its double-barreled actions on indecency and drug lyrics would clear the air and make radio safe for middle America again, it was in for a huge surprise. Between June 1972 and June 1973 the complaints to the Commission concerning "obscenity-indecency-profanity" took a fifteenfold jump, outstripping by over ten thousand the complaints received on all other topics during the period. A new radio format had hit the air, and it was a winner.[33]

This time the problems were not limited to the college stations somewhere on the FM dial. "Topless radio," a live talk show, featured telephone conversations with a male host in which the caller, typically female, would disclose intimate personal and sexual details over the air. It arrived first, as always, in California, but spread like wildfire across the nation. It was popular, too: despite outraged cries from some "listeners," the industry, and a number of U.S. senators, the format would not die—indeed, it was often the top-rated show in its area.

The Commission ordered its staff to monitor several of the "topless radio" shows, and somehow Sonderling Broadcasting's WGLD-FM, in the Chicago suburb of Oak Park, was marked as the licensee to be pounced on. The staff had presented the Commission with a twenty-two minute highlight tape from five hours of airtime of Sonderling's "Femme Forum"; the Commission opened its opinion with its candidate for the best of the best. The topic for the day was oral sex.

Announcer:	OK, Jennifer. How do you keep your sex life alive?
Listener:	Well, actually, I think it's pretty important to keep yourself mentally stimulated most of the time when you are with that person; it's that much better for you.
Announcer:	Uh hum, and how do you do that?
Listener:	Oh, you think about how much fun you're going to be having.
Announcer:	You think about how much fun you are going to be having? That's all it takes?
Listener:	Well, no. (Laughter)
Announcer:	Well, what more does it take?
Listener:	Well, there—well—if that doesn't work there are different little things you can do.
Announcer:	Like?
Listener:	Well—like oral sex when you're driving is a lot of fun—it takes the monotony out of things.
Announcer:	I can imagine.
Listener:	The only thing is you have to watch out for truck drivers.
Announcer:	Uh hum, OK, that sounds like good advice.
Listener:	Try it sometime—you might like it.
Announcer:	Try it—you'll like it! What else, my dear?
Listener:	Oh, well—that's about enough for right now.[34]

The Commission went gunning for this format immediately. The discussion was just too "blatant"—so blatant, in fact, that the Commission considered that the presence or absence of children in the listening audience (a possibility, given that one advertiser was an insurance company targeting the sixteen-to-twenty-year-old driver) was legally irrelevant. The fact that no four-letter words were used did not matter, for this discussion (and presumably all discussions on "topless radio") was obscene, not simply indecent. If Sonderling could air such material, well, anyone could, and turning the dial would be an unsafe exercise for decent people. It is interesting to note that although "topless radio" was rapidly spreading, there were no reports of two such formats in any one market; even Sonderling's top-rated program brought forth no imitators. It is interesting, too, that the Commission did not so note.

The Commission articulated the then-current three-part *Roth-Memoirs* Supreme Court test for obscenity and decided, most conclusively, that the test had been met.[35] However, the Commission erred in its application on each point. First, the dominant theme of the material had to appeal to the prurient interest. The Commission had heard but twenty-two minutes of a five-hour broadcast and had no idea what occupied the other four hours and thirty-eight minutes. A "dominant theme" conclusion could not be made without that information. Furthermore, the Supreme Court's decisions required an exclusive focus on sex, and "Femme Forum" did not quite fit the bill. Second, the material had to be patently offensive by contemporary community standards. As in *Eastern Education*, there was no doubt that the commissioners were offended, as were some listeners. But the Commission made no effort to define the relevant community or to explain why that community's standards were offended. The reason for the omission was simple enough: "Femme Forum" was the top-rated radio program in the Chicago area.[36] Explaining how the number-one show was patently offensive to the community enjoying it would have required the deforestation of large areas of the United States to supply the paper for the analysis. Finally, the Commission did not explain why the program was wholly without redeeming social value, as *Roth-Memoirs* required. It stated that what aired "was not a serious discussion of sexual matters"[37]—but seriousness of discussion had never before been imposed as a requirement.

Sonderling was slapped with a two-thousand-dollar fine and paid it swiftly, thankful to be left on the air. The Commission action killed the format immediately; those stations airing such programs breathed a collective sigh of relief that the sanction had not been more severe. A single fine accomplished enough and allowed the players to continue to rake in profits.

A citizens' group intervened to appeal the decision to the D.C. Circuit, and the court, almost out of habit, sustained the Commission's action. Although conceding that "the Commission does not have a free hand of bureaucratic censorship," the court seemed nonetheless untroubled by the Commission's misapplication of the *Roth-Memoirs* test.[38] The court understood that even the newer *Miller* test, which allowed findings of obscenity based on local community standards and on a lack of serious value on the part of the offending material, would not quite save the action, so it reached deep into the bag of judicial tricks.[39]

First, it solved the "dominant theme" problem by arguing that listening (as opposed, presumably, to watching or reading) was episodic, so anything about sex became the "dominant theme." Next it resurrected *Ginzburg v. United States,* a Supreme Court case holding that nonobscene materials could be found obscene if there were "pandering"—that is, if emphasis were placed on the sexy quality of the materials. The D.C. Circuit thus became the first court to apply that discredited doctrine to any set of facts not involving Ralph Ginzburg. The court, too, had been patently offended.[40]

While *Sonderling* was sitting at the D.C. Circuit awaiting decision, the Commission received another complaint about Pacifica's programming, this time at New York's WBAI. On a Tuesday in late October 1973, Pacifica had been airing a program about attitudes toward language in contemporary society. At about 2:00 P.M. it played a twelve-minute mono-logue from comedian George Carlin's album "Occupation: Foole," which emphasized four-letter words. At one point, Carlin listed seven of them as "words you couldn't say on the public . . . airwaves." Carlin is a superb comedian; he was also a good prophet.

Six weeks later, the Commission received a complaint from a man who, in the words of the Supreme Court, "stated that he had heard the broadcast while driving with his young son, [and] wrote a letter complaining to the Commission. He stated that, although he could perhaps understand the 'record's being sold for private use, I certainly cannot understand the broadcast of the same over the air that supposedly you control.'"[41]

Neither the Commission nor the reviewing courts were aware, nor would they likely have cared, that the complainant was John R. Douglas, a member of the national planning board of Morality in Media. Although only Douglas himself can know, it appears unlikely that he had actually heard the program about which he was complaining. Douglas was not the typical Pacifica listener and would have listened, if at all, only with the aim of finding what he did not wish others to hear. It is also unlikely that it would have taken a member of the national planning board of Morality in Media a full six weeks to complain to the FCC; most complaints follow hard on the heels of the program. Finally, Douglas misrepresented his son's relative age: the son may well have been "young" vis-à-vis his father, but a fifteen-year-old teenager is not "young" within the context of exposure to four-letter words.[42]

Despite its actions against Eastern Education Radio, drug lyrics, and "topless radio," the Commission sat on the complaint against Pacifica for well over a year. There appear to have been two reasons for the delay: the pending appeal in *Sonderling* offered the likelihood of clarifying Commission power to censor; also, the Commission was under strong pressure from both the House and Senate Communications subcommittees to "do something" about gratuitous violence on television, and the problem of indecency on radio became conveniently attached to the violence issue. A threat to cut off FCC funding, should the Commission fail to act, loomed large in the second half of 1974.

Chairman Richard Wiley spent the fall of 1974 jawboning the networks. He saw "dark clouds" on the TV horizon if broadcasters did not show "taste, discretion and decency" in their programming. In February 1975, the Commission took action. It announced to Congress that the networks and the National Association of Broadcasters had agreed to adopt a "family viewing hour" at the beginning of network prime time to make the television airwaves safe for everyone.[43] (This cosmetic change affected programming for about one season. Then, the congressional attention span long since exhausted, things reverted pretty much back to normal.)

The Commission also proclaimed to Congress its victory at the D.C. Circuit in *Sonderling* and announced a clarification of its position on the broadcast of indecent words. The "clarification" was the blunt ruling that the Carlin monologue was banned except for possible late-night broadcast, when the number of children in the audience would be minimal. It mattered not a whit whether the indecent language used in a broadcast had serious literary, artistic, political, or scientific value (part of the new *Miller* test)—it simply could not be aired, no matter who wished to hear it.[44]

News organizations jumped to request further clarification. How would this ruling affect news and public-affairs programming? The Commission tersely informed them that

certain live news events could use the words if there were
no time for editing, but it refused to comment beyond that.
If the news organizations wanted to know more they would
just have to air the offending language and take their chances
with the Commission. In other words, they had better make
sure that offensive language was always edited out.[45]

This time the broadcasters' appeal to the D.C. Circuit met
with success. Judge Tamm found that the Commission action violated section 326, the no-censorship provision of the
Communications Act. Chief Judge Bazelon viewed section
326 as simply coextensive with the First Amendment and
required a determination of whether the speech was protected. He concluded that the monologue was entitled to
protection because the Commission's definition of "indecent" speech was too broad and because the Commission
had incorrectly assumed that material subject to regulation
for children could be banned from broadcast to adults.[46]

In a strained attempt to sustain the Commission order,
Judge Leventhal (author of the opinion sustaining Commission action in *Sonderling*) dissented and introduced a new
theory into the case. Like the court in *Yale Broadcasting*,
Leventhal entirely ignored the factual background of the
case, including the congressional pressure to act. He found
the only issue to be whether the language "as broadcast" at
two o'clock on a Tuesday afternoon could be prohibited. His
opinion emphasized the limited facts of the case, an emphasis that was his own and not the Commission's. He also focused on the compelling nature of the state's interest in the
protection of children.[47]

The Commission sought Supreme Court review and, in
the process, fully adopted Judge Leventhal's reworked theory of the case. The Supreme Court divided five to four in
sustaining the Commission, and Justice Stevens's plurality
opinion bought the new theory hook, line, and sinker. The

decision was limited to the facts of the case: the repeated use of four-letter words at a time when children were likely to be in the broadcast audience.[48]

This view of the "facts" presents two problems in addition to the one posed by the Commission's late, opportunistic embrace of Judge Leventhal's theory. First, the likelihood that the listening audience of a station like WBAI includes children borders on zero. Only the rarest child could comprehend a typical WBAI program, and even then would be, like most adults, bored to death. Second, were one to search for a time when children are least likely to be in the audience, two o'clock on a Tuesday afternoon in October would be a first-rate choice. As preposterous as it seems, the Commission's theory of the case required the justices to disregard an institution called school. Such details, bearing on whether any actual threat was ever present, were of little interest to the Commission, accustomed as it was to winning big at the courthouse. This, then, was but another legal, if not real, victory in the Commission's efforts to purify the air.

Despite the prevalent view, shared by former Vice-President Agnew, that society's ills are in no small part caused by what is seen and heard on the public airwaves, Commission actions over the past two decades have been notably unsuccessful in influencing nonbroadcast behavior. The songs of the Beatles and the Grateful Dead are the occasional golden oldies now, but the war on drugs rages in real life as never before. George Carlin's seven words did not become acceptable fare for the airwaves, although they have gained currency almost everywhere else. The Commission did not, of course, manage to seal off radio and television in a late-1950s never-never land.

Outside of broadcasting, even the Burger Court, reluctantly but completely, held that Americans have the right to express their views in their own ways, not solely in ways that do not offend middle-class sensibilities. The sexual revolution produced the most sweeping changes, removing from television every thematic taboo, including homosexuality and incest, although it has not gone so far as to permit nudity or simulated sex on network television. Ironically, while the taboos have disappeared on television, the sexual revolution has faded in society, pushed back not by the FCC or television but by real-world concerns: venereal disease, the commitment to upward mobility, the need for trust in a relationship. What, then, are we to make of the Commission's attempts of the past two decades to consign radio and television to strict middle-class morality?

Obviously the Commission cannot govern the whole of American culture, no matter how much it would will itself the power to do so. In fact, since the mid-seventies, the Commission has abated its role as guardian of cultural reactionism, perhaps owing to the depolarization of the generation gap that began around that time. But it can censor, and it does censor. When the conventional standards of its members have been offended, the Commission has used its power to bludgeon the offender. The commissioners' middle-class cohorts are never the enemy; it is always the new and the different, and, most typically, the young or the black. In using its power, the FCC has succeeded, not in homogenizing the American airwaves but in limiting the cultural differences that would otherwise have aired. Such a limitation directly contravenes the economic structure of the airwaves, a structure that provides abundant opportunity for diversity. The real issue, then—one too easily forgotten in a period of inactivity—is whether it is appropriate for the FCC to wreak havoc on a diverse marketplace in order to serve its own cultural standards.

IV

THE PRESENT AND THE FUTURE

OVERVIEW

The decision to license brought with it the need to determine who would be privileged to broadcast. As might be expected, favoritism—especially political favoritism—had its influence. More fundamentally, however, censorship, sometimes discreet, sometimes overt, became a part of the process. Richard Nixon's full-scale attack on the broadcast establishment succeeded in toning down opposition to his policies and might well have achieved his overall goal of censorship but for Watergate. Nixon was aberrational only in his intensity.

Part III demonstrated that the party controlling the White House has often fared well in broadcasting decisions that involved politics: a not insignificant advantage of incumbency is a controlling majority on the FCC. That majority sometimes has its own agenda, as we have seen in chapter 10's detailing of the Commission's amazing rearguard actions against offensive countercultural attacks on the dominant middle-class WASP culture. The willingness of the Commission to use every power of censorship at its disposal is notable. Given what most would agree are our rather sturdy traditions of freedom of the press, can such an assault be justified? Must it be continued?

These are the dominant questions addressed in Part IV, which treats legal and intellectual justifications for the present system of broadcast regulation and the future prospects of new technologies. Simply put, as the seventh decade of second-class citizenship for broadcasting approaches, how do we explain severing from the First Amendment protections the very source of news for most Americans? Furthermore, if broadcast dominance of our viewing habits is drawing to a close, how do we intend to treat our new technologies? To what extent does the past govern? What can be learned from it?

Chapter 11 revisits *NBC, Red Lion,* and *Pacifica* (WBAI), which are the sole attempts by the Supreme Court to justify the second-class treatment of broadcasters. Both *NBC* and *Red Lion* assert that broadcast frequencies are scarce in ways that print resources are not. The implications of that conclusion and its failure to satisfy anyone except the Supreme Court justices will be treated first. Then the *Pacifica* case and the concept of broadcasting as an intruder in the home will be discussed. Finally, we will look at a potential outgrowth of *Pacifica* wholly at odds with accepted First Amendment doctrine: the idea that we regulate television because we are afraid of a future we cannot know.

None of the available theories explains the difference between broadcasting and print; it is therefore curious that these theories still exist. The issue for the future is whether the theories that fail to explain one area will be imported into an entirely different one—new technologies—where their explanatory power is even weaker. That is the topic of chapter 12.

This book would not be complete without a look at the future. The days of the total dominance of television, especially VHF, are ending. Newer technologies—cable television, multipoint distribution systems (MDS), direct broadcast satellite (DBS)—will become strong competitors, perhaps supplanting over-the-air broadcasting, just as television superseded radio. But the days of MDS and DBS are well in the future, so for the near and intermediate term, new technology means cable television. Chapter 12 will explore this future as well as cable's past.

About the past there is agreement. Cable was first brought to the Commission's attention in the 1950s and was ignored. Then, during a period of complete industry capture—at least as far as economic issues were concerned—the Commission began to treat cable with a heavy hand. To the applause of the few commentators who cared, the Commission ruled that cable was an adjunct to serve, but not compete with, broadcasters. By the 1970s, it had become clear that the Commission's hostility toward cable was aimed solely at advancing the economic interests of broadcasters. For the first time, then, serious First Amendment questions arose with respect to cable.

About the future there is disagreement. Should cable be treated like broadcasting or like print for First Amendment purposes? Occasionally the response to this question sounds like a trip down memory lane: cable operators certainly don't look like worthy First Amendment people. But the view has not prevailed in quite that form. Instead, two different views of the First Amendment have come to dominate cable regulation. The first is that of the National League of Cities, which rather bluntly concluded that the First Amendment was a hindrance to what they wished to do; therefore, the First Amendment should not be held applicable to cable regulation.

The second view comes from academia and asserts, taking its cue from the broadcast tradition, that we have been wise to separate broadcasting from print and that governmental regulation of broadcasting is the appropriate model for cable. Cable should be denied full First Amendment protections, it says, because the First Amendment print tradition is in fact obsolete, an unfortunate by-product of eighteenth-century thought, inappropriate for our modern society. As broadcasting has shown, government regulation is not that pernicious at all; indeed, it has made for a better actualization of our First Amendment goals and values. Thus it matters not that the original reasons for separating broadcasting from print do not hold for cable. The problem is an outmoded view of what freedom of the press truly means. A changing society needs a changing view of civil liberties. Or does it?

11
THE MODERN RATIONALE
FOR BROADCAST REGULATION

How, with our commitment to freedom and our general belief in the importance of the First Amendment, have we ignored the second-class citizenship accorded broadcasters? And how have we justified it? As Part I detailed, in the beginning broadcasting was assumed to be different from the press, and not much time was wasted worrying about why it was different. But in an era in which most Americans receive the bulk of their information from broadcasting, simply stating that broadcasting is not the press is insufficient. Broadcasting serves the press function, as even the Supreme Court agrees, and can be treated differently only if there is a legitimate justification for the supervision that accompanies our licensing scheme under the Communications Act.

The Supreme Court's entries in the debate, *NBC, Red Lion,* and *Pacifica* (WBAI), have in general failed to impress scholars who write in the field. Perhaps troubled at the overwhelming dissent in the academy, the Court recently dropped a footnote hinting at its own unease in the area, although pointedly looking for other decision makers such as Congress or the Commission to bail it out.[1] Because the issue of justification merits serious scrutiny, this chapter will deal with the various theories—public ownership, scarcity, and pervasiveness—in some detail. If the justifications offered for treating broadcasting differently from print cannot withstand analysis, then it is time to cease accepting blindly the assertion of legitimate differences and instead accord broadcasters the full First Amendment protections they claim.

Every real Texan knows that when you own something, you control it. This tenet is not only an elemental principle of property law; it seems also to be a principle of human nature. If the government owns the airwaves, there ought to be no argument that broadcasters are duty bound to comply with whatever conditions the government wishes to set for their temporary use of the electromagnetic spectrum. This proposition seems so obvious, so inherently right, that a lay reader will undoubtedly wonder why neither *NBC* nor *Red Lion* devoted a word to it. The answer is that the conclusion of absolute control does *not* always follow from the premise of ownership, and the Court knows this full well.

Others do not recognize the distinction, however, and one often finds language dealing with broadcasters stating that broadcasters are trustees of the public, with a fiduciary duty that must be met. These nice legal terms from the law of trusts suggest the high duty of care that a trustee must exercise in handling someone else's property. When used in the broadcasting context, though, the terms are typically thrown in merely to overwhelm any argument the broadcasters might raise about their own rights; the terms add nothing to the debate and can rise no higher than the initial statement that because the government owns the spectrum, it has the power to regulate all aspects of use.[2]

The reason the Supreme Court has never even nodded toward this justification for regulation is that despite its superficial appeal, the justification rests first on a "bootstrap" argument and second on a legal conclusion that has been decisively rejected. The bootstrap is the ownership conclusion. The idea of "ownership" goes something like this: the government owns the radio frequencies because it has power to regulate their use, and the government has power to regulate their use because it owns them. A nifty circle, and it does not break.

Nevertheless, even if the bootstrap argument had validity (and for convenience I have been writing as though it does), it would not, as much of the discussion on public ownership assumes, end all debate there. The government, it so happens, owns lots of things. It owns food stamps, it owns jobs for government workers, it owns parks, and it owns the Post Office, to name just a few. Although the government has occasionally tried to condition welfare benefits (such as food stamps) or government employment on the recipient's promise to forego constitutional rights, the Supreme Court has decisively rejected such attempts.

The government behaves in an unconstitutional manner when it attempts to "purchase" constitutional rights with its handouts. It may ask for many things as quid pro quo, but one thing it is forbidden to request is a citizen's constitutional rights. Whether one turns to speakers in parks or to everyone using the Post Office, the situation is equally clear. Simple ownership of the parks or the Post Office by the government does not provide the slightest power to censor. The government may in fact adopt certain regulations, but these will be tested on the same basis as government regulation of private actors. If the Constitution is a bar, then the regulations fall. Innumerable cases over the past four decades have so held.[3]

Public ownership cannot explain the difference between broadcasting and print, then. Government owns the real property of a park much more obviously than it owns the electromagnetic spectrum, and yet no scheme exists for controlling what is said in parks. The Supreme Court has therefore avoided any reliance on public ownership as justifying broadcast regulation. If the Court moved in that direction, it would face problems of censorship in hundreds of local communities as firmer control over who could use the parks was asserted. Thus the Court, in both *NBC* and *Red Lion*, told its readers that it is because broadcasting is scarce that the government may regulate it in ways that would be inconceivable—and unconstitutional—if applied to the print medium.

The argument of broadcast scarcity has had a talismanic immunity from judicial scrutiny. It is asserted, not explored. When it *is* explored outside the confines of a Supreme Court opinion, scarcity turns out to be rather elusive, in part because the Court is using economic language in a nonsensical way. Broadcast frequencies are indeed scarce; but so are all resources, whether they are trees, ink, or iron ore. The notion of a "nonscarce" resource is simply a contradiction in terms. Probably because of this initial definitional problem, the scarcity argument is hard to pin down. There are a number of different variants of "broadcasting is scarce [and implicitly, print is not]," each of which merits closer analysis.[4]

Only arguments asserting a scarcity that apply to broadcasting but not to print can satisfy the Supreme Court's conclusion. There appear to be five possible types of scarcity argument fitting this formula.[5] The first comes from Justice Frankfurter's *NBC* opinion. Remembering the chaos that occurred after Secretary Hoover abandoned all attempts to regulate stations, Justice Frankfurter noted: "The result was confusion and chaos. With everyone on the air, nobody could be heard." How clearly this situation contrasts with print, where you can write what you wish on your piece of paper, and I can do likewise on mine, and neither of us interferes with the other.[6]

The problem with this form of the argument is that its analogy is wrong. It is true that if everyone broadcasts, no one can be heard. But it is also true that if everyone at a park speaks at the same time, no one can hear and, equally, that if you write your message on a piece of paper and I write mine over it, no one can read your message. In the last two examples, the real-world solutions are that most people listen rather than speak at the park and that our system of property rights prevents the person who does not own the paper from writing over the owner's message. It is not technological scarcity that is at work, but lack of a property mechanism to allocate the right to broadcast.

The drafters of the Radio Act and the Communications Act probably never considered creating a property rights mechanism; indeed, had they thought about it, they would have assumed its impossibility. As late as 1958, CBS President Frank Stanton, the acknowledged intellectual of the industry, stated that he had never considered an auction system for allocation of broadcast rights.[7] Just a year later, Chicago's Ronald Coase demonstrated in a pathbreaking article that just such a system not only would work but was also the typical way of allocating resources.[8] In fact, despite the naive belief that allocation by government is the only sensible way of doing things, a private market in broadcast licenses now flourishes.

During 1984, 782 radio stations and 82 television stations changed hands, for a total price exceeding $2 billion. One must go back to 1975 to find a year in which fewer than two dozen television stations were sold, and to 1972 for a sale of fewer than three hundred radio stations.[9] The government may give the license away initially, but thereafter a free marketplace reigns (subject to pro forma approval of any sale by the FCC). Nothing involving property rights (or scarce property rights, if one prefers) requires a Federal Communications Commission, any more than a property control mechanism with respect to trees and paper requires a Federal Paper Commission. Justice Frankfurter's problem was that he assumed that the normal—in terms of the press, that is, a writer and a reader—was the inevitable. This idea of scarcity is not particularly helpful, for the omission of a property control mechanism for trees and paper would make print just like broadcasting. In other words, the phrasing of the question assumes its answer.

A second form of the scarcity argument also traces its roots to *NBC*. "The plight into which radio fell prior to 1927 was attributable to certain basic facts about radio as a means of communication—its facilities are limited; . . . the radio spectrum simply is not large enough to accommodate everybody. There is a fixed natural limitation upon the number of stations that can operate without interfering with one another." Broadcasting frequencies are inherently limited, but print is not. More trees can be grown; more spectrum cannot be created.[10]

This version of the argument is both right and wrong. It is true that more trees can be grown—but they can't be grown for use *today*. The resources available *now* for print are inherently limited; so are the resources available for broadcasting. Similarly, just as additional trees can be made available for later use, so too can additional frequencies become available. On a single day in 1984 the FCC allocated 684 new FM stations in the lower forty-eight states—two dozen more than the number of stations in the entire country as noted in the Chain Broadcasting Report. We can—and do—add more broadcast stations to service as the technology improves. This aspect of broadcasting development has been rather constant and will continue to be so. The idea of an inherent limitation on broadcasting, with none for print, might have been fine for 1943, but it is untenable today. Furthermore, the FCC has in the past consciously adopted policies that have limited the number of television stations and hindered the development of new technologies that would compete with over-the-air broadcasting. Additional options might have been good for viewers, but the Commission perceived them as harmful to broadcasters. Thus to some extent, the Commission itself can claim some credit for supplying the rationale that keeps its regulation in business.[11]

All other scarcity arguments take *Red Lion* rather than *NBC* as their starting point. One of these uses excess demand as proof that broadcast frequencies are scarce. "Where there are substantially more individuals who want to broadcast than there are frequencies to allocate . . . if one hundred persons want broadcasting licenses but there are only ten frequencies to allocate, . . . only a few can be licensed." Implicitly Justice White was noticing that there is not an excess demand for paper.[12]

Although these are all perfectly accurate statements, they are not helpful, as a few obvious examples will demonstrate. There are also substantially more people who wish to own daily newspapers (or to hold government jobs) than there are newspapers (or government jobs) to go around. The reason that supply and demand are held in balance with respect to newspapers (or simply paper) is that a price is charged for the commodity. VHF television licenses, however, are given away by the government *free*. Because anyone so lucky as to be granted a VHF license can then turn around and sell the license for millions—as the tragicomic story of WHDH so nicely demonstrates—it is hardly surprising that more people want a license than there are licenses to allocate. The same would be true for any valuable commodity—for instance, if the government were to give away paper at no charge, the demand for paper would immediately exceed the supply. This is not voodoo economics; it is a common and sound American tradition to want more for less.

The excess demand vanishes as soon as the licenses to broadcast are in private hands. Broadcast licenses today are bought and sold with much greater frequency than are newspaper concerns, and anyone who wants one—and has the money—can buy one. This market then functions like any other market, with supply and demand finding an equilibrium. Furthermore, as the explication of the next version of the scarcity argument will show, newspapers, because of their scarcity, sell at a greater premium than do broadcast properties.

The next argument, offered with frequency and—given the failure of the other scarcity arguments—ferocity is that whereas anyone can begin a newspaper, not everyone can begin a broadcast station.[13] Like the initial Frankfurter version of the scarcity argument, this one also carries an implicit assumption that answers the very question being asked. Why is it that not everyone can start to broadcast? Simply put, the government will not allow it. In other words, the existing scheme of regulation prevents entry. Under these circumstances, to say that one cannot begin a broadcast station is simply to recite the relevant conclusions of the Communications Act; and to say that anyone can begin a newspaper is to note that there is no Federal Newspaper Entry Act. Thus, this loading of the question fails to advance the analysis. Nevertheless, even with the loaded question it is worth pursuing what would happen in the real world of late-twentieth-century America.

When the co-owned newspapers of Jackson and Hattiesburg, Mississippi, sell for $110 million ($852 per subscriber), one would expect to see new newspapers beginning all the time so that other entrepreneurs could reap similar financial rewards. Even if one could sell a newspaper for just the typical $582 per subscriber (the Sunbelt rate is quite a bit higher), one would do quite nicely. But in fact, new newspapers rarely begin. Anyone can start one, but virtually no one does. Why? The answer is simple: the laws of econom-

ics. Only the largest of cities are able to support two newspapers.[14]

Moreover, daily newspapers are folding, not growing.
Baltimore, Washington, Philadelphia, Cleveland, Buffalo,
and Hartford have recently seen a daily newspaper die.
Other large cities will witness the same event, despite 1970
federal legislation allowing joint operating agreements between newspapers when financial circumstances so dictate.
The most notable recent demise of a newspaper, that of the
Washington Star, came not long after Time, Inc., paid $30 mil-
lion for the ailing paper. Yet even with that investment and
the incredible resources of Time, the paper could not make
a successful go of it.[15]

If keeping an ailing paper afloat is a difficult feat, beginning a new one is even more so. Estimated start-up costs (including plant and equipment) for a paper with a circulation
of sixty thousand are $15–20 million. For a quarter of a mil-
lion circulation, the cost would be $40 million. Yet, if suc-
cessful and then sold for a mere $500 per subscriber, that
investment would yield $125 million, which might seem
worth the gamble—except that it couldn't succeed. In 1978,
the *New York Trib* was started and closed within three months,
with losses of $5 million. The *Philadelphia Journal* lasted four
years, with losses of $15 million. The Unification Church's
new *Washington Times* is reputedly losing $35 million each
year.[16]

Newspapers achieve tremendous economies of scale. It
takes just about as much money to publish the next issue of
an already existing newspaper as it does to publish the first
issue of a new newspaper. Thus, although the costs of production are the same, the large paper can spread its costs
over a broader circulation base. Furthermore, advertisers
have become exceptionally devoted to paying the lowest cost
per thousand readers. A larger newspaper, then, even though

it charges a higher price per line of advertising, can justify that charge by its distribution over a greater circulation. A smaller paper, even with a lower charge per line, still faces the problem of its lesser circulation. It simply costs less to reach each reader of the larger paper. Until these economic facts change, competing newspapers are not going to spring up, whatever the theoretical belief that they will do so may be.[17]

New daily newspapers do, of course, exist. In the mid-1960s, Gannett recognized that the investment in the space program would cause a population explosion around Cape Canaveral, and it entered a market having no daily to create the *Cocoa Today*. Often, too, a weekly or biweekly such as the *Maui News* will move into daily circulation as population grows. But these are small papers facing no local competition. Where there is competition, a bleak future awaits the weaker paper. Wholly unexpectedly, we have reached the situation where a daily newspaper comes quite close to being a natural monopoly.

The prices in newspaper sales quoted above reflect this. One more should be mentioned to bring the point home: although the Ft. Wayne, Indiana, UHF station would have sold for only $5–8 million, the Knight chain paid $40 million for the local newspaper several years ago.[18] The explosive increases in the price of broadcast properties that occurred in the speculative binge in the late spring and early summer of 1985 have narrowed but not closed this gap. Even with this recent jump in broadcast prices, though, the difficulty of entry, if it cuts at all, suggests that newspapers, not broadcast frequencies, are scarce.[19]

Believers in broadcast regulation must be believers in scarcity. That is how the Supreme Court has framed the debate and offered the justification. For the true believer, if the Supreme Court says broadcasting is scarce and print is not, well, it just must be so. Others might be deterred by the collapse of the various scarcity theories, but not those wishing to justify regulation: they simply call forth yet another theory of scarcity. If all the former arguments have proven unable to distinguish broadcasting from print on the basis of broadcast scarcity (rather than print scarcity), one final argument still remains: relative scarcity. There are, when compared to print, too few broadcast outlets.

Relative scarcity invites a look at the numbers of outlets. At the end of 1985 there were 1,220 television stations (of which 654 were VHF) and 9,871 radio stations. On the newspaper side there were about 1,750 dailies and 7,666 weeklies. The number of broadcast outlets expands yearly, whereas the number of daily newspapers has been declining for decades.[20]

How should these figures be compared? If the comparison is between broadcast outlets and daily newspapers, the result is clear: newspapers are scarce; broadcasting outlets are not. If the comparison is broadcast outlets to dailies *and* weeklies, then it is a wash. If only dailies are compared against television, then broadcasting becomes somewhat scarcer. However, if VHF stations only are compared to dailies, the dailies come out ahead by quite a margin.

Thus, only VHF can clearly be seen as scarce with these figures, with a lesser argument that television generally is scarcer. There are, however, two problems with moving from these comparisons to the legal arguments about scarcity: first, *Red Lion* was a radio, not a television case (the same is true for *NBC,* of course); second, no one holding to scarcity wishes to leave radio alone. As long as this is the case, a different basis of comparison is necessary. Indeed, for scarcity advocates it is clear that neither daily nor weekly newspapers can be the relevant comparison with broadcasting. Newspapers generate too few outlets to make the case of broadcast scarcity. But if the comparison is to either all printing presses or all printed matter (community newsletters, handbills, etc.), then broadcasting is overwhelmed and the scarcity case is made.

This version of scarcity does not, however, explain why a handbill passed out near Central Park should be equated with WCBS. Nor does it take account of CB radio. If a handbill can cancel out WCBS, then why can't a CB cancel out the *New York Times* or a book publisher? There are no a priori answers here, which is what makes relative scarcity such an attractive argument.

Proponents are offered two advantages. First, they are free to determine for themselves just what is to be compared to broadcast outlets. Not surprisingly, the selected comparison will always place broadcasting at a disadvantage. Second, it can always be asserted that there are "too few" broadcast outlets, for no one believes that enough exist to serve us. The charm of this argument is its vagueness— there is no way to disprove it. These qualities are best used to keep the faith rather than to expand it, though. Unless people already agree, they are unlikely to be persuaded.

Professor Daniel Polsby noted that only the Supreme Court has had anything good to say about scarcity in the last decade. In the legal literature that is true. Only those born during an era in which scarcity appeared real and permanent have been able consistently to avoid questioning the basis for their conclusions. Outside the legal literature, the belief in scarcity exists—or at least the assertion of scarcity exists—because those who wish to continue broadcast regulation believe that it must exist; otherwise, broadcasters could not be controlled by the government.[21]

This clinging to scarcity does serve a useful purpose. Because the rationale is so untenable, its continued existence demonstrates that there is *something* about broadcasting that leads people to know it must be regulated. The "something" is the reason for continued regulation. We simply await its revelation.

The Supreme Court's affirmance in *Pacifica* of the Commission ban on George Carlin's seven words may have provided a basis for this new theory of media difference. *Pacifica* represents the Supreme Court's sole break from the scarcity rationale. In justifying its decision, the Supreme Court did not state that because broadcasting was scarce it was improper to waste the eleven minutes necessary to hear Carlin's monologue; instead, the Court stated that radio was an "intruder" in the home, "uniquely pervasive," and "uniquely accessible to children."[22]

The latter assertion is puzzling on the one hand and troublesome on the other. Its implication, rather clearly spelled out in the *Pacifica* decision, is that adults may not hear what would be unfit for children. The Court's opinion makes clear that Carlin's monologue would receive full constitutional protection if delivered in a nightclub; indeed, the Court itself filled five pages of the *U.S. Reports* in reprinting the monologue in full. There can be no doubt that it is radio, not the words, that triggers concern.

The factual predicate of the Court's opinion—"uniquely accessible to children"—does not on reflection seem accurate. In just what way is radio "uniquely accessible"? I would guess the Court meant that children can listen to the radio without trouble or supervision. But does that distinguish radio from a newspaper? A child is fully capable of waking before the parent and reading the morning paper unsupervised, or of reading it later in the day before it is trashed. The same can be said for *Time* and *Newsweek*. If the parents work, a child may arrive home and read the mail right after school. Would this mean that the U.S. mail is "too accessible" or "uniquely accessible"?

Equally mystifying is what the Court means by stating that radio is an "intruder" in the home. Whatever else the Court means, it is not true that the FBI or CIA breaks into millions of American homes to deposit the latest Sony radios in bedrooms and living areas. To the best of my knowledge, Americans bring radios and television sets into their homes because they desire them. Furthermore, there is no law requiring that a radio or a television be turned on. Yet this is just what the Court seems to be hinting. The word "intruder" suggests illegality and unwantedness. If homeowners truly believed that radio or television was an intruder, I would expect to see sets out on the streets for garbage collection. Instead, when I read my morning paper I see numbers of full-page ads for these very appliances, suggesting that the merchants believe, contrary to what the Court might think, that Americans desire radios and televisions.

Not only does the Court's statement seem silly, but it also wholly fails to distinguish newspapers, magazines, and books. Each is brought into the home volitionally. Each may contain information both unwanted and offensive to the reader. Are they, too, "intruders" and fit objects for government regulation and censorship? It is impossible to believe that this could be so. Thus far, the Court's statements from *Pacifica* are much like the scarcity conclusion: initially, they may sound good but they cannot provide a distinction that sets broadcasting apart.

The final justification offered in *Pacifica* is that radio is "uniquely pervasive" in our society. Just what the Court means is unclear—and again, this vagueness may prove to be the charm of the argument. Because it is difficult to ascertain what "uniquely pervasive" means, it is difficult to know if the assertion may be refuted. Furthermore, depending on what "pervasive" means, testing the "pervasiveness" of radio, television, newspapers, and magazines may well call for empirical tools that simply do not exist.

It would appear difficult to build an entire theory of regulation on such an undefined assertion. "Uniquely pervasive" might simply refer to radio's existence on beaches and along jogging trails and to the fact that the average home possesses a half dozen radios; or it could be a shorthand way of stating "intruder" or "uniquely accessible to children." Yet it might also be a way of suggesting that radio—and television—are powerful and thus merit regulation.

Like "pervasiveness," the notion of power in this context may prove exceptionally slippery. Discussions of power typically note how many hours a day the average television set is on—a constant trend upward, now exceeding seven[23]—and the fact that most Americans claim to obtain most of their news from television, and then move to the conclusion that television may (or must) be shaping public events. Because existing social science methodology is incapable of shedding light on the assertion, it is impossible to refute, and it thereby holds an advantage identical to that of the "too few" scarcity argument.

The principal example advanced to demonstrate the unique power of broadcasting is the persuasive role televised advertising has in our consumer economy. If American business (which is presumed to be incredibly intelligent on this point) spends billions of dollars on advertising, then that advertising must be effective and powerful in convincing us to do things we otherwise would not do. Although this argument does not justify anything beyond the regulation of advertising, it assumes that the success of advertising demonstrates that television is powerful and that this power can be used in pernicious ways. The argument fails, however, to distinguish television's power from that of other media. We may be becoming more and more of a consumer society, but we were a consumer society prior to the advent of television—indeed, the seeds were sown prior to radio. Moreover, the argument of uniqueness does not adequately explain why so many Americans smoke cigarettes even though cigarette advertising has been banned from the airwaves for a decade and a half.

The power theory has other problems as well. *Pacifica* and *Red Lion* were both radio, not television, cases. Are we really going to assert that radio is a powerful force in American life? Could any living human being believe that WBAI or WGCB (Red Lion) are more powerful than the *Miami Herald,* the newspaper involved in the case rejecting a claim similar to *Red Lion*'s with respect to newspapers? Do CBS and the other networks mold our polity more than the *New York Times* and the *Washington Post* do—or *Time, Newsweek,* the *National Review,* or *The New Republic?* No one can know. But if television is powerful (and print is not), then this question must be answered in the affirmative.

It takes a lot of extrapolation to move from *Pacifica* to a full-blown theory of regulation. Furthermore, the argument that media can be regulated because they are powerful lacks persuasive power and certainly does not find overt support in the Supreme Court. Yet it, or something like it, appears to be the only available construct left to justify continued regulation of broadcasting—and the need to regulate new technologies as they become available. Though not out-and-out embracing a power theory, the most imaginative modern argument for treating broadcasting differently from print supports such a theory even as it rejects any differences between print and broadcasting.

That argument, of course, is the Bollinger thesis, which I discussed in the introduction.[24] Without retreating from my conclusion that the incidents discussed in the prior ten chapters belie Bollinger's argument that regulating broadcasting, but not print, gives us the best of two available worlds, I would note that Bollinger begins his argument by concluding that there are no relevant differences between broadcasting and print—except one: *we think* that there are differences. Because we perceive differences, the argument goes, we may act as though they really exist. I have never escaped the belief that Bollinger represents the Walter Cronkite school of regulation—"that's the way it is." Nevertheless, in this first part of his analysis, Bollinger makes two very strong points: there are no relevant differences between print and broadcasting; but we think and act as though there were. Is there an explanation?

Tradition seems the appropriate beginning. Newspaper people, as I noted early on, know who their ancestors are, and they wear their tradition proudly, even if they fail to live up to it. But, to repeat a quotation from chapter 2, broadcasters are the "lineal descendants of operators of music halls and peep shows."[25] Not a terribly complimentary characterization, but still, a case can be made for it. One ought to remember, though, that Zenger was not a responsible journalist; after all, until the Nixon era and adversary journalism, responsible journalists simply did not get into trouble with their government. Nor was Red Lion's Norris, together with his right-wing crowd, what I would call a responsible broadcaster. But he was someone who took on the powers that be, just as Zenger had. And what did the broadcasting establishment try to do? First they urged him not to fight; then they reluctantly helped; and finally, when the FCC provided them an opportunity, they attempted to substitute an organization, the Radio Television News Directors Association, for Norris. A group with that type of vision may perceive itself as an inheritor of the print tradition, but since it doesn't know what the tradition is, it would be hard put to claim the inheritance.

If broadcasters have not recognized the inheritance, I think government has—a slightly different inheritance, however. We should remember that in its infancy, and for almost two centuries thereafter, print was regulated with varying degrees of strictness in England. First monopolies were given, then they were closely supervised. Why? There was money to be made, and the printing press carried with it enormous potential. The rulers didn't know what to make of this new technology, and the easiest way to make sure it did not get out of hand was to keep it under royal scrutiny. After all, it was "unique" and might well upset the status quo.

So too, I think, with American broadcasting. It radiated fear. It was "pervasive," "unique," an "intruder" in our lives. It was—it is—powerful; indeed, it is almost impossible to read an article on broadcasting that does not make that point. To be sure, nice generalities ring out. We watch more; we read less; we're more violent; we're more passive; events are telescoped to meet our lessened attention span; it changes us in ways we cannot know. But exactly what it does and how it exerts power remain mysteries, even though large numbers of people, many of them very knowledgeable, assure us of its power.

The *New York Times* and the *Washington Post* are powerful, too, but we don't regulate them because of that. Beyond the fact that the Constitution forbids their regulation, the reason we don't regulate is that we have grown used to them. They may be powerful, but we think we know the how and the why. With broadcasting—specifically television (I think we have outgrown the belief that radio is powerful)—we are not as sure what the medium is doing to us, and so we attempt to regulate it to prevent it from doing what we do not know it is doing. We may not know the consequences of introducing television into our homes, but there appears to be a regulatory consensus that we don't want those consequences to get out of hand. We fear broadcasting because

we don't understand it as well as we do print. The fear may
be irrational, but it is there nevertheless. It does not justify
regulation, but it does explain it. It also explains why we can
expect that as newer technologies become available to the
public there will be an intense desire to keep them under
control.

12

TO REPEAT THE PAST: CABLE

Has anything been learned from our more than half a century's experiment in regulating broadcasting? If we could go back to the beginning, would we do it differently and apply the lessons learned? The history of cable regulation, from cable's inception in the late 1940s to the Cable Communications Policy Act of 1984, suggests that the answers are a resounding no. If newer communications technologies become available, the cable history seems to confirm, they will not initially look like participants in the communications system. We will treat them differently, appropriate to our rules, to ensure that they fulfill the necessary requirements of the public interest.

It took a while before the Commission figured out how cable television fit into the scheme of broadcasting, but when it did its attitudes were clear: fear and loathing. The process of dealing with cable carried a perfect parallel with the early days of broadcasting: that is, it was from the start inconceivable that cable television had anything to do with freedom of the press. Cable TV retransmitted entertainment; hence, it could be regulated just as an amusement park could be regulated. The only doubt in all this pigeonholing came from the initial inability of the Commission to figure out just what cable "really" was and what it "really" did.

Cable, or "community antenna television" as it was known until 1972, originated during the Commission's freeze on television licensing between 1948 and 1952. A local cable system (simply meaning the company that selects and provides the stations on the channels available to subscribers) would use one of two possible methods to bring television to communities otherwise unable to get it. Typically, a large master antenna was erected in a propitious place and then homes wishing the service were wired from it. Master antennas were most useful in communities that had local television but where hilly or mountainous terrain made reception poor. In communities without any local service, a microwave relay system was created to bring distant signals across the miles to the cable system. In neither case is there any technological interference with any spectrum user. This aspect is the key to cable technology: more can always be added without that interference which has plagued over-the-air broadcasting.

Because microwave relay systems are common carriers—that is services that must be open, on a first come, first serve basis, to all who wish to use them—they need approval from the Commission to operate. As common carriers, however, they are covered under a different part of the Communications Act (Title II) than that which applies to broadcasters (Title III).

The necessity of Commission approval of microwave relays is what first brought cable onto the Commission docket. It was 1950, and very few cable systems were in existence. Although there was no doubt that the Commission had jurisdiction over all microwave relay systems, it did not follow that that jurisdiction continued any further, to attach to the subsequent use of the relayed materials. That is, the Commission had power to decide whether the microwave system was necessary (essentially a routine approval), but having so decided it could not tell the end user—the cable system—how to operate its business. Yet that was the question cable seemed to pose. Should the Commission assert jurisdiction

over cable systems using microwave as a delivery mechanism and treat those systems, too, as common carriers? The
decision in 1950 was to defer action "pending consideration" of cable.[1]

As an aid to the consideration of jurisdiction, all the
Commission's senior staff, the general counsel, chief engi-
neer, and heads of both the Broadcast and Common Carrier bureaus, concluded in a memorandum sent just before
the end of the freeze in 1952 that it did not appear that "the
Commission can defer for very long taking a position with
respect to its jurisdiction" over cable. Accordingly, they set
forth their views on the issue at length. Even though there
was "no question" that Congress had not considered cable in
1934, the senior staff recommended regulation as a common carrier. A common carrier under Title II had to meet
four requirements: (1) the communications must be interstate; and (2) the service must be a communications service
that is (3) open to the public and (4) for hire. It was "not
unreasonable" to conclude that cable met all four tests.[2]

Having determined that the Commission should assert
jurisdiction, the memorandum turned to what that assertion would entail. The senior staff saw cable completely in
traditional common-carrier terms of supplier-consumer relations; thus the needed regulatory approach was to limit
the charge for cable service to a just and reasonable rate,
prevent discrimination in service, and protect against dis-
continuance of service. When looked at with the hindsight
of three decades, the memorandum is amazing. The problem that would fixate the Commission's attention on cable
was how to protect broadcasters from competition. Yet this
initial memorandum does not advert to that problem and
instead assumes just the opposite: that as more broadcasters
go on the air, cable will be squeezed and tempted to discon-
tinue service to those who might otherwise need it.

Despite the senior staff's call for action, the Commission

did nothing. Annual reports simply and duly noted that the Commission was continuing its study. The reason for the inaction was that designating cable a common carrier would have added significantly to the burdens of the Commission. Common-carrier regulation takes both time and effort, and the Commission lacked the staffing to supervise cable as the senior staff had suggested it should. Furthermore, by 1954 the only pressure on the Commission to deal with cable was coming from broadcasters who wished protection from a service that might cut into their audiences. Throughout the 1950s the Commission held that it could not and would not protect any broadcaster from competition, and thus an assertion of jurisdiction over cable would have made no sense: it could not have given broadcasters what they wished— suppression; and it would have added significantly to the Commission's workload.

In 1957 the senior staffers changed their minds. Although they noted that "certain reasonable assumptions" would make cable a common carrier, they no longer wished this result. The realization that the only reason to regulate cable was to protect broadcasters from competition, which the Commission could not do, forced the conclusion that regulation made no sense.[3] In 1958 the Commission so held in *Frontier Broadcasting v. Collier:* cable was not a common carrier in the "ordinary" sense of the term because the subscriber did not "control" the programming that was sent over the cable.[4] The senior staff memo in 1952 had recognized this problem, but skirted it by defining the cable system as more of a passive conduit sending signals to its subscribers. *Frontier* instead conceptualized the cable operator as picking and choosing among signals for transmission to subscribers. The importance of this conclusion was that it allowed the Commission to decline a burdensome and unnecessary obligation to regulate.

Although the Commission reaffirmed its *Frontier* conclusion a year later, pressure was building for the Commission to protect broadcasters from the unwanted competition of cable television.[5] The switch came in mid-1959, when the Commission overturned a routine grant of an application by a private microwave common carrier to construct a system to supply a subscriber cable system; the Commission ordered a hearing examiner to build a record on the application.

In the short year since *Frontier* there had been both legal and political changes. The D.C. Circuit had overturned (in another context) the Commission's long-standing doctrine that it could not protect a broadcaster from competition (by another broadcaster) and concluded that under some circumstances a community might receive better service from one broadcaster than it would from two.[6] In the Senate, Warren Magnuson's Commerce Committee was excoriating the Commission for its failure to come up with a policy that would assist struggling UHF stations in the West. Thus, reversing *Frontier* would now make sense legally and, regardless, made overwhelming sense politically. All the Commission had to do was wait for the hearing examiner's determination on the subscriber cable system case.

Finally the hearing examiner submitted his conclusion: the application should be granted. The Commission bluntly reversed his determination. Without going back on its conclusion that cable was not a common carrier, the Commission asserted a jurisdiction to control the end uses of the microwave relay common carrier. It concluded that outside signals on the cable system in Lander, Riverton, and Thermopolis, Wyoming, would result in the demise of Riverton's VHF station, KWRB. Accordingly, unless the Riverton station gave its approval, the microwave system could not import any broadcast signals.[7]

The time to go to the D.C. Circuit had arrived. Quickly, the court brought out its rubber stamp. The judges even refused to admit that the Commission had changed its position since *Frontier,* although they did opine that even if the Commission had done so, it had supplied "convincing reasons" for its action here, the reasons being the postulated demise of KWRB.[8] The few commentators in legal journals who took note of the decision agreed with both court and Commission. This was an example of regulatory policy at its best: seeing the problem of the potential loss of a community's television station and working to prevent it. Unanswered, because unasked, was whether the Commission could have prohibited live theater or the importation of books if that, too, would have made the existence of KWRB shaky. Moreover, if only KWRB *or* cable could survive in Riverton, why was the FCC (rather than the viewers) to decide which would go and why KWRB should be the chosen survivor?

With the judicial go-ahead secured, the Commission then announced that it would consider the "fundamental question" of whether the Commission should impose conditions on microwave relay systems "designed to limit and regulate" the manner in which cable would be allowed to compete with over-the-air broadcasting "to which it [cable] is an adjunct." A footnote contained an assertion of an equal jurisdiction over master-antenna cable systems even though they did not use microwave relay. Although the Commission offered no explanation for this assertion, the rationale was clear: if cable was to be appropriately limited as an adjunct, it made no sense to leave any system unregulated.[9]

And limit the Commission did. First it told cable systems what they must carry: each and every local station. There was no way cable homes were going to be forced to unhook their cable to watch programs on local TV. More significantly, there was no way the Commission was going to expose those local stations to the risk that cable subscribers might miss their programming by *not* unhooking the cable system. This position was bluntly reinforced by the compan-

ion do-not-show rule: no cable system could offer an alternative time or channel for any program available on local
television. It was clear that cable would be no more than an
"adjunct." But lest anyone lose sight of this, the Commission
froze the top one hundred television markets (encompas-
ing virtually every urban area in the nation) for cable. No
system in those markets could "import" a signal not otherwise available in the market. For these markets, the "must
carry" rules created both the floor and the ceiling.[10]

The rules, while not declaring cable illegal, came as close
as the Commission thought possible to hamstringing cable
completely. Attacks were mounted in cases from the West
Coast to the Midwest to, naturally, the D.C. Circuit. The
Commission lost in the West and won, as always, in the D.C.
Circuit; then, while the midwestern suit was pending, the
Supreme Court settled the regulatory issue. In *United States
v. Southwestern Cable,* an opinion that came as quite a surprise
to the industry, the Court fully sustained the Commission's
regulatory authority:[11] even though the 1934 Congress
could not have anticipated cable and so the Communications Act did not cover cable, the FCC could regulate it anyway, as long as such regulation was "reasonably ancillary"
to the Commission's regulation of broadcasting. Then the
Court noted (although it did not pass on the specific regulations) that the Commission's goal of protecting independent
UHF stations from the possibility of losing audiences—and
revenues—because of an attractive cable offering was "reasonably ancillary" to the Commission's tasks.

The Court in conclusion tried to soften its blow by noting that in the "circumstances," permission for the cable system to add new signals was only being delayed "pending appropriate hearings." Presumably, if the hearings failed to
show a danger to the San Diego UHF station (Southwestern
Cable's "rival"), the cable system would be allowed to bring
in additional signals. But presumption and reality are dif-

ferent things. For the nine months that *Southwestern Cable* had waited at the Supreme Court, the FCC had been sitting on the hearing examiner's analysis of the San Diego market, which concluded, based on a broad inquiry, that there "is no evidence that CATV-produced competition, to date, has had any effect whatsoever on the service offered to the public by the San Diego television stations, or the ability of those stations to continue to offer that service." One week after the Supreme Court ruled, the Commission overturned the hearing examiner's determination. Cable was a competitor and would be held in check regardless of the impact (or lack thereof) its competition had on broadcasters.[12]

Taking advantage of the seemingly free rein offered by the Supreme Court, the Commission members sat back to think. They put everything relating to cable under "rule making" and began for the first time to think seriously about how cable and broadcasting interrelated. The Commission would "explore the broad question of how best to obtain, consistent with the public interest standard of the Communications Act, the full benefits of developing communications technology for the public." Commission edicts began with a dribble in 1969 and concluded in February 1972 with a gusher of rules known as the "Consensus Agreement" because of the alleged consensus of all major parties—broadcasters, cable operators, the White House Office of Telecommunications Policy, and of course the Commission—that this was an appropriate compromise given the respective strengths and weaknesses of their economic, political, and legal positions. The Consensus Agreement dealt with virtually every facet of cable operations, from allowing a system to have as many educational (PBS) stations as it wished to specifying when a more distant nonmarket station could be "leapfrogged" over a closer nonmarket station.[13]

The initial order from the Commission required cable systems with thirty-five hundred subscribers to begin putting on their own programming. A system that takes broadcast signals (the definition of a cable system) must, the Commission said, do more than transmit these signals to subscribers' homes; it must affirmatively add to the diversity of viewing by creating programming of its own. Since independent programming would, a fortiori, require local production facilities, the Commission, without missing a beat, ordered the systems to acquire them. Why someone who did not wish to program at all would nevertheless program well remained unexplored and unexplained. If the Commission thought the public would need or like local programming, then the public interest demanded the Commission see that it was provided.

A year later the Commission shifted its concern to the premium cable channels, those for which subscribers pay an additional monthly fee. Here the Commission's concern was that the subscribers were getting too much of what they wanted. The new pay-cable rules limited (to 90 percent of total programming) the number of hours a premium channel could devote to sports and movies; in the remaining time the channel was ordered to show something else, whether anyone wanted it or not. The Commission rationalized this series of rules by the belief that they would force, as did the origination rules, cable systems to come up with their own programming, possibly something new, and by the conflicting view that it did not want pay cable channels "siphoning" good programs from "free" television.

The Consensus Agreement "did something" about lots of things. With respect to programming, it continued the Commission's policy of limiting cable's opportunities to offer serious competition for local broadcasters, although it did cautiously open the way for cable systems to provide more outside channels. The agreement also vigorously continued the policy of ordering cable to offer programming that would not otherwise appear on over-the-air television. The

Commission "finally" solved its distant-signal problem by tying the number of distant signals that could be imported to market size: three for the big markets (the top fifty); two for the medium ones (the next fifty); and one for the small markets. The grant was not without limitations, for the Commission not only defined where a system had to look for its distant signals but also ordered that any of those stations' programs that were under contract locally (even if aired at different times or not at all) be deleted from the cable system's offerings.

The pre-1970 rules had looked to a future where once UHF stations became viable, cable would be an unnecessary and uneconomical adjunct to broadcasting—in other words, its future was oblivion. The Consensus Agreement rules were better only in that they did not look to cable's demise. They would accept a status quo with cable frozen in its proper place of subservience.

Thus, little diversity could be offered because of the distant-signal limitation. In that era before video cassette recorders, moreover, the rules prohibited one of the genuine benefits cable offered: time shifting. Denying cable subscribers the obvious aspects of diversity, the Commission instead offered them a different diversity. Access channels would be made available to the public and to local government and educational institutions. Diversity would come via community programming and the offerings of a local soapbox; it would not come from a national, and therefore homogenizing, source. This aspect of the rules was not without irony.

The Commission had never favored public access (absent fairness violations) to broadcast airtime. In one of the Vietnam cases discussed at the beginning of chapter 9—*BEM*—the Commission had ruled that the Communications Act precluded general access. The D.C. Circuit had then reversed. When the Consensus Agreement came down with its requirement of access to cable systems, the Commission was seeking Supreme Court review of the D.C. Circuit's *BEM* decision. The Commission wished to guarantee that broadcasters need never provide access (as opposed to fairness) to anyone unless they wished to do so.[14] What could never be considered for broadcasters could easily be done to cable systems. No amount of adverse regulation could be too much.

Just because *Southwestern Cable* held that the Commission had statutory grounds for asserting power over cable did not mean that all assertions would pass constitutional muster. The Commission had, as usual, won a stunning victory on the jurisdictional question and had exploited that victory with a regulatory broadside never attempted—and never considered—with respect to broadcasters. Everywhere cable operators turned, a Commission rule told them what they must and must not do. This situation opened three avenues of possible constitutional challenge. First, does the First Amendment authorize Commission licensing of cable systems? Second, is a prohibition on what a cable system wishes to carry censorship within the meaning of the First Amendment? Third, does the demand that a system carry certain channels or become a programmer itself violate the First Amendment by forcing the system to say what it does not wish to say?

Southwestern Cable had not involved any constitutional issue. Nevertheless, it would have made no sense for the Court to stretch to find statutory jurisdiction only to turn around and say that the stretching was unconstitutional overreaching. In reality, the only question was how the courts would explain why Commission regulation of cable was constitutional. The first attempt came in the case still waiting in the Midwest. In August 1968 in *Black Hills Video Corp. v. FCC*, the Eighth Circuit found the question hardly worth the bother.[15]

Black Hills was a master-antenna system and thus, but for the Commission's brute assertion of jurisdiction, would have had no reason to come before the Commission (unlike microwave relay systems, which do use spectrum, albeit not in the broadcast bands, to bring programs to their communities).[16] The Eighth Circuit handled the constitutional question in a single paragraph. The quarter-century-old decision in *NBC* answered all the questions, and the court quoted from that decision's key paragraph: "The right of free speech does not include, however, the right to use the facilities of radio without a license. . . . Denial of a station license on that ground [public interest, convenience, or necessity], if valid under the Act, is not a denial of free speech."[17]

Whatever the problems with this analysis in *NBC*, the problems become geometrically magnified here. As applied to a master-antenna cable system, the court's reasoning, simply put, was that if Congress requires a license, the First Amendment is satisfied if the Commission applies the appropriate standard in refusing the license. The identical reasoning could justify licensing a newspaper in the Black Hills: Congress requires the license, and denial of the license on the ground that reading might interfere with watching television is not a denial of free speech; therefore, the newspaper may not print.

Why didn't the analogy jump out? Because this was 1968. Even *Red Lion* was a year away. How could anyone think that cable television, which simply added to the entertainment available within a market, could claim First Amendment rights? A perceptive observer of the constitutional status of broadcasting had, in the early 1960s, quite correctly noted that *NBC* was "generally regarded as having sounded the death knell for the argument that government regulation of broadcasting violated the licensee's right of free expression."[18] If broadcasting did not have such rights, how could a mere "adjunct" claim them? And since the adjunct would lose anyway, why waste time thinking about the problem?

Red Lion, of course, would not by itself provide assistance to cable until a change in the perception of cable occurred —until cable was no longer conceptualized as an adjunct to, and therefore part of, broadcasting. Furthermore, even that step might not help if, as mentioned late in chapter 3, *Red Lion* turned out to rest on a new First Amendment theory applicable to all mass communications media. *Tornillo* answered the latter concern negatively in 1974. When combined with *Red Lion,* it suggested an inquiry focusing on whether the medium considered was more like the "scarce" broadcasting or like the definitionally "nonscarce" print medium.

Two years before *Tornillo* clarified the future inquiry, the Supreme Court took one more crack at cable. At issue was the Commission's requirement that larger cable systems begin cablecasting programming whether or not that was what they wished. Midwest Video most emphatically did not so wish. In *Midwest Video [I]* a sharply divided Supreme Court upheld the cablecasting requirement as being within the jurisdiction of the Commission. From the Court's perspective, the Commission sought "only to ensure that [a cable system] satisfactorily meets community needs within the context of their undertaking." Although no constitutional question was presented in the case, the Court favorably cited *Black Hills Video,* and citations to *NBC* abounded throughout the opinion—suggesting that even the Court had not yet given thought to the dimensions of the constitutional problems its jurisdictional conclusions were producing.[19]

The next case of significance was decided in 1977. It was a challenge by Home Box Office to the pay cable rules, which forced HBO to create or acquire programming other than movies and sports; the rules also required HBO to make some programming available without the fee, and they prohibited commercials. Fortuitously for HBO, this litigation became intertwined with a long-running battle between the D.C. Circuit and the Commission over classical music radio stations. Although the two problems hardly seem related, both involve the owner's choice of format.

The radio situation involved stations that were the sole source of a given format in their market. Some unique formats do well financially; others, such as classical music, do rather poorly. If a station with a money-losing (or simply insufficiently profitable) unique format is sold, the buyer will typically change the format to something that is likely to generate more profits. Writing that "we do not doubt that, at our present level of civilization, a 16 percent ratio between devotees of classical music and the rest of the population is about right," the D.C. Circuit began ordering the Commission to prohibit changes away from classical music if the station was able to make money with the format. In a startling reversal of roles, the Commission told the court it would not obey and, rubbing this conclusion in, went on to lecture the D.C. Circuit about how the court's conclusion violated the First Amendment.[20]

HBO came to the D.C. Circuit before it had a chance to slap the Commission on that unique-format conclusion. Furthermore, in the posture of *HBO,* the unique-format ruling had placed the Commission in the exceptionally vulnerable position of claiming that it could dictate cable formats while denying that it could do the same for radio. *HBO* was like leading a lamb to slaughter. The court hammered the Commission and invalidated the rules with a vengeance on each of three different grounds.

First of all, the Commission could not do to cable what it cannot do to broadcasting. Because the Commission itself had held that it lacked power to regulate radio formats, the court found that logic dictated it could not regulate cable formats. Second, the package of rules was wholly unsupported by evidence of harm done to over-the-air broadcasting (the predicate from *Southwestern Cable* and the Commission's asserted justification for the rules).

Finally, the Commission was to learn who had the say about the First Amendment. The rules in question were content rules. The Commission told HBO that only so many movies and sporting events could be shown each week; then the rules demanded that HBO program something else. Unlike all prior challenges to cable rules, HBO's presented the classic First Amendment case: the government had demanded that a speaker cease saying what he or she wishes to say. Because of its intertwining with the radio format, and because it was so recognizable as a traditional case, the D.C. Circuit was not confused by the new-technology issue. It ruled that even if the rules were supported by evidence and did fall within Commission jurisdiction (which they did not), they violated the First Amendment.[21]

The First Amendment point naturally focused on *Red Lion* and *Tornillo*. Physical scarcity, as in *Red Lion,* would justify regulation. Economic scarcity, as in *Tornillo,* could not. Cable systems might be economically scarce, but the whole point of cable is abundance. The "physical interference and scarcity requiring an umpiring role for government is absent." The decision was an incredible judicial change. There was no ambiguity: for constitutional purposes, cable was not broadcasting. It was entitled to the print First Amendment.

This case marked the earliest time that a constitutional challenge by a new communications technology not only received a serious airing but in fact won. A court was finally able to grasp the elemental point that merely because something was new did not mean that it was fair game. Whether the court would have done so without the fortuitous intertwining with the radio-format battle may be problematical, but given the D.C. Circuit's traditional blinders in the broadcast area, anything that adds to its understanding should be applauded.

Suddenly the First Amendment issue seemed clear, even in the Eighth Circuit, home of *Black Hills Video*. That circuit invalidated the Commission's access rules as intruding on a cable system's First Amendment rights in a way that the Commission would not intrude on broadcasters, thus relegating *Black Hills* to a footnote dealing with jurisdiction. The Supreme Court then agreed to review the Eighth Circuit case, and in 1979 it affirmed the decision. *Midwest Video [II]* knocked out the Commission's access rules in reasoning similar to that of the D.C. Circuit's *HBO*. The access rules imposed common carrier–like obligations on a system, and because the Commission by statute was barred from imposing such rules on broadcasters, it followed that the rules could not be "reasonably ancillary" to broadcast regulation. Because it had invalidated the rules, the Court did not reach the constitutional point, but instead simply noted in a concluding footnote that a First Amendment challenge had also been raised and that the challenge was "not frivolous."[22]

Further challenges to Commission regulations were not forthcoming, because the Commission had entered an entirely unprecedented phase in its history. Under chairmen appointed by presidents Carter and Reagan, the Commission overthrew its cable rules almost as quickly as prior Commissions had promulgated them. Suddenly viewers, not broadcasters, mattered, and competition among media sources was the new order of the day. With the single exception of the "must carry" rules, restrictive cable rules vanished in the hope of fostering more contented viewers.[23] *HBO* and Commission deregulation, especially in the areas of distant-signal importation and entry restrictions on earth station receivers, resulted in the explosive growth of cable during the late 1970s and first years of the 1980s. Freed of Commission hostility, cable was successful in finding its niche in the consumers' hearts and market.

This deregulatory drive had the effect of deflecting the constitutional issues. Had the Commission not repealed its rules, constitutional challenges would have been forthcoming at a time when the courts were finally appearing receptive. Thus the Commission's deregulatory actions had somewhat the effect of a preemptive strike.

Just because the Commission was withdrawing did not mean that the issue of cable regulation was going away. Participants may change; issues seldom do. Into the regulatory vacuum leaped the National League of Cities, advocating that cable regulation was appropriately a local matter in which each affected city could make its own decisions about what type of cable system, including offerings, it wished.

A two-front battle emerged. On the local level, each time a city decided that it would award a franchise it pitted its demands against the estimates and greed (and, all too frequently, questionable ethics) of the would-be franchisees. This was really no contest. The awarding city was quite literally the only game in town, and its terms would prevail.

Nationally, however, the situation was different. Here the National League of Cities and the cable trade organization, the National Cable Television Association, both attempted to control pending legislation dealing with cable television. In the process, the First Amendment was left elsewhere. The position of the NLC was articulated well by Mayor Charles Royer of Seattle when he stated that the First Amendment was not the cities' concern.[24] Nor was it to be Congress's. When Congress passed the Cable Communications Policy Act of 1984, not a single member rose to object to the fundamental premise of the bill, that cable was not entitled to the First Amendment protections afforded a newspaper.

Both the cities and the cable industry desired legislation

clarifying their relationship as well as the overall status of cable. The NCTA needed this legislation much more, though; it was thus in no position to stand on principle. Furthermore, the National League of Cities had a potential ally in the wings should the broadcasting industry view the occasion as one for risking political capital in another attempt to hamstring cable. The NCTA knew it had to give in order to get. As is the case with all diplomatic negotiation, the final settlement conformed to the realities of armed forces on the ground. There were ebbs and flows, and often it looked as if no legislation would be forthcoming, but compromises by each finally resulted in passage.

The principal compromises, not surprisingly, involved money. A cable company and the franchising city typically become joint-venturers, with the city guaranteeing a freedom from cable competition in return for a percentage of the company's gross revenues. The Cable Communications Policy Act of 1984 continued this arrangement, although with safeguards for each party. Cities could continue imposing franchise fees of up to 5 percent of gross operating revenues, the FCC's ceiling under the Consensus Agreement. In turn, cable operators achieved their primary desire: the right, beginning in 1986, to control the fees they charged subscribers (unless the FCC makes a determination that the market lacks sufficient competition). The trade-offs here were easy and obvious. Cable companies were largely freed from the specter of rate regulation (although they are subject to market constraints because of competition from all sources of entertainment, especially video rentals), and cities obtained the right to request substantial annual fees that might substitute for unpalatable tax increases.[25]

Closely related to money, in both substance and importance, was control. Cities demanded and obtained the right to select their cable operator. Furthermore, when a franchise expired, the city could select again. Although cable operators would have liked to contest the former right, they really could not. But the right to refranchise could put a serious damper on the initial victory. What happens to the capital equipment if a different company is selected at the end of the franchise period? Here the NLC compromised. Should an operator be ousted, it would receive fair market value for its capital equipment. Forced-sale financial ruin would not be in the cards.

Renewal itself represents the most obvious—and ambiguous—compromise position between the cities' desire for a free hand and the cable operators' wish for automatic renewal. The section encourages, but does not mandate, renewal. Should a city not wish to renew, then an administrative hearing will determine (1) whether the company has substantially complied with its important franchise promises, (2) the quality of service the company renders the community (defined to exclude programming questions), (3) the company's financial ability to meet new promises, and (4) whether the operator's proposal is reasonable to meet future cable-related needs of the community. After the hearing, the city, if it still wishes to deny renewal, must provide written reasons relating to the issues at the hearing, and judicial review is available to the operator. Should the losing cable operator go to court, the city can only prevail if the findings at the hearing are supported by a preponderance of evidence (legalese for more likely than not). While it is impossible to tell how this scheme will work, the basic idea seems clear: cities should renew and save everyone the trouble of going through what would otherwise be a lengthy and uncertain process.[26]

The cities prevailed completely on access issues. Before *Midwest Video [II]*, the FCC rules had required the cable operator to set aside a number of channels for the use of the public, local government, and local education. Invalidation by the Court did not slow the process, because the cities had in the meantime come to view access concessions as one of their perks. In the major franchises that had been awarded at the end of the 1970s and into the early 1980s, the cities had routinely demanded and received access channels. The 1984 act codified this practice. Furthermore, the act requires that a certain number of channels be available for commercial uses not affiliated with the cable system. These leased-access channels range from 10 percent of capacity in a system with thirty-six to fifty-four channels, to 15 percent of the channel capacity in the larger systems.[27]

Finally, the act deals with obscenity and indecency in two different ways. An operator must provide, by either sale or lease, a lockbox for subscribers who wish to be able to control children's use of their sets. And speech that is "obscene or otherwise unprotected by the Constitution" may not be transmitted by a cable system. No definitions are provided in the section.

Passage of the legislation did not erase the problems courts were beginning to recognize in the late 1970s. The act instead provides a focus for analyzing the constitutional issues. Essentially, there are two major and one subsidiary First Amendment issues. The major issues are content regulation of cable programming and the ability of municipalities to grant cable franchises, typically exclusive ones. The subsidiary issue is the requirement of access channels. Legislatively, the cities prevailed on all three points. What remains to be seen is the amount of deference courts will accord that legislative determination as the courts come face to face with First Amendment issues in the cable context.

The most familiar of the constitutional issues is that of content regulation. Without very good reason government cannot control the content of the communications of any speech source unless the speech itself lacks constitutional protection. Thus obscenity can be prohibited in magazines, books, movies, and cable systems.[28] But that is not an important issue here. The issue that typically arises in the cable context is whether soft-core sex, nudity, or sexual innuendo can be banned in movies or programs that would be rated either X or R. Just as the Supreme Court's *Miller* test could be seen as aimed at the then-popular movie *Deep Throat,* the cable problem can be conceptualized as banning, at a minimum, the Playboy Channel. The argument for prohibition is that such programming is unsuitable in the given community and that *Pacifica* (WBAI) authorizes prohibition.

The argument from *Pacifica* has several strands. That decision had emphasized the pervasiveness of broadcasting. But why should pervasiveness be limited to radio? Cable, after all, is evolving rapidly as a major part of modern mass communications, and for those homes with cable it is interchangeable with radio and television; indeed, from the viewers' perspective it is the same. Like radio, cable is watched in the home, and nowhere else are the viewers' privacy interests—in this case the right not to be affronted by programming that offends—greater. Finally, cable, again like radio, is accessible to unsupervised children.[29]

Yet this argument wrenches *Pacifica* from its facts. Justice Stevens's opinion had emphasized the factual basis of a massive, concentrated dose of assaultive vulgarities spoken during midday. To apply *Pacifica* to the category of nonobscene sex removes the shock-value concept from the case. Justice Stevens's opinion was not written in isolation from all other First Amendment cases decided over the years. It was designed to cover a specific factual problem, not to authorize wholesale censorship of all mass communications on the ground that programming that offends one group should therefore be unavailable to every other group. Furthermore, even if the parallel between dirty words and soft-core pornography is sufficiently precise to bring part of *Pacifica* into play, there still would remain the question of whether cable can be subjected to rules drawn up in the context of radio.

Just how well do the rationales offered in *Pacifica* to split radio from print fit cable? Off the top, the ineffectiveness of warnings used by WBAI does not fit. The multitude of extensive program guides available provides ample testimony to the well-known fact that viewers read before they watch. The guides alert the reader-viewer to whether a particular program will have materials that may offend. Thus, no viewer need be surprised by what is on the screen. If the concern instead is children who would either inadvertently or, worse still, intentionally view inappropriate programming, then lockboxes will solve the problem. Furthermore, R- and X-rated programming is invariably shown at night (or at least in the evening), when parental supervision is more likely to be available.

The weakest of the analogies is in the "intruder" argument. Cable is a subscription service; it is connected only after a request and payment of an installation fee have been made. Admission to the home is thus voluntary, and the decision to admit is reaffirmed monthly by the payment of fees. If viewers wish to end any intrusion, all they need do is cancel the subscription (or cease paying the bill). If they wish an instant end to the intrusion, the cable outlet may be disconnected with relative ease. Furthermore, cable is not like a radio, which if not used is worthless; cable is a wire to a television set—should the viewer disconnect the wire, there would still be other uses for the set. It stretched credulity to call radio an intruder in *Pacifica;* it would be too Orwellian to state that a service that need not be taken and costs money to continue intrudes on our lives in such a way that government must censor it.

Nevertheless, some argue that cable and its many offerings have become so important—so pervasive, in *Pacifica's* terms—that we *must* continue it, whether or not it offends. Cable, so the argument runs, is too important in our modern society (given what it can deliver) to require a person to be without it. Yet once cable is in the home, the viewers' privacy interests predominate. And they do so in such a way that those who wish to have their privacy respected claim they must dictate what others will not see. This argument asks far too much, as those who wish to have both cable and privacy also demand the right to control the options of all other subscribers. Given what the argument asks and the familiar nature of the issue, it is really not surprising that all federal courts that have faced this issue have recognized it for what it is—censorship—and invalidated the legislation.[30]

The 1984 act authorizes the grant of exclusive cable franchises, and this authorization, conforming to the typical practice of municipalities, presents the other major constitutional question raised by cable. A single franchise is awarded because this allows the city and cable company, as joint-venturers, to exclude competition and therefore achieve higher revenues than might otherwise be available. From the cities' perspective, the ability to grant an exclusive franchise is the ability to maximize franchise fees and give-backs such as access channels, studio facilities, and other goodies.

To combat the cities' demands, cable operators have attempted to cloak themselves in the image of "electronic publishers." To listen to them is to see a cable operator actively picking and choosing among vast numbers of available offerings to find the appropriate mix of entertainment and information necessary for its subscribers. It sounds just like a newspaper[31]—until you think about it. An operator does select WTBS, for example, but there it stops; the operator certainly does not get credit for picking each and every program WTBS selects—especially in circumstances in which WTBS changes its programming after it is on the cable system. The problem, as former FCC commissioner Professor Glen Robinson has so aptly noted, is that the "argument seems overambitious and underconvincing."[32] Yet just because the cable operators' argument is overly rhetorical does not mean that the conclusion is wrong. Cable is, beyond dispute, a medium of communications.[33] As such, and consistent with the First Amendment, it may only be regulated for a sound reason.

Ever since *Red Lion* and *Tornillo,* it has been apparent that to justify regulation there must be a sufficient explanation of why a medium should not be treated in the same way as print. And lest anyone miss the obvious point, no matter how well loved a city's newspaper may be, the Constitution presents an unassailable barrier to the idea that a city could grant an exclusive franchise to a newspaper. How then are such grants to cable systems justified?

There is no Supreme Court support for any justification except scarcity, and yet, as *HBO* and the Eighth Circuit in *Midwest Video [II]* have correctly stated, scarcity is foreign to cable because cable is the medium of abundance. This is not to say that no one will assert that cable, too, is scarce. If scarcity is the necessary predicate for regulation, and if someone wants to regulate, you can safely bet that scarcity will be asserted. Thus a federal district judge in Rhode Island sustained cable franchising requirements precisely because—you guessed it—cable is scarce. The judge offered two different, albeit related, concepts of scarcity. First, because it costs so much to create a cable system—$7 million in the case before him—there is economic scarcity. Residents lacking $7 million are "shut out," whereas for just pennies they could write a leaflet. Second, cable is a natural monopoly—that is, only one *system* (forget the number of channels, because to consider them undermines the argument) can survive in an area—which is a fortiori scarce. And traditionally, government regulates all natural monopolies.[34]

In *Tornillo,* identical arguments had been offered to bring newspapers within the scarcity rationale. The Court rejected them. Although it would be nice to suggest that this news had not permeated Rhode Island, the better explanation is that the judge knew full well he was relying on paper-thin arguments but used them nevertheless because he thought they were the best available for the result he wished to reach.

The natural-monopoly argument is as close as cable can be pushed to the procrustean bed of scarcity. It has been a favorite of the cities, which in most cases have proceeded to make it a self-fulfilling prophecy by granting an exclusive franchise. Three strands of the argument merit mention. First, factually the argument is unproven; in some markets competing cable systems exist. Second, if the city grants an exclusive franchise, then any argument about natural monopoly begs the question—and, if an excluded company wishes to wire the city, the natural-monopoly argument goes on to answer the question incorrectly. Third, the argument focuses on the scarcity of cable systems, not on choices available to subscribers to cable channels. The search for scarcity is clearly forced.

Once cable scarcity is seen as the phantom it is, it becomes easy to explain why cities have been able to franchise cable companies. Cities own their streets, and laying cable wires is disruptive to traffic. No one, not even the local newspaper, can go out and dig up city streets without permission, and cable companies have had to go to the city to obtain permission. And that permission has come in the form of a bargained franchise. If permission is withheld, digging up the streets would render the cable company both civilly and criminally liable. Before proceeding to discuss what this means, however, it is worthwhile to pause and consider, not a cable company, but a newspaper.

Suppose a city with a great morning newspaper were informed that a new daily wished to begin publication. The city cannot grant an exclusive franchise, nor could it accomplish the same thing by rejecting a second newspaper on the grounds that the city was well served by the existing newspaper. The laws of economics may justify one-newspaper cities; the Constitution would not.

To begin publication, the newspaper needs a building in which to edit and print. The city could not deny a building permit on the gound that one newspaper already served the population well. Building permits may be denied on appropriate grounds, such as zoning, but the fact that the applicant is the press is not an appropriate ground. Nor could the city condition the building permit on payment of a press franchise fee. The paper can be made to pay all taxes generally applicable to all businesses but cannot be singled out for special taxes. Indeed, this latter point is so important that in 1983 the Supreme Court invalidated a Minnesota newsprint tax that applied only to newspapers (which were otherwise exempt from an even higher use tax).[35]

Once the plant is constructed and the presses are running, the newspaper must distribute its product. Papers are delivered by truck to various substations; then carriers handle home delivery, typically by car. Street vendors or street vending machines may also be used. The city may not single out the paper's trucks, the carriers' cars, or the vendors or vending machines for individualized treatment. If commercial trucks as a class present problems, then the paper's trucks can, to the extent they fall within those problems, be covered *as* commercial trucks. Similarly, if street vending is a problem, then a general law covering vending may be applied to the newspaper. But a law dealing just with newspaper trucks or vending is unconstitutional. To use another example, the cafeteria of the *Washington Post* may be regulated by public health authorities even if Richard Nixon is president—but the ability to regulate what is served up in the cafeteria does not allow regulation of what is served up in the pages of the newspaper.

All of this is obvious, indeed elemental. Now suppose, though, that the newspaper finds that the best way to deliver its news to its subscribers is by a wire from the newspaper plant into the subscribers' homes. How many of these points change? None. If the paper needs an addition to its plant, the building code still applies, but a provision exclusively regulating newspapers using wire does not. The same can be said for trucks, vendors, and the cafeteria. Only general laws may be applied to the newspaper; special laws may not. As long as we remember that this is a newspaper, the requirement of general laws is remarkably easy.

Suppose, however, that the city turns to the newspaper and says distribution in the old way is fine, but if you are going to distribute your paper in a more modern fashion, we want 5 percent of your revenues. Further suppose that only a newspaper distributing itself in this new fashion is covered. Although the case is novel, because the means of distribution would be novel, the principles to be applied are not novel. They have been around for over forty years.[36] The city can regulate noncommunicative activities of the press by general laws that rest on legitimate city concerns and that are applicable to everyone. Thus, the city could conclude that laying the wire would be too disruptive; if the city has an ordinance dealing with this type of disruption (or simply adopts one as soon as the paper presents the problem) and the application fits within the ordinance, then the paper may not lay its wire. But that prohibition comes not because the offender is a newspaper, but because a general law dealing with disruption of city streets exists.

This newspaper analysis should be clear and hardly startling. The next point should be obvious as well. It applies to cable, too.

In 1986 the Supreme Court spoke obliquely to this situation. The case was *Los Angeles v. Preferred Communications.*[37] Los Angeles had divided itself into several zones, for each of which an exclusive franchise would be awarded. Preferred, however, decided to bypass Los Angeles's normal process of selecting cable franchisers; instead it requested permission of both the phone company and the Department of Water and Power to lease excess space on poles and underground conduits to construct a system. Both entities refused, citing Preferred's lack of city approval. But when Preferred requested city permission, that too was refused. The courthouse became the next scene of the drama.

Initially Los Angeles won without trial, but the Ninth Circuit, in a scholarly opinion by Judge Sneed, reversed, finding that because there was excess physical capacity, *Tornillo* was controlling.[38] The Supreme Court then granted review, but in a unanimous opinion by Justice Rehnquist it indicated that it wanted to know a lot more before tackling the cable constitutional issue. "More detailed views" await "a fuller development of the disputed issues in the case [traffic delays, hazards, and esthetic unsightliness]. We think that we may know more than we know now about how the constitutional issues should be resolved when we know more about the present uses of the public utility poles and rights-of-way and how [Preferred] proposes to install and maintain its facilities on them."[39]

In short—indeed in what for the current Court is a spectacularly short opinion—the Court ducked. That the Court was serious about avoiding constitutional issues relating to cable became even more evident a week after *Preferred,* when the Court refused to review the D.C. Circuit's determination that the "must carry" rules violated the First Amendment.[40] For the time being, at least, the Court has no intention of entering what it perceives as a new and novel First Amendment area.

Three justices not only joined the *Preferred* opinion but

also offered a one-paragraph addition of their own that hark-ened back to the earlier days: "Different communications media are treated differently for First Amendment pur-poses."[41] That is, neither the print model of *Tornillo* nor the broadcast model of *Red Lion* may be appropriate for cable. Rather, the Court should, once again, start all over, avoid analogies, and fashion principles uniquely appropri-ate for cable. As has typically been the case, nothing in the broadcast experience suggests to the justices that fashion-ing principles means creating the ability for government to abuse the licensing powers that the Court may find appro-priate.

Nevertheless, the newspaper example demonstrates that while cable may be novel, the problems it presents are not. Nor does the cable industry need the nine justices to sit back and decide how many novel principles must be fashioned so that cable will be treated "just right" with an appropri-ate balance of freedom and responsibility—whatever that would be.

Instead, the newspaper example I offered points to an-swers worked out over a forty-year period. Applying this example to cable, it becomes clear that—as with other me-dia—although the city may regulate and charge fees, its ac-tions must be related to the disruption of its property and nothing else. Thus it may charge cable companies a fee for the right to dig up streets, but this fee must be related to the city's expenses, not the cable company's revenues. That is, a cable system must pay the taxes that others pay; special franchise fees unrelated to direct costs to the city and apply-ing exclusively to cable are, however, unconstitutional. Pre-venting disruption of streets, although important, authorizes nothing beyond a determination of how much disruption to allow.

Once a city makes the choice of how much disruption it is willing to live with, issues of franchising become clear. If a city will have no disruption, then no cable system can enter, because the wires must be laid underground.[42] As a result some form of satellite distribution system will probably come to serve that municipality. If a city chooses to allow some disruption, then an exclusive franchise cannot be allowed if a second system can lay its cable at no additional disruption to the city. Finally, there is no need to worry about renewals of a franchise, for once the cable is laid the city's legitimate interests have ended. If there is no further need to lay cable, the city has no further legislative interest.

A city may protect its streets, but it may not control who sends messages or what messages are sent. Only the fact that cable is a newer technology could mystify this truth. Tying city powers into city interests and traditional First Amendment analysis goes virtually all the way toward answering the constitutional questions about the demands for free access-channels from the cable operator. No one pretends that a new newspaper could be forced to provide an op-ed page for public access. If the paper thought it could better use that page for its own choices of information, it would do so. The same holds for cable. What does access mean, after all? Access is an assertion that someone whom the cable operator would not put on a channel can use that channel anyway (because that use is, theoretically at least, in the public interest).

The only new argument on access that is not involved with franchising is that, unlike a newspaper, before the cable system exists, nothing exists. Thus the access channels never were those of the cable operator, who loses nothing by ceding them initially. But the op-ed page never "was" the newspaper's before the paper started, and a building permit could not be conditioned on the creation of an access op-ed page. Unless some meaningful distinction between cable systems and newspapers is available—and no one has suggested one—the demand of free access-channels is simply an unconstitutional outgrowth of the city's legitimate power to protect its roadways.

Leased access—the 10 percent and 15 percent set-aside channels demanded by Congress in the 1984 act—presents a different question. In essence, the cable system is being made a common carrier for these channels. There seems little doubt that Congress could have declared cable a 100 percent common carrier and left every channel available for others to use.[43] Common carriers are simply conduits, and no First Amendment rights have ever been found to be violated by saying that if someone wishes to enter a common-carrier industry, it must be a common carrier.

The new question with respect to leased-access channels is whether an entity can be part communicator and part common carrier over the same system. There is no logical reason why this status should not be constitutional, but before rushing into such a conclusion one should note that there are differences between a cable company and traditional common carriers. Normally, the sender of common-carrier transmissions has a specific intended receiver. This situation would not hold with cable, however, as the sender would have no idea who, if anyone, would be on the receiving end. Although this does not appear to be a distinction of any substance, it serves to alert us that old concepts are being used in newer ways and that in the process strains may well be placed on them.

Cable, unlike even newer technologies, has had an eventful history. Many difficult constitutional issues have been discussed, although most remain unresolved. This lengthy overview of cable's history is an attempt to shed light on the choices being made. It also fully illustrates the reluctance of decision makers to ask constitutional questions. Instead, those questions are left to judges who will bend over backward to sustain whatever status quo government legislates. Cable nicely illustrates the observation of Lee Bollinger that "new technologies of communication are both new battle-grounds for renewed fighting over old first amendment issues and focal points for reform efforts."[44]

Some of the First Amendment issues posed by cable regulation after enactment of the Cable Communications Policy Act—such as attempted bans on offensive programming—are quite familiar. Others, such as franchising, *should* be familiar, but technology often dazzles us, making the problem seem all too novel and complex. Still others, such as whether an entity can be partly a full communicator and partly a common-carrier conduit, are genuinely novel. If we can remove technology's blinders, we may be able to avoid the slapped together legislative compromise that leaves the First Amendment somewhere in the judges' chambers, to be taken out only after decades upon decades of regulation. Otherwise the history of broadcasting, and now of cable, will in all likelihood simply be replayed again and again with newer technologies.

Conclusion

This book has been written against the background of Lee Bollinger's seminal thesis that a press half free and half tethered provides us both the uninhibited reaching and the balance necessary to serve First Amendment goals. This book, quite obviously, is my dissent. The evidence I have presented demonstrates that the licensed half of the press has been subject to political abuses wholly inconsistent with a concept of freedom of expression. I do not believe, therefore, that Bollinger's thesis can stand. At a minimum I believe the complacency of Bollinger's followers in the academy is unfounded.[1]

In the process of questioning Bollinger's thesis, I have also unintentionally questioned an even more strongly held thesis in constitutional law: that the federal courts exist (in both theory and reality) to enforce the civil-liberties protections of the Constitution. No fair reading of the broadcast experience I have detailed leaves doubt that the federal courts—both the D.C. Circuit and the Supreme Court— have operated largely as rubber stamps for the Federal Communications Commission. In the process they have provided legitimacy for some of the most blatant political abuses of the Commission. That the federal courts have not understood the broader perspective in which Commission actions were taken may serve as an excuse, but it is not a justification. Not actively seeking to understand the full context in which governmental actions operate is inconsistent with the premise that federal judges act as the key guardians of the Bill of Rights.

One rejoinder to what I have said is that large media corporations ought not to be seen as having civil liberties. Yet even this rejoinder must be qualified in at least two ways. Many of the abuses I have described were perpetrated on very small broadcasters such as Pacifica and Red Lion. Furthermore, I doubt if many, reflecting on Richard Nixon and the *Washington Post,* really wish to hold that large corporations cannot claim the protections of the Bill of Rights. This second point leaves only a return to the distinction, so much discussed in this book, that print properly enjoys the full protections (whatever they may be) of the First Amendment, but broadcasting does not.

The heirs of the print tradition might not dissent on the appropriateness of this distinction. They have rarely seen broadcasters as relations, even slightly disreputable ones. The interests of the two media were theoretically dissimilar: broadcasters pursued obscene profits; print explained the events of the nation and the world to an audience desiring information. To a large extent this durable perception of difference has proven correct. Only briefly, once with the Hutchins Commission in the late 1940s[2] and then immediately before and for about five years after *Red Lion,* has the image of broadcast regulation been seen as a possibility for improving the public-interest function of the American press. The Supreme Court put the kibosh on this in *Miami Herald v. Tornillo* in 1974, and little has been heard since.

The heirs of the print tradition have been lucky. It was not inevitable that the outcome would occur as it did. *Red Lion* might have been the model of a similar conclusion in *Tornillo.* That it was not speaks amply for the depth of the distinction in our American consciousness—especially for those (including each member of the Supreme Court) who were raised in the days of the crystal set. But future Supreme Court justices will be familiar not only with the vacuum tube, but with computers, fiber optics, and satellites as well. For them, print may seem unique only in being largely irrelevant. As the duality between print and broadcasting vanishes into technological obsolescence, will there be claimants to a print tradition—one grounded in the conclusion shared by both the framers of the First Amendment and the best of the scholars of freedom of expression[3]—that views government as the principal source of possible abuses of freedom of communications?

When Ithiel de Sola Pool's *Technologies of Freedom,* an important book suggesting appropriate legal responses to newer technologies, appeared in 1983, the major legal reviews provided some answers about how the current generation of scholars is viewing the First Amendment and the future. Book reviews in legal journals are almost exclusively vehicles for the reviewer to write an essay about the subject of the book under consideration, with the book typically used only for illustration and contrast; the four major reviews of Pool's book are essentially in this tradition. Of these four, two are major because they are written by two of the nation's most important First Amendment scholars, David Anderson and Frederick Schauer. The other two are important because of place: they occupy pages of the *Harvard Law Review* and the *Yale Law Journal,* the two most prestigious journals of American law.

Anderson and Schauer are both traditionalists, although their reviews demonstrate that in viewing new technologies there are two important traditions to consider. For Anderson, "the printing press is our metaphor for freedom of expression, a metaphor blessed with the very words of the First Amendment."[4] First Amendment rights should be parceled out based not on which medium is being used but rather on the function the medium performs. Broadcasting performs the functions of print and should be accorded like protections. So too should the newer technologies as they come on line.

Schauer is not so sure. Although no summary will do

justice to Schauer's highly nuanced position, two separate
thrusts dominate his conclusions. The first is that the First
Amendment is only one of many important interests within
the United States. The second is that more is not necessarily
better; a lean and mean First Amendment, protecting little
but protecting what is truly important, is better than a First
Amendment that is used to solve all issues of communication and communicators.

Schauer notes that some forms of harm normally associated with speech may well be magnified by mass-communi-
cations technology. Thus it is possible that "we might want
to respond by decreasing the amount of first amendment
protection" rather than by increasing it, as Pool suggests.
Furthermore, courts should be wary in offering First Amendment protection to novel communications technology, because it is a "mistake . . . , often with unseen but hard consequences, to extend the first amendment to cover that
which it ought not cover." Once it becomes plain that First
Amendment coverage is appropriate, as Schauer now concludes it is with broadcasting and cable, then courts will act.
The "history of first amendment doctrine provides considerable cause for optimism. While the reactions have not
always been as fast as many would like, and have been too
fast for others, the courts have in the past demonstrated the
ability to adapt first amendment doctrine to new forms of
technology."[5]

Anderson and Schauer represent the two basic First
Amendment traditions. Anderson's view, amply supported
by this book, is that our "press" cannot be separated from
First Amendment protections without serious risks. Schauer
instead holds, as supporters of broadcast regulation have
held, that each technology presents different problems and
that "first amendment responses should be every bit as novel
as the technology they are attempting to track."[6]

Even Schauer's cautious hedging becomes libertarian when

compared with the Harvard review. The reviewer, Mario Baeza,[7] found that the "primary problem" with Pool's analysis lay in the fact that Pool "largely ignores the legitimate concerns that a complex, modern society may have about the unregulated introduction of new mass media technologies. Sensitivity to these concerns has led to the current state of the law." Baeza has few concerns about the potential dangers of regulation, which, according to him, Pool overstates, or about the current state of the law.[8]

Local regulation of cable is analogous to federal regulation of broadcasting. "Indeed, local regulation represents both a return to the regime of the 1920's and 1930's and a march ahead into new complexities that derive from technological advances and from the greater legal protection for individual rights that exists in contemporary society." But the "greater protection for individual rights" has a catch: there must be affirmative government action to regulate in the public interest. That there is no scarcity is irrelevant. The pervasiveness of mass communications and the viewers' privacy interests require affirmative government regulation. To the arguments that *Pacifica* (WBAI) was both wrongly decided and in any event inapplicable to cable, Baeza responds: "Formalistic legal reasoning, however, will not prove helpful on this issue. . . . A sensitive application of the first amendment to the electronic media must account for pervasiveness and privacy issues as key challenges for the future."[9]

The approach of the Yale reviewer, Stephen Carter,[10] could not have been more different, although he too supports extensive regulation of new technologies. The "public's fears of the power of the media are not wholly irrational. Left unregulated, the modern media could present serious threats to democracy." This statement jumps off the page. Traditional First Amendment theory has uniformly held that government regulation of the press would be a serious threat to an open democracy. Carter inverts the theory: an unregulated press becomes the threat to democracy.[11]

Yet Carter's review fairly abounds with traditional First Amendment viewpoints, such as the necessity of an open flow of information—which creates an informed citizenry —to sustain democracy. *Context* is different. Modern society needs a First Amendment that can keep pace with the explosive changes around us. Change and wealth will distort the market. The "critical problem" of the modern First Amendment is the "unequal access wealth can buy." That our mass media are privately held exacerbates the access problem. Large private interests are thus now capable of doing what before only a government might have done: censor, mold, and shape a false consensus; furthermore, given their special privileges in our society, they have the interest to do so. "We are moving into a world . . . in which the information is controlled increasingly by those who are not totally disinterested in the outcomes produced by the system."[12]

With the media concentrated in fewer hands and wealth being the exclusive entrée, the system is loaded to support the status quo. "Those who lack the money lack access to [spread their messages]; their principal First Amendment right is to listen." They will hear too little diverse information because "those who challenge deeply entrenched interests are treated as freaks or ignored." Instead the media put forth messages largely supportive of a centrist capitalist position; the underlying assumptions of the system are simply not questioned. Thus, if "free and open debate on issues of public importance is necessary for the healthy functioning of a democracy, then as the power to shape opinion (or decide which opinions are heard, which amounts to the same thing) is concentrated in fewer hands, the democracy may grow less and less healthy."[13]

Carter reluctantly supports government regulation as a

check on private power and as a hope for the needed cor-
rectives. "The First Amendment is intended to promote the
free discussion of public policy, not permit special interests
to manipulate that discussion or prevent it from taking
place." To assist free discussion he supports the continuation of the fairness doctrine and equal-time provisions for
broadcasting and would, in fact, carry them over to newer
technologies, specifically cable. Access channels are a necessity, because they provide a means of bringing otherwise
unheard messages to a larger audience. Finally, in some unspecified way he would authorize censorship if it were shown
that certain harmful (and hateful) messages were being too
frequently heard and thus were likely to have an effect.[14]

The Harvard and Yale reviews, especially the latter, represent a fundamental break with Anderson and even Schauer.
Mass communications will cause new problems and will
need new solutions. The Yale review, which is both powerful
and persuasive, argues for what I have described elsewhere
as the "newer First Amendment." The leading advocate
of this newer First Amendment has been Judge J. Skelly
Wright of the D.C. Circuit. His view is that our society must
return the focus to the individual and prevent inequalities
of wealth from dominating the ideas on the democratic
agenda. The marketplace of ideas may be overwhelmed by
the wealthy with their access to all mass communications
and to the homes of everyone. The ideas of the financially
privileged would prevail not because of merit but because of
pervasiveness. From this perspective it matters not a whit
whether one talks about newspapers, television, or cable.
What is necessary is a First Amendment that recognizes that
society has changed, a First Amendment adapted to the
problems of our times, not to those of two hundred years
ago. Although I fully sympathize with the concerns of the
"newer First Amendment" advocates, I believe that the

older First Amendment, which rejects an affirmative government role as being fundamentally inconsistent with an open democracy, has served us well and ought not to be discarded.[15]

Justice Douglas had been on the Court thirty-four years when the FCC–D.C. Circuit conflict on whether broadcasters had to allow paid access to those who sought it came before the Supreme Court. He recognized that within the argument for paid access was an idea different from that traditionally associated with First Amendment litigation, and he offered the following comments:

> What kind of First Amendment would best serve our needs as we approach the twenty-first century may be an open question. But the old-fashioned First Amendment that we have is the Court's only guideline; and one hard and fast principle which it announces is that Government shall keep its hands off the press. That principle has served us through days of calm and eras of strife and I would abide by it until a new First Amendment is adopted.[16]

He knew, of course, that the First Amendment need not have a fixed meaning and that the Court was fully capable of fashioning a First Amendment fit for the twenty-first century. It is, after all, perfectly legitimate to demand that the Constitution keep up with the times; it must. Douglas's not-too-subtle point was that the new First Amendment position then being advocated would not serve our society as well as the old-fashioned one of distrust of the government.

The choices he faced then will be with us constantly as new technologies appear and change the way we communicate with one another, because with each new technology we will refight old battles about the meaning of freedom of speech. We did this in the early days of broadcasting and at the same time successfully preserved the print tradition. I doubt, however, that we can pull the same coup twice.

There is a tremendous difference between a conclusion that even though the old tradition is sound, a new technology (radio) has nothing to do with the old, and a conclusion that the old tradition is no longer viable in meeting the needs of our society. As the belief in the uniqueness of broadcasting necessarily evaporates, there will come a tension about how to deal with an unknown future. The claim will be made that keeping the Constitution up with the times requires a newer tradition, one looking to, rather than away from, the government. As we hear this claim, we should recall the lessons of licensing, whether in seventeenth-century England or twentieth-century America. If we do, the old-fashioned tradition of freedom won't look so bad.

Notes

INTRODUCTION

1. *New York Times v. United States,* 403 U.S. 713, 717 (1971).

2. Id. at 717.

3. S. Ungar, THE PAPERS AND THE PAPERS 128–29 (New York: Dutton, 1972).

4. H. Kalven, *Broadcasting and the First Amendment,* 10 Journal of Law and Economics 15, 18 (1967).

5. M. Hughes, ed., J. Milton, COMPLETE POEMS AND MAJOR PROSE 746 (New York: Odyssey Press, 1957).

6. D. Anderson, *The Origins of the Press Clause,* 30 UCLA Law Review 455 (1983).

7. L. Levy, EMERGENCE OF A FREE PRESS 95 (New York: Oxford University Press, 1985).

8. The standard work on the English experience is Fredrick S. Siebert's FREEDOM OF THE PRESS IN ENGLAND, 1476–1776 (Urbana: University of Illinois Press, 1952). A fresh look, from both a broader perspective and a narrower time-frame, is overdue. A beginning is in P. Hamburger, *The Development of the Law of Seditious Libel and the Control of the Press,* 37 Stanford Law Review 661 (1985).

9. J. Barron, *Access to the Media—A New First Amendment Right,* 80 Harvard Law Review 1641 (1967).

10. *Miami Herald v. Tornillo,* 418 U.S. 241 (1974).

11. L. Bollinger, *Freedom of the Press and Public Access,* 75 Michigan Law Review 1 (1976).

12. Id. at 36.

13. Id. at 27, 36.

14. Id. at 32–33.

15. L. Tribe, AMERICAN CONSTITUTIONAL LAW 697–700 (Minneola, N.Y.: Foundation Press, 1978).

16. This aspect of the theory helps explain not only the imme-

diate acceptance of Bollinger's theory but also its transformation from theory to "fact." Because those adopting Bollinger's theory typically came from constitutional law rather than from broadcasting, they simply assumed that the regulated regime of broadcasting worked well—as Bollinger had theorized it would. An example is Professor Tribe's AMERICAN CONSTITUTIONAL LAW at 700. Tribe, unlike others, had the clear excuse that his treatise was about constitutional law, not broadcasting. His imprimatur, however, allowed others to mistake theory for fact.

CHAPTER 1

1. *Los Angeles Times,* October 14, 1932.

2. C. Orbison, *"Fighting Bob" Shuler: Early Radio Crusader,* 21 Journal of Broadcasting 459, 470 (1977).

3. Id. at 460–62.

4. Id. at 465.

5. Id.

6. L. Caldwell, *Freedom of Speech and Radio Broadcasting,* 177 Annals of the American Academy of Political and Social Sciences 201 (1935).

7. *Trinity Methodist Church v. FRC,* 62 F.2d 850, 851 (D.C. Cir. 1932).

8. 62 F.2d at 851.

9. 62 F.2d at 852, 853.

10. Cert. denied, 288 U.S. 599 (1933).

11. *Near v. Minnesota,* 283 U.S. 697 (1931).

12. Fred Friendly recounts the story of the *Saturday Press* in MINNESOTA RAG (New York: Random House, 1981).

13. 283 U.S. at 704.

14. Id. at 706.

15. Id. at 711.

16. Id. at 713.

17. Id. at 716.

18. Id. at 719–20.

19. V. Blasi, *Toward a Theory of Prior Restraint,* 66 Minnesota Law Review 11 (1981).

CHAPTER 2

1. *FRC v. Nelson Bros. Bond & Mortgage,* 289 U.S. 266, 271 (1933).

2. FRC, Second Annual Report 161 (1928).

3. G. Carson, THE ROGUISH WORLD OF DOCTOR BRINKLEY 143 (New York: Rinehart, 1960).

4. Id. at 10.

5. Id. at 76.

6. Id. at 38.

7. Id. at 77.

8. Id. at 85.

9. Id.

10. Id. at 89.

11. Id. at 99–100.

12. Id. at 100–101.

13. Id. at 103.

14. Id. at 146.

15. *KFKB Broadcasting Association, Inc. v. FRC,* 47 F.2d 670, 672 (D.C. Cir. 1930).

16. Carson at 166.

17. Id. at 153.

18. Id. at 238.

19. Id. at 249–50.

20. *Mutual Film Corp. v. Ohio Industrial Commission,* 236 U.S. 230 (1915); *Mutual Film Corp. v. Industrial Commission of Ohio,* 236 U.S. 247 (1915); *Mutual Film Corp. v. Kansas,* 236 U.S. 248 (1915). Justice Holmes was a member of the Court that decided these cases and, like all others, joined the opinion.

21. *Diversity of citizenship* simply means the plaintiffs are citizens of one state, the defendants citizens of another. In such situations the case may be brought in either federal or state court.

22. In 1915 only the part of the Fifth Amendment forbidding the taking of property without payment of compensation had been found to apply to the states (*Chicago, Burlington, and Quincy Railroad v. Chicago,* 166 U.S. 226 [1897]), and the Court was clear that no other guarantees in the Bill of Rights were restraints on

the states (*Twining v. New Jersey,* 211 U.S. 78 [1908]). As late as 1922 the Court expressed doubt that the First Amendment could be applicable to the states (*Prudential Insurance v. Cheek,* 259 U.S. 530 [1922]). Only after *Gitlow v. New York,* 268 U.S. 652 (1925), did this change.

23. 236 U.S. at 243.

24. Id. at 243, 244.

25. Id. at 251, 258.

26. A. Meiklejohn, FREE SPEECH AND ITS RELATION TO SELF-GOVERNMENT (1948) revised as POLITICAL FREEDOM 78–89 (New York: Oxford University Press, 1960).

27. Quoted in A. Boyan, *The Ability to Communicate,* in H. Clor, ed., THE MASS MEDIA AND MODERN DEMOCRACY 137, 140 (Chicago: Rand McNally, 1974).

CHAPTER 3

1. *NBC v. United States,* 319 U.S. 192 (1943).

2. *Red Lion Broadcasting v. FCC,* 395 U.S. 367 (1969).

3. Report on Chain Broadcasting, Docket No. 5060 (May 1941).

4. *Broadcasting,* December 22, 1980, at 98.

5. Id. at 99.

6. E. Barnouw, THE GOLDEN WEB 169 (New York: Oxford University Press, 1968).

7. United States Code Annotated §303 (1986 Supplement) is a grab-bag section, consisting of a listing of the Commission's many powers and duties.

8. Justices Black and Rutledge did not participate in the decision.

9. 319 U.S. at 192, 213, 218, 219.

10. Id. at 219.

11. Id. at 223.

12. Id. at 226.

13. NBC Brief at 36–37.

14. 319 U.S. at 226–27.

15. Justice Douglas did not participate.

16. FRC, Third Annual Report 32 (1929).

17. 395 U.S. at 377.

18. Id. at 380, quoting 319 U.S. at 219.

19. Id. at 388–89.

20. Id. at 388–89, 396–97.

21. *New York Times v. Sullivan,* 376 U.S. 254 (1964).

22. H. Kalven, *The New York Times Case: A Note on the "Central Meaning of the First Amendment,"* Supreme Court Review 191 (1964).

23. *Speiser v. Randall,* 357 U.S. 513 (1958).

24. 395 U.S. at 390.

25. A. Meiklejohn, POLITICAL FREEDOM 26 (New York: Oxford University Press, 1960).

26. Meiklejohn at 24–28.

27. 395 U.S. at 390.

28. *Whitney v. California,* 274 U.S. 357, 375–77 (1927) (concurring opinion).

29. 395 U.S. at 390. This argument had been recently and forcefully presented in a seminal article by Jerome Barron, *Access to the Press—A New First Amendment Right,* 80 Harvard Law Review 1641 (1967).

30. 395 U.S. at 393.

31. The conclusion of unconstitutionality was in fact reached five years later in *Miami Herald v. Tornillo,* 418 U.S. 241 (1974).

32. Meiklejohn at 78–89.

CHAPTER 4

1. E. Barnouw, A TOWER IN BABEL 64–65 (New York: Oxford University Press, 1966).

2. Id. at 67.

3. Id. at 68.

4. Id.

5. Id. at 69. Westinghouse needed a license, and Conrad did not, because the Radio Act of 1912 (see note 8 below) only required licensing of commercial operations.

6. Barnouw at 70–71.

7. Wireless Ship Act, 36 Stat. 629 (1910).

8. Radio Act, 37 Stat. 302 (1912).

9. Barnouw at 91.

10. G. Archer, HISTORY OF RADIO TO 1926 249 (New York: American Historical Society, 1938).

11. Id. at 269.

12. Id. at 280.

13. Id. at 249.

14. Id. at 158.

15. H.R. 5889, 67th Cong. 1st sess. (1921).

16. White to Hoover, April 12, 1921, White Papers, Library of Congress, Box 15.

17. Much to my surprise, I learned that newspapers have pre-death "obituaries" ready for even young public officials in the best of health. The information here comes from an undated "obituary," likely written in 1934, in the files of the *Seattle Times* library.

18. Ironically, Dill's radio "expertise" became the vehicle for his head start. In late 1930, General Electric invited him to travel to Schenectady to see its new development—television. While planning the trip he took into account his pet project, hydroelectric power for the Northwest. He requested a meeting with the governor of New York, reasoning that any man twice elected governor of New York was a potential candidate for president. During the six-hour meeting, Dill raised to Franklin Roosevelt the subject of a dam at Grand Coulee and obtained his support. "I don't suppose I'll ever be President, but if I am, I'll build your dam" is Dill's account of FDR's agreement (*Seattle Times*, January 3, 1971).

Yet despite his relative youth and his legislative successes, Dill retired in 1935, probably to avoid public scrutiny during an especially messy divorce from his wife of eight years, the millionaire former suffragette "General" Rosalie Gardner Jones. After a successful remarriage, Dill again tried electoral politics, only to be defeated for the governorship in 1940 and for Congress two years later. Frustrated in his political ambitions, he retired to a Spokane law practice from which he would speak out on communications issues for the next thirty-five years, until his death at the age of ninety-three.

19. Archer at 281.

20. Id. at 293–94.

21. Barnouw at 121.

22. *Hoover v. Intercity Radio Co., Inc.*, 286 F. 1003 (D.C. Cir. 1923).

23. Barnouw at 122.

24. Archer at 312.

25. J. Herring and G. Gross, Telecommunications: Economics and Regulation 243 (New York: McGraw Hill, 1936).

26. Archer at 356.

27. H. Hoover, The Memoirs of Herbert Hoover: The Cabinet and the Presidency, 1920–1933 142–43 (New York: Macmillan, 1952).

28. Barnouw at 180.

29. *United States v. Zenith Radio Corp.*, 12 F.2d 614 (N.D. Ill. 1926).

30. 67 Congressional Record Part II, 12352, 69th Cong. 1st sess. (1926).

31. 35 Opinions of Attorneys General 126 (1926).

32. *NBC v. United States,* 319 U.S. 190, 212 (1943).

33. Id. at 212.

34. 44 Stat. 1162 (1928).

35. 67 Congressional Record 5479.

36. *Seattle Post-Intelligencer,* November 7, 1976.

37. FRC, First Annual Report 6 (1927).

38. Barnouw at 199.

39. Id. at 211.

40. Id. at 214.

41. 45 Stat. 373 (1928).

42. L. Schmeckebier, The Federal Radio Commission 31 (Washington, D.C.: Brookings Institution, 1932).

43. Barnouw at 216.

44. L. Caldwell, *Appeals from Radio Decisions,* 3 Journal of Air Law 296 (1930).

45. Barnouw at 219.

46. *Reading Broadcasting Co. v. FRC,* 48 F.2d 458 (D.C. Cir. 1932).

47. *FRC v. Nelson Bros. Bond & Mortgage,* 289 U.S. 266 (1933).

48. E. Barnouw, The Golden Web 13 (New York: Oxford University Press, 1968).

49. Communications Act, 48 Stat. 1093 (1934).

50. 49 Stat. 1475 (1936).

CHAPTER 5

1. E. Barnouw, THE GOLDEN WEB 28 (New York: Oxford University Press, 1968).

2. Id.

3. 67 Congressional Record II, 12352, 69th Cong. 1st sess. (1926).

4. O. Graham and M. Wander, eds., FRANKLIN D. ROOSEVELT: HIS LIFE AND TIMES 125 (Boston: G. K. Hall, 1985).

5. Roberts understood the charge that he had changed his voting because of politics (the "switch in time that saves nine") and vehemently denied it. His explanation, offered by Justice Frankfurter (*Mr. Justice Roberts,* 104 University of Pennsylvania Law Review 311 [1955]), is not convincing, however.

6. W. Douglas, GO EAST, YOUNG MAN 463 (New York: Random House, 1973).

7. H. Johnson, "Who is Public Enemy No. 1?" *Collier's,* May 25, 1940, at 78.

8. See A. Schlesinger, THE POLITICS OF UPHEAVAL 211–443 (Boston: Houghton Mifflin, 1960); and W. Leuchtenburg, FRANKLIN D. ROOSEVELT AND THE NEW DEAL 143–66 (New York: Harper and Row, 1963). I use *supposed* in the text because the new body of literature on Justice Brandeis, such as P. Strum's LOUIS D. BRANDEIS (Cambridge, Mass.: Harvard University Press, 1984), is casting doubt on how "truly" Brandeisian the second New Deal was.

9. Interview with Joseph Rauh in Washington, D.C., October 22, 1982.

10. Barnouw at 170.

11. 6 Federal Register 1580 (1940).

12. 6 Federal Register 3302 (1940).

13. *Stahlman v. FCC,* 126 F.2d 124, 127 (D.C. Cir. 1942).

14. Id. at 128.

15. Id.

16. 9 Federal Register 702 (1944).

17. Id.

18. H. Ashmore, FEAR IN THE AIR 114 (New York: Norton, 1973). I wonder, however, about the accuracy of Porter's recollection, given Roosevelt's failing health and the limited time FDR was alive while Porter was chairman.

19. Sixth Report and Order, 41 FCC 148 (1952).

20. J. Graham and V. Kramer, Appointments to the Regulatory Agencies 30 (1976) (Senate Commerce Committee Print).

21. Id. at 64—65.

22. Amazingly, Doerfer appears to have been headed for the Federal Power Commission, but a mixup in the cover memos of his file and that of Jerome Kuykendall resulted in their appointments being announced backwards and Doerfer going to the FCC (id. at 34, 35).

23. Id. at 60.

24. Id. at 39, 41, 42.

25. The metaphor is from Senator John Pastore, Surgeon General's Reports by the Scientific Advisory Committee on Television and Social Behavior, Senate Commerce Committee, 92d Cong. 2d sess. 231 (1972).

26. Barrow Report, Network Broadcasting, H.R. Report no. 1297, 85th Cong. 2d sess. 61—62 (1958) (letter to House Committee on Interstate and Foreign Commerce from John C. Doerfer, August 30, 1956).

27. H. Friendly, THE ADMINISTRATIVE AGENCIES 58 (Cambridge, Mass.: Harvard University Press, 1962).

28. "How President's Wife Built $17,500 into Big Fortune in Television," *Wall Street Journal,* March 23, 1964, at 1, 12. The station was an overnight success. It had wrapped up network affiliation even before Mrs. Johnson was awarded the license, and advertisers flocked to Austin. The October 27, 1952, issue of *Broadcasting* reported that advertising sales were such, a month before the station went on the air, that "Austin's Bringing in a Gusher" (quoted in E. Barnouw, THE IMAGE EMPIRE 5 [New York: Oxford University Press, 1970]).

29. *McClatchy Broadcasting v. FCC,* 239 F.2d 15, 18 (D.C. Cir. 1956).

30. 10 RADIO REGULATION 1224 (1955).

31. 11 RADIO REGULATION 1113 (1956).

32. 13 RADIO REGULATION 507 (1957); and L. Jaffe, "The Scandal in TV Licensing," *Harper's,* September 1957 at 77.

33. 9 RADIO REGULATION 719 (1954).

34. Id. at 770i.

35. 10 RADIO REGULATION 77 (1954).

36. Id. at 92, 138.

37. Jaffe at 77.

38. B. Schwartz, THE PROFESSOR AND THE COMMISSIONS (New York: Knopf, 1959), and *Comparative Television Licensing and the Chancellor's Foot*, 47 Georgetown Law Journal 655 (1959).

CHAPTER 6

1. Hearings before the Subcommittee on Communications of the Senate Commerce Committee on S. 2004, 91st Cong. 1st sess., pt. 2, 398, 412 (1969).

2. *FRC v. Nelson Bros. Bond & Mortgage*, 289 U.S. 266, 282 (1933).

3. Cullman Broadcasting had originally written to the Commission to request clarification of its fairness obligations (25 RADIO REGULATION 895 [1963]).

4. F. Friendly, THE GOOD GUYS, THE BAD GUYS, AND THE FIRST AMENDMENT 48–49 (New York: Random House, 1975).

5. 32 Federal Register 10303 (1967).

6. 32 Federal Register 11531 (1967).

7. Quoted in Friendly at 54.

8. 33 Federal Register 5362 (1967).

9. *RTNDA v. FCC*, 400 F.2d 1002 (7th Cir. 1968).

10. *Red Lion Broadcasting v. FCC*, 395 U.S. 367, 373 (1969).

11. 8 FCC 2d 381 (1967); and *Banzhaf v. FCC*, 405 F.2d 1084, 1086 (D.C. Cir. 1968). The decision came during the era of *Valentine v. Chrestensen*, 316 U.S. 52 (1942), in which the Supreme Court had ruled that commercial speech was wholly outside the protection of the First Amendment. In 1976 this status changed, and accurate commercial speech gained constitutional protection (*Virginia Pharmacy Board v. Virginia Consumer Council*, 425 U.S. 748 [1976]). It is interesting to note, however, that the premise of *Banzhaf* was that the ads were not commercial speech but rather statements about a controversial issue. If this premise is taken seriously, *Banzhaf* presents the same constitutional issue as *Red Lion*.

12. *Office of Communication of United Church of Christ v. FCC*, 359 F.2d 994, 998, 999 (D.C. Cir. 1966).

13. Friendly at 89.

14. 359 F.2d at 1008, 999.

15. Id. at 1007, 1008.

16. *Office of Communication of United Church of Christ v. FCC*, 425 F.2d 543, 550 (D.C. Cir. 1969).

17. 4 RADIO REGULATION 2d 697, 699 (1965).

18. 24 FCC 2d 18, 21, 23 (1970).

19. Friendly at 80, 81.

20. 24 FCC 2d 42, 51 (1970); *Brandywine–Main Line Radio v. FCC* 473 F.2d 16, 69–70 (D.C. Cir. 1972) (Chief Judge Bazelon dissenting).

21. 24 FCC 2d 18 (1970).

22. 473 F.2d 16, cert. denied, 412 U.S. 922 (1973).

23. This summary comes from the D.C. Circuit's final look at the case, *Greater Boston Television Corp. v. FCC*, 444 F.2d 841 (D.C. Cir. 1970).

24. 1 FCC 2d 393 (1965).

25. 17 FCC 2d 856, 873 (1969).

26. 444 F.2d at 860.

27. *Broadcasting*, April 5, 1982, at 36, and July 27, 1981, at 27.

28. 16 FCC 2d at 28 (1969).

29. L. Jaffe, *WHDH: The FCC and Broadcasting License Renewals*, 82 Harvard Law Review 1693, 1700 (1969).

CHAPTER 7

1. FRC, Third Annual Report 32 (1929).

2. Id. at 36.

3. FRC, Second Annual Report 155 (1928).

4. E. Barnouw, THE GOLDEN WEB 52 (New York: Oxford University Press, 1968).

5. Elliott Roosevelt, the president's son, continued to present his own opinions on the arms embargo over Mutual and took the four Hearst-owned Texas State Network stations, of which he was president, out of the NAB.

6. *Broadcasting*, December 8, 1980, at 88.

7. *The Mayflower Broadcasting Corp.*, 8 FCC 333, 338 (1940 proposed findings of fact), 339 (1941 decision and order).

8. Id. at 339.

9. Id. at 340 (emphasis added).

10. Id.

11. *Broadcasting,* December 22, 1980, at 98.

12. Editorializing by Broadcast Licensees, 13 FCC 1246 (1949).

13. F. Friendly, THE GOOD GUYS, THE BAD GUYS, AND THE FIRST AMENDMENT 6 (New York: Random House, 1975). Friendly is the individual who brought the actual facts of *Red Lion* to light, and the legal community owes him a great debt for doing so. The facts in this section are taken entirely from his excellent account.

14. Id. at 7.

15. Id. at 4.

16. Id. at 34.

17. 40 FCC 576 (1963).

18. Friendly at 33.

19. Id. at 33, 34.

20. Id. at 37.

21. *The Nation,* May 25, 1964, at 525.

22. Friendly at 38. Cook's autobiography, MAVERICK (New York: Putnam's, 1984), chap. 23, not unnaturally paints a somewhat different portrait and contends that it was Cook's idea, not the DNC's, to do both the Goldwater "biography" and the "Hate Clubs" piece. Cook bristles at Friendly's argument that Cook's writings were simply part of the DNC effort, countering that he was essentially a loner throughout who received some, but not that much, help from the DNC.

The two stories are remarkably similar—much more so than Cook would probably realize or like. I suspect, although I cannot prove, that Friendly's broader perspective is the more accurate, even if Friendly did not get all the details of Cook's relationship with the DNC precisely correct. Furthermore, autobiographies are notoriously self-serving, and it is not even clear that Friendly was not precisely correct in all those details.

23. Friendly at 39, 41.

24. Id. at 36.

25. Id. at 42.

26. Id. at 44, 45.

27. 26 FCC 2d 591 (1969).

28. *Broadcasting,* September 13, 1976, at 28.

29. Friendly at 176–77, and chap. 11.

30. *American Security Council Education Foundation v. FCC*, 607 F.2d 438, 448, 467, 463 (D.C. Cir. 1979), aff'g 63 FCC 2d 366 (1977).

31. This statement by Whitehead has been in my teaching notes for years, but I was unable to find its source. In a letter to the author dated April 26, 1985, Whitehead confirmed that the "quote to which you refer was indeed from me." But he noted that few of his speeches were published, and he could not remember where he had said it, either. Richard Salant informs me that Whitehead's comment was made in the course of an informal breakfast with reporters.

CHAPTER 8

1. M. Barrett, ed., 1969–70: YEAR OF CHALLENGE, YEAR OF CRISIS, The Alfred I. duPont–Columbia University Survey of Broadcast Journalism 31 (New York: Grosset and Dunlap, 1970).

2. R. Nixon, RN, THE MEMOIRS OF RICHARD NIXON 409–11 (New York: Grosset and Dunlap, 1978).

3. Id. at 410.

4. J. Spear, PRESIDENTS AND THE PRESS 122 (Cambridge, Mass.: MIT Press, 1984). Spear is by far the best available treatment of the Nixon assault on the press. His only serious omission is a failure to realize just how out of line the FCC decision involving the O'Brien "Loyal Opposition" speech was, and thus he gives it but passing note. I discuss the O'Brien speech in full in chapter 9.

5. W. Safire, BEFORE THE FALL 352 (Garden City, N.Y.: Doubleday, 1975).

6. W. Porter, ASSAULT ON THE MEDIA 255–62 (Ann Arbor: University of Michigan Press, 1976) reprints this speech as well as most of the significant documents relating to the Nixon assault on the press.

7. Quoted in Nixon at 412.

8. Porter at 244–49.

9. Id. at 245.

10. Id.

11. Safire at 341.

12. Spear at 116–17.

13. YEAR OF CHALLENGE, YEAR OF CRISIS at 36–37.

14. Spear at 117.

15. Porter at 263–65.

16. Id. at 274–77.

17. Id. at 274.

18. Id. at 275.

19. Id. at 276. Paley was bothered, however, by a recent "Loyal Opposition" program by Democratic National Committee chairman Lawrence O'Brien and "wanted to make it very clear that it would not happen again and that they would not permit partisan attacks on the President" (id. at 275).

20. Id. at 276.

21. Spear at 153, 154.

22. M. Barrett, ed., MOMENTS OF TRUTH? The Fifth Alfred I. duPont–Columbia University Survey of Broadcast Journalism 128–29n (New York: Thomas Y. Crowell, 1975).

23. Spear at 155.

24. Broadcasting in America, 42 FCC 2d 1–172 (1973). (The Johnson study dealt only with the top fifty markets and thus did not include Jacksonville.)

25. Porter at 61.

26. H. Ashmore, FEAR IN THE AIR 116 (New York: Norton, 1973).

27. Spear at 133.

28. Id. at 132–33.

29. Id. at 150.

30. Porter at 167–68.

31. 23 FCC 2d 382 (1970); 25 FCC 2d 318 (1970).

32. Quoted in Porter at 157.

33. Id. at 173–74.

34. *Broadcasting,* May 18, 1961.

35. 76 Stat. 150 (1962).

36. Porter at 302–4.

37. Id. at 303.

38. Id. at 304.

39. Safire at 365.

40. Quoted in Spear at 191.

41. Id. at 173.

42. MOMENTS OF TRUTH at 4n.

43. Id. at 4.

44. The documents are reproduced in id. at 216–19, 231.

45. M. Barrett, ed., 1970–71: A STATE OF SIEGE, The Alfred I. duPont–Columbia University Survey of Broadcast Journalism 43 (New York: Grosset and Dunlap, 1971).

46. F. Powledge, THE ENGINEERING OF RESTRAINT 34 (Washington, D.C.: Public Affairs Press, n.d.).

47. Id. at 35.

CHAPTER 9

1. T. Reeves, THE LIFE AND TIMES OF JOE MCCARTHY 561–62 (New York: Stein and Day, 1982).

2. Had the personal-attack doctrine, used in *Red Lion,* been more fully developed, then McCarthy, but not someone from the Republican National Committee, might have been the appropriate source of the response to the Stevenson speech.

3. F. Greenstein, THE HIDDEN-HAND PRESIDENCY 194 (New York: Basic Books, 1982).

4. 25 FCC 2d 216, 242, 275, 283 (1970).

5. *Nicholas Zapple,* 23 FCC 2d 707 (1970); and *Cullman Broadcasting,* 25 RADIO REGULATION 895 (1963).

6. 25 FCC 2d at 275, 283.

7. A huge footnote collecting the literature appears in D. Lange, *The Role of the Access Doctrine in the Regulation of the Mass Media,* 52 University of North Carolina Law Review 1, 2–3n.5 (1973).

8. 25 FCC 2d at 242.

9. Id. at 307.

10. Id. at 296–98.

11. Id. at 283, 299–300.

12. *CBS v. FCC,* 454 F.2d 1018, 1020 (D.C. Cir. 1971).

13. Letter from Chairman Rosel H. Hyde to Hon. Wayne Hays, Commission Reference No. 8330-S, C2-105 (1968).

14. 454 F.2d at 1027.

15. 25 FCC 2d at 299–300.

16. Id. at 300 (emphasis added).

17. 25 FCC 2d 739, 742, 745, 746n.16 (1970).

18. 454 F.2d at 1031.

19. 25 FCC 2d at 309.

20. *DNC v. FCC*, 460 F.2d 891 (D.C. Cir. 1972).

21. Lar Daly, discussed in Senate Report No. 562, 86th Cong. 1st sess. (1959).

22. 14 RADIO REGULATION 720 (1956).

23. Id. at 722.

24. *New York Times*, November 6, 1956, at 71.

25. H.R. 6810, 84th Cong. 1st sess. (1955).

26. 3 RADIO REGULATION 2d 647, 651 (1964).

27. Id. at 648.

28. *McCarthy v. FCC*, 390 F.2d 471 (D.C. Cir. 1968); *DNC*, 34 FCC 2d 572 (1972); *Carter-Mondale*, 74 FCC 2d 631, 645n.20 (1980).

29. T. White, THE MAKING OF THE PRESIDENT 1960 293–94 (New York: Atheneum, 1961).

30. S. 204, 87th Cong. 1st sess. (1961).

31. H.R.J. Res. 247, 88th Cong. 1st sess. (1963); 110 Congressional Record 19413 (1964).

32. 55 FCC 2d 697 (1975). Although it could be argued that this ruling was consistent with the exceptions to section 315 and that it certainly made sense to have debates, the FCC was forced to overturn an administrative interpretation rendered fairly contemporaneously with the statute's enactment in order to achieve the desired results. And contemporaneous administrative interpretations have a favored place in administrative law.

33. 54 RADIO REGULATION 2d 1246 (1983), aff'd *League of Women Voters Education Fund v. FCC*, 731 F.2d 995 (D.C. Cir. 1984).

34. 47 United States Code Annotated §312(a)(7) (1986 Supplement).

35. *CBS v. FCC (Carter-Mondale)*, 453 U.S. 367 (1981).

CHAPTER 10

1. *Washington Post*, November 3, 1974, sec. K.

2. The hearings are listed in T. Krattenmaker and L. Powe, *Televised Violence*, 64 Virginia Law Review at 1126 (1978).

3. *Mile High Stations, Inc.,* 28 FCC 795 (1960).

4. *Palmetto Broadcasting,* 33 FCC 250 (1962).

5. Id.

6. *Robinson v. FCC,* 334 F.2d 534 (D.C. Cir. 1964).

7. 36 FCC 147 (1964).

8. Id. at 152.

9. 2 FCC 2d 1066 (1965).

10. Hearings before the Subcommittee on Communications of the Senate Commerce Committee on S. 2004, 91st Cong. 1st sess., pt. 2, 346–49 (1969). At the pages just cited, both Commissioner Robert E. Lee and Commissioner Cox refer to a dissenting opinion by Lee wherein he reprinted the poem. Yet I have found no such published opinion in either of the two possible sources, the FCC Reports or RADIO REGULATION. The poem is reproduced, however, in the Harvard Law Review: Note, *Morality and the Broadcast Media,* 84 Harvard Law Review 664, 668–69 (1971).

11. *Jack Straw Memorial Foundation,* 21 FCC 2d 833 (1970), and 24 FCC 2d 266 (1970).

12. 21 FCC 2d at 842.

13. 24 FCC 2d 408, 416–17 (1970).

14. Id. at 410.

15. Id. at 411.

16. Id. at 409n.2.

17. Id. at 422.

18. The factual discussion that follows is largely taken from an excellent student Note, *Drug Lyrics, the FCC, and the First Amendment,* 5 Loyola of Los Angeles Law Review 339 (1972), which in turn was based on the files of the lawyer representing Yale Broadcasting in the litigation over the Commission's ban.

19. Address, September 14, 1970, quoted in id. at 352.

20. "Acid Queen" by Peter Townsend, copyright 1969, Essex Music; quoted in id.

21. 5 Loyola at 352.

22. Krattenmaker and Powe at 1288–92.

23. 28 FCC 2d 409 (1971).

24. Id. at 411, 412, 413, 417.

25. *Complaint of Anti-Defamation League against KTYM,* 6 FCC 2d 385, 398 (1967).

26. 5 Loyola at 348, 366.

27. *Yale Broadcasting v. FCC*, 478 F.2d 594, 603 (D.C. Cir. 1973) (Chief Judge Bazelon dissenting from denial of motion for rehearing en banc).

28. 5 Loyola at 357n.159.

29. "The Pusher," words and music by Hoyt Axton, copyright Lady Jane Music, 1964, used by permission; quoted in id. at 363–64.

30. 32 FCC 2d 377 (1971).

31. Hearings before the Subcommittee on Monopoly of the Senate Select Committee on Small Business, on the Effect of the Promotion and Advertising of Over-the-Counter Drugs on Competition, Small Business, and Health and Welfare of the Public, 92d Cong. 1st sess., pt. 2, 734–36 (1971).

32. 478 F.2d at 599.

33. FCC News Release (August 2, 1973), quoted in L. Powe, *Cable and Obscenity*, 24 Catholic University Law Review 719, 732 (1975).

34. 27 RADIO REGULATION 2d 285, 286 (1973).

35. *Roth v. United States*, 354 U.S. 476 (1957); *Memoirs v. Massachusetts*, 383 U.S. 413 (1966).

36. 41 FCC 2d at 924 (Commissioner Johnson dissenting).

37. Id. at 920.

38. *Illinois Citizens Committee for Broadcasting v. FCC*, 515 F.2d 397, 407 (D.C. Cir. 1975).

39. *Miller v. California*, 413 U.S. 15 (1973).

40. 515 F.2d at 405, 406; *Ginzburg v. US*, 383 U.S. 463 (1966).

41. *FCC v. Pacifica Foundation*, 438 U.S. 726, 730 (1978).

42. *Broadcasting*, July 10, 1978, at 20.

43. Krattenmaker and Powe at 1129–30, 1215–16.

44. 56 FCC 2d 94, 98.

45. 59 FCC 2d 892 (1975).

46. *Pacifica Foundation v. FCC*, 556 F.2d 9 (D.C. Cir. 1977).

47. 556 F.2d at 30–37.

48. 438 U.S. 726 (1978).

CHAPTER 11

1. *FCC v. League of Women Voters*, 104 S.Ct. 3106, 3116n.11.

2. For the reasons given in the following paragraphs, this argu-

ment does not appear in the legal literature and is now used exclusively as an unthinking reflex by occasional advocates of broadcast regulation. Nevertheless, at one time even Justice William O. Douglas adhered to the public-ownership argument (W. Douglas, THE RIGHT OF THE PEOPLE 76–77 [Garden City, N.Y.: Doubleday, 1958]). When he faced the issue in real life, however, he concluded that broadcast regulation was unconstitutional (*CBS v. DNC*, 412 U.S. 94, 148 [1973]).

3. E.g., *Hague v. CIO*, 307 U.S. 496 (1939). See, generally, W. Van Alstyne, *The Demise of the Right-Privilege Distinction in Constitutional Law*, 81 Harvard Law Review 1439 (1968); and C. Reich, *The New Property*, 73 Yale Law Journal 733 (1964).

4. One type of argument about "scarcity" that is often heard can immediately be shown to be invalid. A recent example, published in *Access*, a monthly paper for antimedia activists, presented a study of the almost four thousand communities in the United States that have a broadcast facility licensed to them (R. Jennings, "Scarcity Still an Issue," 178 *Access* 2, 6 [February 1985]). The study found scarcity all over. First, it refused to count *any* broadcast signal the community receives from "other places," thereby ensuring that the bulk of the communities would have but one signal. Then it noted that two-thirds of these communities have no daily newspaper; thus there are insufficient media outlets, and "scarcity" is obvious. Beyond choosing a methodology guaranteed to cook the data to achieve the desired result, the argument typifies too much of the scarcity debate: a belief that if *anything* is scarce, broadcasting can be regulated. Not surprisingly, an almost infinite number of similar Alice in Wonderland scarcity arguments are available, but there is no point in searching further for them. All of them are backward-looking, having already decided that regulation is a great idea and simply trying to find something that is "scarce" so that the Supreme Court's incantation can be satisfied. Their failure is that the desire to regulate overwhelms the desire to analyze. The Supreme Court has used scarcity in but one sense: broadcasting is scarce, but print is not. It is this sense that allows regulation of broadcasting in ways that would be unconstitutional if applied to print.

5. Although I have been writing on this issue for a decade, beginning with *"Or of the [Broadcast] Press"* (55 Texas Law Review 39

[1976]), I found that my own thinking was clarified by reading in draft Matthew Spitzer's SEVEN DIRTY WORDS AND SIX OTHER STORIES (New Haven, Ct.: Yale University Press, 1986). (A shorter version appears as *Controlling the Content of Print and Broadcast,* 58 USC Law Review 1349 [1985].)

    6. *NBC v. United States,* 319 U.S. at 212 (1943).

    7. I. Pool, TECHNOLOGIES OF FREEDOM 138 (Cambridge, Mass.: Harvard University Press, 1983).

    8. R. Coase, *The Federal Communications Commission,* Journal of Law and Economics 2 (1959).

    9. *Broadcasting,* January 28, 1985, at 46.

    10. 319 U.S. at 213.

    11. Docket 80–90 (1984); *Broadcasting,* December 31, 1984, at 36–37; Freedom of Expression, Hearings before the Committee on Commerce, Science, and Transportation, U.S. Senate, 97th Cong. 2d sess., Serial 97–139 at 3–65 (1982) [hereafter Packwood Hearings]; Powe, *"Or of the [Broadcast] Press"* at 55.

    12. *Red Lion Broadcasting v. FCC,* 395 U.S. at 388–89 (1969).

    13. Id. at 386.

    14. Packwood Hearings at 140.

    15. Id. at 146.

    16. Id. at 139; "Times of Washington Is Attaining Credibility But Not Profitability," *Wall Street Journal,* December 17, 1985, at 1.

    17. Packwood Hearings at 141.

    18. Id. at 156–57.

    19. At the peak of the speculative binge a Los Angeles VHF station was reportedly sold for $510 million (*Broadcasting,* May 20, 1985, at 39). While this amount staggers my imagination, several months earlier the Des Moines Register and Tribune Co., owner of the *Des Moines Register* and the *Jackson (Tennessee) Sun,* sold for over $200 million (AP Wire Service, February 14, 1985). On a market rather than a media basis it is hard, if not impossible, to explain why Des Moines and Jackson can approximate 40 percent of Los Angeles without a reference to the types of properties being sold. One can only imagine what the *Los Angeles Times* would fetch. Undaunted by such queries was longtime broadcast regulator Henry Geller. Grasping at the giddy $510 million figure for the Los Angeles VHF station, he created yet another scarcity argument. This time broadcast *prices* demonstrated scarcity—why

else would anyone pay so much? (*Broadcasting*, June 17, 1985, at 40). This is simply further demonstration that the number of scarcity arguments that omit a comparison with print is as elastic as necessary. See also note 4 above.

20. 1986 BROADCASTING–CABLECASTING YEARBOOK A-2 (Washington, D.C.: Broadcasting Publications, 1985); Packwood Hearings at 143. Another 285 television stations and 532 radio stations are licensed but not operating (*Broadcasting*, February 18, 1985, at 84).

21. D. Polsby, *Candidate Access to the Air*, Supreme Court Review 223 (1981).

22. *FCC v. Pacifica Foundation*, 438 U.S. at 748, 749 (1978); see T. Krattenmaker and L. Powe, *Televised Violence*, 64 Virginia Law Review at 1221–37 (1978).

23. 1986 BROADCASTING–CABLECASTING YEARBOOK at A-2.

24. L. Bollinger, *Freedom of the Press and Public Access*, 75 Michigan Law Review 1 (1976).

25. Quoted in A. Boyan, *The Ability to Communicate*, in H. Clor, ed., THE MASS MEDIA AND MODERN DEMOCRACY 137, 140 (Chicago: Rand McNally, 1974).

CHAPTER 12

1. L. Powe, *A Silver Anniversary Look at Frontier Broadcasting*, 10 Media Law Notes No. 4 at 4 (1983).

2. The memo, dated March 25, 1952, is reproduced in Review of Allocations Problems, Special Problems of TV Service to Small Communities, Hearings before the Senate Interstate and Foreign Commerce Committee, 85th Cong. 2d sess. 3490 (1958).

3. Interoffice memorandum, July 25, 1957, reproduced in id. at 4142, 4146.

4. 24 FCC 252 (1958).

5. Statement of Commissioner Loevenger, Regulation of Community Antenna Television, Hearings before the House Subcommittee on Communications and Power of the House Committee on Interstate and Foreign Commerce on H.R. 7715, 89th Cong. 1st sess. 41 (1965).

6. *Carroll Broadcasting v. FCC*, 258 F.2d 440 (D.C. Cir. 1958).

7. *Carter Mountain Transmission Corp.*, 32 FCC 459 (1962).

8. *Carter Mountain Transmission Corp. v. FCC*, 321 F.2d 359, 364 (D.C. Cir. 1963).

9. *Rules re Microwave-Served CATV*, 38 FCC 683, 684, 685 (1965).

10. *Second Report and Order*, 2 FCC 2d 725 (1966).

11. *United States v. Southwestern Cable*, 392 U.S. 157 (1968), was one of two cable cases on the docket. The other, *Fortnightly Corp. v. United Artists Television* (392 U.S. 390 [1968]), involved the question of whether master-antenna transmission of copyrighted programming violated the Copyright Act. The assumption at the time was that cable would win the jurisdictional issue in *Southwestern Cable* but lose the copyright issue in *Fortnightly*. Instead just the opposite occurred.

12. 392 U.S. at 181; *Midwest Television*, 11 RADIO REGULATION 2d 273, 303 (1967); 13 RADIO REGULATION 2d 698, 724 (1968).

13. 15 FCC 2d 417 (1968); 34 FCC 2d 143 (1972).

14. *Business Executive's Move for Vietnam Peace v. FCC*, 450 F.2d 642 (D.C. Cir. 1971), rev'd sub. nom. *CBS v. DNC*, 412 U.S. 94 (1973).

15. 399 F.2d 65 (8th Cir. 1968).

16. For the part of the spectrum used in microwave relay there are neither existing nor foreseeable "scarcity" problems (FCC Network Inquiry Special Staff, VIDEO INTERCONNECTIONS 49–51, 95–105 [1980]).

17. 399 F.2d at 69.

18. J. Barron, *The Federal Communications Commission's Fairness Doctrine*, 30 George Washington Law Review 1, 2n.6 (1961).

19. *United States v. Midwest Video*, 406 U.S. 649, 670 (1972). There were four dissenters on Commission jurisdiction, and Chief Justice Burger, although he voted to sustain the Commission, opined that this case had just about reached the limit.

20. The beginning case, from which the myopic 16 percent conclusion is taken, is *Citizens Committee v. FCC*, 436 F.2d 263 (D.C. Cir. 1970). The Commission expressed its constitutional conclusions six years later, in 60 FCC 2d 858 (1976). Not surprisingly, the D.C. Circuit would have none of that and reversed (610 F.2d 838 [D.C. Cir. 1979]). The Supreme Court finally ended the de-

cade of warfare by siding with the Commission, stating that the Communications Act did not require the Commission to impede the change of formats (*FCC v. WNCN Listeners Guild,* 450 U.S. 582 [1981]).

21. *HBO v. FCC,* 567 F.2d 9 (D.C. Cir. 1977).

22. *FCC v. Midwest Video [II],* 440 U.S. 689, 709n.19 (1979), affirming 571 F.2d 1025 (8th Cir. 1978).

23. "We have consistently found [viewer preference] insufficient to overcome the policies of our mandatory signal carriage rules" (Quincy Cable TV, 89 FCC 2d 1128, 1137 [1982]). The D.C. Circuit subsequently found the rules unconstitutional on appeal (*Quincy Cable TV v. FCC,* 768 F.2d 1434 [D.C. Cir. 1985], cert. denied, 106 U.S. 2889 [1986]).

24. "I don't believe the First Amendment—and this is a harsh thing to say—I don't believe it is the primary concern of the cities" (*Wall Street Journal,* October 15, 1984, at 30). In a letter to the author dated June 13, 1985, Mayor Royer stated that the quotation "probably" came in the context of the early political discussions of the legislation. Nevertheless, he is of the view that "there was no substantive conflict between [the] First Amendment and [the] legislation." As the following text indicates, his First Amendment is quite conducive to municipal power.

25. Cable Communications Policy Act of 1984, 98 Stat. 2779, establishing "Title VI—Cable Communications" to the Communications Act.

26. 47 United States Code Annotated §546 (1986 Supplement).

27. 47 United States Code Annotated §§531, 532 (1986 Supplement).

28. I have no intention of attempting to define obscenity. Nor am I concerned about the community-standards aspect of the Supreme Court's *Miller* test.

29. The analysis in this paragraph and those that follow on this topic is taken from T. Krattenmaker and M. Esterow, *Censoring Indecent Cable Programs,* 51 Fordham Law Review 606 (1983).

30. *Cruz v. Ferre,* 571 F. Supp. 125 (S.D. Fla. 1983), aff'd 755 F.2d 1415 (11th Cir. 1985); *Community Television of Utah v. Roy City,* 555 F. Supp. 1164 (D. Utah 1982); *HBO v. Wilkinson,* 531 F. Supp. 987 (D. Utah 1982). These cases stand on increasingly strong

ground as the battle over "soft-X" takes on a more anachronistic sound with the prevalence of video cassette recorders. With a VCR anyone can legally acquire a nonobscene but sexually explicit program and see it in the home. No cable subscriber—or anyone else—can do anything to prevent this. Using the Playboy Channel instead of a video store to acquire the programming makes no constitutional difference, as no one is forced to subscribe.

31. G. Shapiro, P. Kurland, and J. Mercurio, Cablespeech 80–89 (New York: Law & Business, 1983).

32. G. Robinson, *Cable Television and the First Amendment,* 6 Communications and the Law at 60–61 (1984).

33. *Los Angeles v. Preferred Communications,* 106 U.S. 2034 (1986).

34. *Berkshire Cablevision v. Burke,* 571 F. Supp. 976 (D. R.I. 1983).

35. *Minneapolis Star and Tribune Co. v. Minnesota Commissioner of Revenue,* 460 U.S. 575 (1983). See also *Grosjean v. American Press,* 297 U.S. 233 (1936).

36. *Schneider v. State,* 308 U.S. 147 (1939), is the beginning of this line of cases holding that government may regulate the time, place, and manner, but not the content, of speech. Specifically, *Schneider* held that a law prohibiting leafletting in order to prevent littering is unconstitutional. If the state wishes to prevent littering, then it must pass a law dealing with litter, not speech.

37. 106 U.S. at 2034 (1986).

38. *Preferred Communications v. Los Angeles,* 754 F.2d 1396 (9th Cir. 1985). Judge Sneed's excellent opinion parallels the argument made in the text that a city's interest in disruption of traffic allows it to regulate traffic, not cable systems.

39. 106 U.S. at 2038.

40. *Quincy Cable TV v. FCC,* 768 F.2d 1434 (D.C. Cir. 1985), cert. denied, 106 U.S. 2889 (1986).

41. 106 U.S. at 2038.

42. Given the existing problems of sewer repair, road construction, and new building, I believe that the traffic disruption most municipalities allow will guarantee cable entry. See *United States v. Grace,* 461 U.S. 171 (1983); but cf. *Metromedia v. San Diego,* 453 U.S. 490 (1981).

43. My instincts tell me that this conclusion represents yet another example of not considering First Amendment aspects of technological development. Hence I suspect it merits some serious study.

44. L. Bollinger, *Freedom of the Press and Public Access,* 75 Michigan Law Review 1 at 24 (1976).

CONCLUSION

1. Bollinger recognized not only the potential pitfalls of licensing but also specifically that it may have been abused—or, as he put it, suffered "unintended consequences" (*Freedom of the Press and Public Access,* 75 Michigan Law Review 1 at 32n.98 [1976]). I am unaware of any citation to this limitation in the literature adopting his thesis.

2. The Hutchins Commission's official title was The Commission on Freedom of the Press. It published its findings as A FREE AND RESPONSIBLE PRESS (Chicago: University of Chicago Press, 1947).

3. D. Anderson, *The Origins of the Press Clause,* 30 UCLA Law Review 455 (1983); V. Blasi, *The Checking Value in First Amendment Theory,* American Bar Foundation Research Journal 523 (1977); V. Blasi, *The Pathological Perspective and the First Amendment,* 85 Columbia Law Review 449 (1985); T. Emerson, THE SYSTEM OF FREEDOM OF EXPRESSION (New York: Random House, 1970); F. Schauer, FREE SPEECH: A PHILOSOPHICAL INQUIRY (Cambridge: Cambridge University Press, 1982); M. Yudof, WHEN GOVERNMENT SPEAKS (Berkeley and Los Angeles: University of California Press, 1983). But see L. Bollinger, THE TOLERANT SOCIETY (New York: Oxford University Press, 1986).

4. D. Anderson, 17 UC Davis Law Review 731 (1984).

5. F. Schauer, 84 Columbia Law Review 558, 565–72 (1984).

6. Schauer qualifies that sentence by stating it is an idea that "has at least surface appeal" (id. at 568).

7. M. Baeza is a partner at Debevoise & Plimpton in New York and a part-time lecturer at the Harvard Law School.

8. M. Baeza, 97 Harvard Law Review 584, 591 (1983).

9. Id. at 592, 593, 594.

10. Carter was at the time of his review an assistant professor and is now a professor at the Yale Law School.

11. S. Carter, 93 Yale Law Journal 581, 583 (1984).

12. Id. at 581, 600.

13. Id. at 582, 600, 602, 603.

14. Id. at 604.

15. Wright's position was initially set forth in *Politics and the Constitution: Is Money Speech?* 85 Yale Law Journal 1001 (1976); he elaborates it in *Money and the Pollution of Politics*, 82 Columbia Law Review 609 (1982). Carter's Yale review of Pool indicates that the position will have a persuasive advocate in the academy for years. My rejoinder was published as *Mass Speech and the Newer First Amendment*, Supreme Court Review 243 (1982).

16. *CBS v. DNC*, 412 U.S. 94, 160–61 (1973) (Justice Douglas concurring).

Index

Compositor:	G&S Typesetters, Inc.
Printer:	Vail-Ballou Press
Binder:	Vail-Ballou Press
Text:	11/13 Baskerville
Display:	Baskerville